ASSASSINATION

Political Murder Through the Ages

Xavier Waterkeyn

NEW
HOLLAND

*To Fidel, who knows so much more about the
subject of assassinations than I ever will.*

First published in Australia in 2007 by
New Holland Publishers (Australia) Pty Ltd
Sydney • Auckland • London • Cape Town

www.newholland.com.au

Unit 1, 66 Gibbes Street Chatswood 2067 Australia
218 Lake Road Northcote Auckland New Zealand
86 Edgware Road London W2 2EA United Kingdom
80 McKenzie Street Cape Town 8001 South Africa

National Library of Australia Cataloguing-in-Publication Data:
Waterkyn, Xavier.

Assassination: Political Murder Through the Ages

ISBN 978 1 74110 5667 (pbk.).

1. Assassination - History. 2. Political crimes and
offenses - History. 3. Assassins - History. I. Title.

364.1524

Publisher: Fiona Schultz
Production: Linda Bottari
Project Editor: Michael McGrath
Editors: Belinda Castles, Kirsten Chapman
Designer: Jeff Gordon
Cover Concept: Greg Lamont
Printer: McPherson's Printing Group, Maryborough, Victoria

Contents

Introduction

Who hasn't thought of murdering a politician at least once in their lives?
Go on, admit it, you know you have.
I know I have, but I also have to get real and to face the fact that I'd be
unlikely to go through with it.
I have my reasons:

• Assassins fail more often than they succeed. Kings, emperors and their modern equivalents prime ministers and presidents are usually well guarded and with good reason—you can't please all of the people all of the time.

• Assassination is strictly for the committed amateur, for professionals, for those who are so passionate that they don't care what happens to them afterwards or for nutcases who kill because the aliens from Zmerdost IV are telling them to.

• Even when they succeed, assassins usually don't get away with it. For some reason the people who depended on the political leader get very upset when the supplier of the gravy for all the gravy trains gets bumped off. The manhunt—assassins are nearly always men—is usually intense, with no expense spared.

• Assassination doesn't often change anything real. Assassins are simplistic people. They tend to believe that one person is the cause of all their trouble. This is only true in some dictatorships. If you really want to change things you have to start a civil war, since the problem—whatever the problem is—is usually systemic. To change a system you need to remove or kill a whole bunch of people in power. However, what most assassins and lots of other people never understand is that the

8

problem is usually widespread. It comes down to the individual decisions of millions of people who are complicit in maintaining the status quo either because the system works for them, or because they're too afraid to risk something. In desperate countries, people are afraid of losing their lives. In the developed world, people are afraid of losing their spa baths. Either way, people get the governments they deserve.

I find the usual definitions of assassination inadequate so here is the one that I have formulated in order to set the bounds of this book: assassination is the murder of a prominent person who is or was active in politics. The murder arises out of primarily political, moral or ideological reasons but may also be called assassination when such murder has serious political consequences, regardless of the motives of the assassin.

By 'prominent person who is or was active in politics' I mean: kings, emirs, shahs, emperors, tsars or whatever you want to call the head of a hereditary monarchy or the head of state in the language of your choice.

Presidents, prime ministers, viziers, dictators or whatever you want to call the head of the executive branch of a government in any system, be it democratic, communistic, despotic or otherwise.

Within these pages are also a smattering of journalists, writers, freedom fighters and other passionate busybodies whose job or life mission of meddling in politics led to making someone angry enough to kill them.

It's largely irrelevant whether the political person is aspiring to office, is in office or has 'left politics', since the reasons for political killings are complex and anger and revenge know no bounds.

The phrases 'political, moral or ideological reasons' and 'when such murder has serious political consequences' require a little clarification. Most of the time, people kill political leaders for political reasons. I define politics as 'the art of resource management'. I call it an art because it sure as hell isn't a science. The whole point of government is to decide who makes the cake, who slices the cake, who gets the big pieces with the icing on top and who gets the crumbs. The assassin usually figures that killing the head cake slicer will result in a more even distribution of cake—as if there wasn't another slicer waiting to assume the mantle of power slicing. However, in rare cases the assassin kills for personal reasons, and the fallout is a side effect of an act of murder, rather than something the assassin or his accomplices may have envisaged. Nevertheless, the assassination itself is still a death with major political ramifications—even if they are only superficial ones.

There's one more stipulation. Assassination means premeditated killing outside of a judicial process, so state sanctioned executions don't normally count; however, to a great extent I think that this is quibbling over historical niceties. The killing of the Romanovs in Russia was an assassination in all but name and it would be hard to define the execution of Nikolae and Elena Ceausescu in Romania as having followed due process, so in some cases I've allowed my own judgement to define 'assassination'.

Feel free to disagree with me if you have nothing better to do.

The currency used in the book is contemporary (as at 2007) US dollars unless otherwise stated.

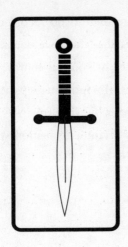

Ancient Assassinations

It was a common belief in ancient military dictatorships that the afterlife was pretty much the same as the 'beforelife', only with better booze (no hangovers), better women (no resistance) and better warriors (no disobedience).

Assassination is older than history, but since there is no record of the first caveman to break the skull of a tribal chief, we depend on the first written records to tell us about early political murders. Unfortunately, the oldest written records are Mesopotamian palace ledgers that are about as exciting to read as stock control forms.

For the earliest accessible account of an important assassination we need to look to the Egyptians.

Egypt

1962 BCE

We know very little of Amenemhat I—or Amememhet I, because Egyptian hieroglyphs don't include vowels the true pronunciation of the oldest of ancient Egyptian names will always be a guess. His name means 'Amen is in front'. We do know that he usurped the previous pharaoh, Mentuhotep IV, in 1991 BCE, and in doing so established the Twelfth Dynasty—the first Dynasty of the Middle Kingdom period— and that he moved the Egyptian capital from Thebes to Itjtawy. We don't know where Itjtawy is any more, but scholars think that it's somewhere south of Memphis.

Amenemhat ruled for almost twenty years before making his son Senusret I (also Senwosret I) his co-ruler and thus established the first co-regency in Egyptian history. Ten years later, while Senusret was on campaign in Libya, the assassins struck.

An unknown scribe wrote down an account of the assassination during the reign of Senusret. It is fascinating because it is written from the point of view of the murdered king, talking to his son about what happened. One evening in the 31st year of his reign, Amenemhat had lain down to sleep with his bodyguard nearby, but he hadn't counted on a conspiracy from the bodyguards and his harem:

It was after supper, when night had fallen, and I had spent an hour of happiness. I was asleep upon my bed, having become weary, and my heart had begun to follow sleep. When weapons of my counsel were wielded, I had become like a snake of the necropolis. As I came to, I awoke to fighting, and found that it was an attack of the bodyguard. If I had quickly taken weapons in my hand, I would have made the wretches retreat with a charge! But there is none mighty in the night, none who can fight alone; no success will come without a helper. Look, my injury happened while I was without you, when the entourage had not yet heard that I would hand over to you when I had not yet sat with you, that I might make counsels for you; for I did not plan it, I did not foresee it, and my heart had not taken thought of the negligence of servants.

The pharaoh's assassination also inspired a poem: *The Story of Sinuhe*. It tells of the eponymous hero and how he discovers who killed the pharaoh and who plotted to ensure that Senusret didn't inherit the throne. Instead of warning his king, however, Sinuhe escaped to Libya and married the daughter of a chieftain, becoming rich and powerful. Years later Senusret, who had survived the plot, invited Sinuhe to return, forgiving him for his lapse and taking him into royal service. Scholars now believe that the poem is entirely a work of fiction but they continue to regard it as a masterpiece of ancient Egyptian literature. If you'd like to read the poem yourself there is a translation at: *http://jennycarrington.tripod.com/JJSinuhe*.

Amenemhat was buried in the necropolis of Lisht. His pyramid is a ruin and looks like an isolated sand hill rising out of the desert plain.

Senusret I rushed back from Libya upon hearing of his father's death and survived any plot against him. He would reign for another 36 years, becoming one of the most powerful pharaohs in Egypt's history. He is also buried in his own ruined pyramid just south of his father's at Lisht. The burial chambers of both pyramids were built below the water table and are now flooded. Archaeologists have never seen them.

Amenemhat's own seizure of power from Mentuhotep IV outlines an interesting problem in defining assassination. When one ruler murders another ruler and takes his place, historians don't usually consider this to be an assassination as such. However, such an act certainly fits the description, so you can consider usurpation to be a special form of assassination reserved for those who not only want to make history, but who also want to *be* history. So depending on how you look at things: Amenemhat I was either the first recorded victim of an assassination, or he was the first known assassin.

1334 to 1320 BCE

The final years of Egypt's Eighteenth Dynasty are cloaked in speculation and rumour.

Let's start with Amenhotep IV. Better known by his adoptive name of Akhenaton, this pharaoh is generally considered by scholars to be the world's first monotheist. He established the cult of Aten, worshipping the disc of the Sun, at a time when even the Jews hadn't fully accepted the idea that there was only one god.

Even though Akhenaton was Pharaoh and his word was law, his introduction of a new religion turned Egyptian society on its head and made him plenty of enemies, especially among the priesthood who had spent centuries cashing in on their myriad gods. Politically the cult of Aten was a bit of a disaster. To make matters far worse, in around the mid 1330s BCE Egypt suffered a plague of what some scholars now think was the world's first outbreak of influenza.

The Egyptians didn't know it at the time, but the flu virus may have migrated from pigs. They may have had their suspicions about this—that might even explain one of the origins of the 'unclean' status of pigs among Semitic peoples. Such speculations aside, the plague didn't help establish legitimacy for the cult of Aten. The gods appeared to be having their revenge and quite a few humans joined in too.

We don't know how Akhenaton actually died since no one has ever found his body, but he died c.1334 BCE while still a relatively young man. This may not be so suspicious, but there did follow a period of considerable instability and finagling to find a pharaoh who would restore the old gods and toe the line. First up was a mysterious pharaoh called Smenkhare who may or may not have actually been Akhenaton's widow, the famously beautiful Nefertiti. Smenkhare lasted two years before Tutankhamen came along. Here the confusion intensifies because the face that the modern world associates with Tutankhamen may actually belong to Smenkhare.

Tutankhamen was actually born Tutankhaten so in his time he went from being the 'Living image of Aten' to the 'Living Image of Amun'. We don't know if this gave him an identity crisis. To us his identity is even more obscure although he was probably the son of Akhenaton and his less famously beautiful minor wife Kiya.

The great irony of King 'Tut' is that he is far more famous in death than he ever was in life.

The great irony of King 'Tut' is that he is far more famous in death than he ever was in life. He lasted nine years on the throne (1333–1324 BCE), but hardly any of them counted, as he was too young to really rule. By the age of eighteen, he was dead.

According to a team of Egyptian scientists, who conducted a computerised tomography (CT) scan of his body in 2005, Tutankhamen sustained a severe break in his left leg. Gangrene set in relatively quickly afterwards and the young Pharaoh died. We have no way of knowing if the leg broke because of an accident, or if the accident was in some way set up.

The person who had most to gain immediately from Tutankhamen's death was the commander of the army, Horemheb, whom the young Pharaoh had named Deputy of the Lord of the two Lands and whom everyone thought was the boy king's successor.

But Horemheb had to wait a little longer. Tut's regent and vizier, Ay, managed to outmanoeuvre him. Ay had been at the centre of power a little too long, he may even have been Nefertiti's father, and he wasn't about to give up the opportunity of being a living god. It is likely that he saw his chance and took it. We know this from an extraordinary letter that archaeologists found in the ruins of Hattusa, the capital of the Hittite Empire. Although the letter is unsigned, it seems the writer was Ankhesenamum, the third daughter of Akhenaton and Nefertiti and the widow of Tutankhamen.

She wrote: 'My husband has died and I have no son. They say about you that you have many sons. You might give me one of your sons to become my husband. I would not wish to take one of my subjects as a husband.'

Nothing like this had ever happened before. The Egyptians had a famous cultural superiority complex, but the end of the Eighteenth Dynasty was a time when anything might have happened. As it turned out, after getting an envoy to investigate the legitimacy of the appeal, the Hittite monarch Supiluliuma I sent his son, Zannanza to Egypt. While on the way, Ay probably had the prince murdered and consolidated his position by marrying Ankhesenamum. Ay, however, was an old man who only lasted four years and had named his adopted son Nakhtmin to succeed him. In hindsight, Nakhtmin never stood a chance. Horemheb probably had him murdered and may also have played a part in speeding up Ay's death.

It's been well over 3000 years now and we may never know the truth, but it's possible that Horemheb's eventual succession to the throne was the culmination of a program that had begun fourteen years previously, and had led to the deaths of everyone who had ever had anything to do with the cult of Aten. If it *was* a systematic pattern of assassination, it paid off. Horemheb ruled Egypt for about 28 years and though childless himself, picked an extraordinary successor, his vizier Ramses I, who went on to found Egypt's Nineteenth Dynasty. Ramses I ruled for only two years (1292–1290 BCE) and his son Seti for eleven years (1290–1279 BCE), but his grandson Ramses II, Ramses the Great, ruled for an incredible 66 years (1279–1213 BCE) and many historians still regard his reign as Egypt's Golden Age.

History almost totally forgot Akhenaton's bold experiment. After his death his successors returned to the old ways and the records of his reign were all but obliterated. The new capital city that he built, Akhetaten (Tel-el-Amarna) is now a ruin—a virtually flat plain on a barren east bank of the Nile that is almost unrecognisable as ever having been the site of a city.

Greece

514 to 461 BCE

Although the modern English word 'tyrant' means a particularly nasty authoritarian ruler, the original Greek word, tyrannos, means 'someone who took power by force'—think military coup. That doesn't necessarily mean that the tyrant was unwanted. In fact when Peristratos of Athens (c.607–528 BCE) took over the city in 561 (and again in 559–556 BCE and again in 546–528 BCE), he did so with popular support, and his sons Hippias and Hipparchus continued the family trade of ruling Athens. It wasn't politics that did in Hipparchus though, but love.

Hipparchus became infatuated with a young man called Harmodius. The trouble was that Harmodius was already in love with Aristogeiton. Harmodius told Hipparchus he wasn't interested, and humiliatingly told his lover about Hipparchus's approach. Hipparchus then took his spite out on Harmodius' sister. He invited her to perform rites at a religious festival then disqualified her on the grounds that she wasn't a virgin. This was the sort of insult that used to get people killed. Although Aristogeiton and Harmodius hatched a carefully orchestrated plan to kill Hipparchus, becoming involved in a plot to revolt. At the moment of truth they panicked and rushed in too early, leaving themselves no means of escape. They stabbed the tyrant to death with daggers and were stabbed in turn by Hipparchus's bodyguards.

Hippias became more tyrannical in the modern sense after the death of his brother and in 508 BCE the Athenians revolted. Hippias fled to Persia where he enlisted the support of Darius I to invade Greece. The Greeks, however, soundly defeated the Persians—at the famous Battle of Marathon on the road to Athens—and had the pleasure of finally killing Hippias in 490 BCE.

The assassination of Hipparchus had forced the expulsion of Hippias and ultimately led to the foundation of democracy in Greece. As a result Harmodius and Aristogeiton became martyrs to the cause of freedom. Athens commissioned the sculptor Antenor to create a statue to the men to stand in the Athenian Agora. Although the original masterpiece was lost, many copies were made and you can see one today in the Museum of Naples.

Predictably, the road to democracy ran neither straight nor true. The Athenian reformer Ephialtes widened the scope of Athenian democracy in the year 462 BCE, only to run afoul of an oligarchal plot in 461 BCE, when he was assassinated by a rich aristocrat named Arisodicus of Tanagra. The death of Ephialtes, though, paved the way for his political ally Pericles to inherit his mantle. Pericles would later die in the Great Plague of Athens, but not before establishing democracy as a lasting institution and leading Athens into a Golden Age of 30 years of prosperity and military victory—before the Athenians screwed everything up with the Peloponnesian War.

China

465 to 423 BCE

In spite of the evidence of the bloodthirsty nature of European and Egyptian rulers of the ancient world, it would be a mistake to think they had the monopoly on assassinations. People everywhere will kill to gain power, or at least give assassination a good attempt.

A survivor's tale

The man we now know as Qin (pronounced "Chin") Shi Huang Ti was born with the given name of Zheng in 260 BCE. He would eventually become the first warlord to unify a large part of China. In fact the name China itself comes from the ancient Chinese state of Qin. The Chinese themselves have usually referred to their country as Chung Kuo (pronounced "Jung Guo") – the Middle Kingdom.

Zheng was born as a prince of the kingdom Qin in Handan, capital of the Zhao in the state of Zhao. It was common practice under feudalistic regimes for the princes of vassal states such as Qin to be held hostage by their overlords. Keeping the sons hostage was an effective way of keeping the fathers in line and Zheng was such a hostage under an agreement between Zhao and its vassal, Qin. During his time there he made friends with fellow hostage Dan, the crown prince of Yan. Zheng, as heir to the state of Qin eventually ascended the throne in 247 BCE at the age of around 12 but he remained under the thumb of a regent until he staged a palace coup in 238 BCE when he was about 21. Henceforth, throughout his subjects referred to him as the King of Qin.

It wasn't long before he began his policy of expansion and invaded the territory of his friend Dan of Yan. At the time Dan was playing host to several people, including two gentlemen by the name of Tian Guan and Jin Ke and an out-of-favour former general of the King of Chin, one Fan Yu Qi. Dan realised that he was too weak to fight Qin's army so he was gratified when Tian Guan suggested that Jin Ke could kill Qin, but they needed a pretext to see the young king. Fortunately they persuaded Fan Yu Qi that he had no hope of surviving and the general killed himself. This provided Jin Ke with a head of an enemy that he could present to Qin. Dan also provided Jin Ke with a strategic map of Yan – an offering that would lure Qin into a false sense of trust. The map would go in a case, in which Jin Ke could conceal a poisoned dagger.

Jin Ke and a youth of Yan called Qin Wu Yang then left for Qin disguised as envoys. The ruse worked and the King of Qin received them – Jin Ke carrying the head and Qin Wu Yang the map case.

Qin was paranoid even then and because having armed men in his presence made him feel nervous his guards were some distance away. Nevertheless, during the audience Qin Wu Yang began to perspire and shake while his face went white. Jin Ke acted, perhaps too quickly. He grabbed the map case, removed the dagger, grabbed one of Qin's sleeves and attempted to stab the king. Qin wrestled with the would-be assassin while struggling to unsheathe a long and unwieldy ceremonial sword. Eventually Qin succeeded in drawing the sword and seriously wounding Jin Ke before tearing away and escaping. Jin Ke threw the dagger but missed.

By now the palace guards had fallen upon the two men and Jin Ke and Qin Wu Yand entered into legend as the unsuccessful assassins of China's first emperor. Had they succeeded the nation would, undoubtedly, have been saved 17 years of war and bloodshed. The history of China might well have turned out very differently. By 221 BCE the King of Chin was 38 years old and had completed his unification program. He reigned for eleven years as emperor, but still simply called the King of Qin. During his reign he standardised weights and measures, currency and even road dimensions and the axle widths of vehicles using those roads. Most importantly, he standardised Chinese script so that educated people—who spoke entirely differently languages in his huge realm—could read and write to each other intelligibly. On the down side, he burned any books that he didn't approve of en masse, and he massacred large numbers of scholars to prevent conspiracies from people who might be tempted to outsmart him.

The King's paranoia was his undoing. As first emperor, he had intended that his realm would last ten thousand generations, but on his death on, 10 September 210 BCE, he had centralised so much power to himself that he left no strong heirs and the kingdom fell apart in civil war. He had, however, set a pattern of unification that would last for millenia. One man had proven that it could be done and the repeated unification of China would be the first goal of any aspiring dynasty worthy of the name. Eight years later, former peasant Liu Bang went on to establish the Han Dynasty, which would remain in power for over four hundred years, until 220 CE.

Throughout his life the King of Chin had tried every immortality concoction that any quack might have given him, but he prepared for death anyway. Just how thoroughly no one would know for a long time. No one knew the exact site of his mausoleum for over two thousand years. Then, in March 1974, local farmers drilling a water well in the vicinity of the ancient capital of Xian, broke through to a huge subterranean chamber. Inside were 8099 life-size terracotta warriors and horses. Scholars estimate that it

Throughout his life the King of Chin had tried every immortality concoction that any quack might have given him.

must have taken roughly three quarters of a million workers some forty years to complete Qin Shi Huang's 'virtual army'. To date the exact location of his tomb remains unknown.

Qin Shi Huang survived an assassination attempt, failed to survive death, but he nevertheless managed to achieve some sort of immortality.

The Saga of Rome

Given the serious shortcomings of the system of hereditary rule, it's hardly surprising that assassination became the primary way of removing the bully-at-the-top. In fact, there's hardly any other way of deposing him. You can't vote him out. If you tell him that you want him to go, he's likely to send the boys around and say, 'Yeah, who's gonna make me? You and whose army?' This is a fair enough question, but who can afford an army? Who has the time to round one up? It's much easier to find the right moment for a quick stab in the dark or a bit of poison.

Love them or loathe them the Romans were extremely influential. Long after the death of their empire we continue to feel the touch of their culture and history reaching out to us from the grave of their civilisation. The words that you're reading right now are written in the Roman alphabet. If the language that you speak or think in is Portuguese, Spanish, English, French, German or Italian (or any of their related languages) then you're living your life using a language that is either a direct descendant of, or heavily influenced by, Latin. A quarter of the world's population speaks such a language.

The cultures that Rome created have played major roles in the world we inhabit today.

The story of Rome lasted for over 1200 years and historians generally divide it into three major periods—Monarchy, Republic and Empire. It's a history in which the players paid for their great triumphs with the blood of the high and the low, and it's littered with millions of corpses of the nameless and hundreds of corpses of the mighty and the powerful.

Unfortunately, practically all the knowledge that we have about early Roman history comes from sources dating no earlier than the late Republican period. Writers then, as writers now, had to eat, and the rich and powerful commissioned these works to make Rome and their own families look good. Chroniclers and historians weren't about to spoil things for themselves by recording politically inconvenient facts; history, then as now, tends to be written by the winners.

It's impossible to know how much real knowledge we've lost but what has survived gives us—if nothing else—some good stories. What is clear from what survives is that assassination was one of Rome's most enduring traditions, beginning with the foundation of the city itself.

The foundation of Rome

According to legend, after the fall of Troy in 1184 BCE, the Dardanian Prince Aeneas fled the doomed city, taking with him a group of Trojan exiles including his father, Anchises, and his son, Ascanius. His wife, the Trojan princess and sister of Hector and Paris, Creusa, died in the escape. By about 1182 BCE Aeneas and the surviving Trojans had made it to the Italian peninsula. There, Aeneas became the ally of Latinus, the king of the Latins. After marrying Latinus's daughter Lavinia, Aeneas conquered the Rutuli tribe and founded the city of Lavinium. Thirty years later, in about 1150 BCE, his son Ascanius founded the city of Alba Longa. Ascanius had a son called Aeneas Silvius who also went by the name of Iulus. Iulus became the ancestor of the gens (family of) Julia, which would eventually produce Julius Caesar.

Almost 500 years later Numitor, a descendant of Iulus, inherited the throne of Alba Longa and his brother Amulius inherited the treasury. Amulius figured that since he had his hands on the purse strings he had the power, so he decided to overthrow his brother and forced Numitor's daughter, Rhea Silvia, to become a vestal virgin priestess to prevent her from having any children who might one day challenge him. Amulius, however, didn't count on the gods—and here history meets myth.

Around 772 BCE, the god Mars raped Rhea and the union produced twin sons, Romulus and Remus. Amulius ordered Rhea to be buried alive and ordered the assassination of the twins as well. The servant who was ordered to kill the infants couldn't go through with it and abandoned them in a basket on the banks of the river Tiber. The river's god, Tiberinus, flooded the river and carried the basket away to safety beneath a fig tree. There they were suckled by a she wolf, fed by a woodpecker and found by the shepherd Faustulus, who with his wife Acca Larentia raised the boys as their own in the town of Gabi, some twenty kilometres east of the future site of Rome.

As the twins grew they impressed the general populace with their beauty, strength, nobility and sense of justice—winning attributes in the ancient world. Eventually, when the young men were eighteen, they came to the attention of Numitor and Amulius. It didn't take long for everyone to work out the truth of who they were and what had happened. People generally detested Amulius and the twins had been popular even before people knew that they were the rightful heirs to the Alban throne. The twins acted quickly and killed Amulius in a lightning-fast popular uprising and coup. In a gesture of grand-filial piety, they refused the crown of Alba Longa as long as Numitor was alive and after a long overdue ceremony honouring their dead mother they left Alba Longa to found a new city.

They took with them misfits, fugitives, runaway slaves, the dispossessed and the disenfranchised. In one sense the legend of the founding of Rome is one that is similar to American and Australian history of a nation founded by people whom others had shunned.

What happened later is therefore somewhat of a pity.

Romulus wanted to build the new city on a hill called the Palatine; Remus wanted to build on the more easily defended Aventine hill, and each brother had his own group of supporters. The twins then held a competition to see into the future. The result was that Romulus saw twelve vultures in a vision, while Remus only saw six, indicating that Romulus had the support of the gods. The twelve eagles also implied that with Romulus as founder, Rome would last for 1200 years.

When Romulus began to mark the foundations of the new city's walls, Remus contemptuously jumped over the mark. The gesture was both an insult and a bad omen, implying that an enemy would easily breach the city. Romulus, furious, killed Remus on the spot. In the ensuing fight between the two groups of supporters Faustulus died too and that day Romulus buried both his brother and his adopted father. Such is the legacy of being a true son of the God of War. Romulus named the new city—officially founded on 21 April 753 BCE—after himself. He created the Roman Legions and the Senate and propagated a healthy genetic and cultural mix by encouraging the Roman men to abduct and rape the women of the neighbouring Sabine tribes.

The legend of the foundation of Rome gave a flavour of what was to follow in subsequent centuries. It is interesting to speculate that if Remus had won, the Eternal City might have been called Rema, and we would have had the Remian Empire. But would things have really turned out any differently?

From Monarchy to Republic

There would be seven kings of Rome. History knows very little about them and for all practical purposes we can consider them to be legendary. One thing is certain, early Romans tired of their kings very early and overthrew the last Roman King, Tarquinius Superbus, in 509 BCE. The overthrow resulted in the formation of the Roman Republic and consuls replaced the kings. The first consuls were named Brutus and Collatinus, and Rome would maintain a system of dual consuls for centuries—Brutus's first act was to make the Roman people swear that they would never again allow any man to be a king in Rome. It was a promise that they managed to keep in law, if not in fact, for 427 years.

The transition to empire

When you think about it, over 400 years of republicanism is about twice as long as any modern republic has actually lasted so far, so the system worked well for a long time.

As Rome grew bigger, however, it became unstable. Consuls were originally only elected for a year at a time and it became increasingly obvious that in order to have any continuity of policy or direction, you'd have to reelect the same consuls on a regular basis. Of course if a consul was too popular for too long, the Romans would become suspicious and political factions would start to fight among themselves. Infighting, of course, only made things worse. It took a while but the Roman Republic, in the form in which it was established, became untenable, and Roman government degenerated into a protracted civil war. Eventually, the Roman people in general just wanted someone to step in and make everything all right—someone strong, someone who wasn't afraid to take charge, someone who had an army behind him to keep those pesky senators—the rich white men of their day—in line. Plus ça change …

First some background:

Marcus Tulius Cicero, Gnaeus Pompeius Magnus, better known as Pompey and Gaius Julius Caesar were born within seven years of each other and died within five years of each other in the last century BCE. Their lives were interwoven in a tight mesh of destiny and loyalty and their deaths were testaments to betrayal. The stories of these three men and their assassinations marked the end of the Roman Republic and the beginning of the Empire.

Cicero had been a bright student and eventually built up a successful law practice. In a rather obvious move for a lawyer, he wanted to go into politics, but had the liabilities of being a both a commoner and a distant relative of Gaius Marius Gracchus, the general who had run foul of the establishment by supporting a form of democracy that gave more power to the people—a questionable idea at best.

History, however, was beginning to turn things upside down for Rome. Marcus Livius Drusus the Younger, Tribune of the People in 91 BCE, had fought, in the spirit of Gracchus, for the full citizenship of Roman provincials who were being taxed, but had no say in how the Senate spent their taxes. Unfortunately he was outmanoeuvred, his reforms declared invalid, and supporters of the status quo assassinated him in 91 BCE. The allied provincials revolted and started the Social War of 91–88 BCE. By the end of the Social War, the Consul Lucius Julius Caesar III (c.135–87 BCE—a distant relation to *the* Julius Caesar) enfranchised all the cities that had not taken part in the war. The move created an Assembly that could, in theory, rival the Senate and this shifted the balance of power somewhat.

General Gaius Marius and General Lucius Cornelius Sulla Felix had achieved important victories against the rebel cities, but the Senate was worried about Marius. He had already been Consul for an unprecedented six terms and some thought that his ambition would have no end. Just as the Social War ended, Mithridates VI, king of Pontus decided that he wanted to take Greece from the Romans. The Senate then had to choose between sending Marius or Sulla to stop him. The Senate chose Sulla.

Publius Sulpicius Rufus, however, was now Tribune of the People and deeply in debt. He cut a deal with Marius. Sulpicius would arrange for the Assembly to vote that Marius would fight Mithridates. In exchange, Marius would pay off Sulpicius's debts. The scheme worked and, when the Senate tried to oppose the bill authorising Marius to fight, both the general and the Tribune started a riot. The Senate feared for their lives and caved in. Sulla was furious and marched upon Rome, an unprecedented event. No Roman general with a standing army had ever entered the city, and the gesture panicked Marius and Sulpicius.

Marius tried to form an ad hoc army of gladiators, but they were no match for Sulla's legions. Marius and Sulpicius lost and both men fled. The Senate annulled Sulpicius's law authorising Marius to fight Mithridates, and in short order the Senate-supported soldiers found Sulpcious, ran him through with a sword, cut off his head and sent it to Sulla. Marius fled to Africa and Sulla marched to Greece to confront Mithridates.

In Rome, Gnaeus Octavius (an ancestor of the later Octavius Caesar) now represented Sulla's interests and Lucius Cornelius Cinna represented those of Marius. Although both men were elected Consul, fights broke out between the two factions. Marius raised an army in Africa and marched back on Rome. Sulla had created a dangerous precedent. Marius' troops went on a rampage, killing Sulla's supporters, including Octavius, and put their heads on display in the Roman forum. After five days of bloodshed Cinna's troops finally killed Sulla's troops. One hundred dead Roman nobles later the terrified Senate passed a law exiling Sulla and appointing Marius to the eastern campaign, but within a month the 71-year-old general was dead from causes that may or may not have been natural.

Sulla had a war to fight, and it wasn't until the Battle of Orchomenos in 83 BCE that he won a decisive victory for Rome which gave Asia Minor to Rome for hundreds of years and would eventually allow the transformation of Byzantium to Constantinople. All that, however, was in the distant future. Sulla marched on Rome with the help of Marcus Licinius Crassus Dives and a 24-year old Pompey against forces loyal to Cinna, who, as Consul, was still in control. Cinna didn't last long and died, assassinated in a mutiny before Sulla even came close.

Sulla secured an easy victory and in the emergency both the Senate and the Assembly appointed him Dictator—a title only bestowed in extreme crisis—in early 82 BCE. Dictators were only supposed to hold power for six months, but Sulla's appointment had no time limit and it effectively broke the promise against kingship that the Roman people had made 427 years earlier.

Sulla was no knight in shining armour. His dictatorship was a reign of vengeful terror that saw the murder of at least 1500 of the Roman nobility. One of the targets to escape was the Consul Cinna's seventeen-year-old son-in-law Julius Caesar. Caesar was married to Cinna's twelve-year-old daughter, Cornelia Cinna—known as Cinnila. Sulla demanded that Caesar divorce Cinilla, but Caesar chose love and Sulla confiscated Caesar's rather modest fortune as a result. Not long after Caesar and his wife fled Rome, Cinilla gave birth to Caesar's only legitimate Roman child, Julia.

His dictatorship was a reign of vengeful terror that saw the murder of at least 1500 of the Roman nobility.

Sulla regretted not killing Caesar outright. The historian Suetonius related that Sulla said: 'In this Caesar there are many a Marius.' Ironically, in disinheriting Caesar, Sulla also created him. Caesar's ancient lineage had set him up to be a Priest of Jupiter and this office barred him from military service. With his fortune confiscated and his birthright gone, Caesar had nothing left to lose and joined the army.

Two years later Sulla abruptly resigned the dictatorship. The decision stunned Rome, but they elected him Consul anyway. The next year he resigned from politics and, as a final whammy in his last speech to the Senate, he revealed that he had had a life-long, homosexual love affair with a Greek-born actor Metrobius. This is a bit like a retired President of the United States admitting that he'd had a life-long relationship with a male Hollywood film star.

By the following year the 60-year-old ex-dictator was dead from cirrhosis and his funeral was a huge state affair. Historians remark that Sulla's whole reign-of-terror was designed to teach Rome a terrible lesson about absolute power and that Sulla believed that Rome would never allow such a thing to happen again. If that is true then Sulla failed completely. Rome probably couldn't have had a better teacher, but Rome was an amazingly stupid student.

Pompey had risen fast under Sulla and continued to rise after his death. He distinguished himself in the campaign to recapture Spain. A Marian General, Quintus Sertorius, had become virtual ruler of Hispania, but in 72 BCE he was assassinated at a banquet by one of his own officers Marcus Perperna Vento. Strangely this didn't impress Pompey who killed Vento later in 72 BCE before finally consolidating his hold on Hispania in 71 BCE. The next year—a full seven years before the usual legal qualifying age—Pompey was elected Consul by overwhelming popular support, much to the disgust of his fellow Consul, Crassus.

Meanwhile Caesar had spent time in the east, spending time in the court of Nicomedes IV of Bithynia, so long in fact that rumours about

Caesar and Nicomedes led later enemies of the Romans to call him the 'Queen of Bithynia'. It didn't help the rumours that, when Nicomedes died in 74 BCE, he left his kingdom to Rome.

On the death of Sulla, Caesar returned to the capital, where he gained a reputation for fine oratory. Even Cicero was impressed. Here in the early 21st century the populace has a very different relationship to the spoken word and, after a lifetime of television, many people have the attention span of only one and a half music videos. Two thousand years ago, however, people valued great oratory and a man with a golden tongue could rule the world.

Caesar wasn't just a good talker, he was a doer, and he continued his rise in the military and in public life. In 69 BCE his wife Cinilla, for whom he had given up so much, died in childbirth, along with the baby. Caesar then married Pompeia, one of Sulla's granddaughters, but she was implicated in an affair with Publius Clodius Pulcher.

In 63 BCE, amid his enemies' allegations of bribery, Caesar succeeded in being elected to the post of 'Pontifex Maximus' or 'Greatest Bridge Builder', the chief priesthood in Rome and a title that carried a great deal of power and prestige. Pompeia had become a liability and Caesar divorced her, leading him to remark famously, 'Caesar's wife must be above suspicion'.

In the same year, Cicero secured the Consulship for himself and uncovered a conspiracy to overthrow the Republic, which Cicero then actively suppressed with the aid of the Senate. Cicero then publicly admonished Publius Clodius Pulcher's attempted affair with Pompeia. Clodius resented Cicero's remarks and Cicero soon fell out of favour, a victim of Clodius's increasing popularity with the common people of Rome, the plebeians. Cicero went into exile. In his capacity as Tribune of the People, Clodius confiscated Cicero's property and burnt his villas. Cicero would not return to Rome until 57 BCE when Cicero's friend, Titus Annius Papianus Milo, became Tribune of the People and after Clodius's methods of wielding power had turned opinion among the upper classes somewhat against him.

On Cicero's return the Senate passed a resolution restoring the orator's property and his houses were rebuilt at public expense. This didn't stop Clodius from personally attacking the workmen assigned to the project. Milo fought back. Clodius attempted to impeach Milo but in the general confusion of the time the matter wasn't resolved until five years later.

In 60 BCE, three years before Cicero's return, Caesar had become Senior Consul of the Roman Republic, but he had been making enemies fast. He needed a powerful ally and found one in Pompey. Pompey had become hugely popular on account of a successful campaign against piracy in the Mediterranean and dealing finishing blows to both the Seleucids and to Mithridates. The triumphs weren't just military. Pompey's conquests increased the Republic's annual tax revenues from 50 million to 85 million drachma—a rise of 70 per cent. Caesar formed an alliance with both Crassus and Pompey, forming the First Triumvirate, and Caesar sealed his relationship with Pompey by marrying off his only daughter to him.

All the ancient sources agreed that Julia and Pompey were devoted to each other in spite of their arranged marriage and 23-year age difference. But their happiness didn't last.

In 55 BCE Julia was pregnant when a crowd of rioters surrounded Pompey and stained his toga with blood. On seeing the bloody gown Julia went into shock then premature labour and lost the baby. Her health never recovered. Pregnant again the next year, the 28-year-old darling of the Roman people died in childbirth in August and her child (sources conflict on the gender) died after only a few days. She was buried on the field of Mars by special Senatorial decree.

Caesar in the meantime had partly completed his famous conquest of Gaul and was in Britain at the time of Julia's death.

In spite of Julia's personal popularity, political opposition to the Triumvirate had grown to the point where only massive bribery and corruption could secure the reelection of Crassus and Pompey. Clodius was still around and the situation was a powder keg waiting to explode. It finally did on 18 January 52 BCE when Milo and Clodius accidentally met on the Via Appia near Bovillae. Milo's gang clashed with Clodius's gang and Clodius died. In spite of Cicero's masterful defence of Milo (the surviving speech is called *Pro Milone*) the orator was playing to a hostile crowd and he wasn't able to save his friend. Milo went into exile at Massilia (modern-day Marseilles).

The murder of Clodius sparked riots that led to the burning of the Curia, the Senate House. The Senate charged Pompey with the task of suppressing the violence. When Pompey managed to restore order the Senate appointed him sole Consul—a desperate half-measure that avoided turning Pompey into a dictator.

Although Pompey had Rome, he realised that nothing was going to stop Caesar, whose military conquests and popularity were beginning to acquire a life of their own. Pompey then played a waiting game. He didn't have to wait long.

On 10 January 49 BCE General Gaius Julius Caesar, his second-in-command Marcus Antonius (Mark Antony) and his armies—victorious from their campaigns in Gaul—crossed the Rubicon River in the north east of Italy. The river marked the border between the provinces of Italia and Gallia and, in illegally crossing the border with a standing army, Caesar made it clear that he was going to invade Rome. He had reached the point of no return. As he said: 'the die is cast'.

Instead of confronting Caesar directly, Caesar's former ally and son-in-law, ordered the evacuation of Rome and his legions retreated to Brundisium in the south. Bizarrely, the Senate forgot to take the treasury with them, so Caesar confiscated it from the Temple of Saturn. Pompey and Caesar fought it out, first at Brundisium, where Pompey lost, and then at Dyrrhachium, where Caesar lost 1000 men.

Pompey failed to press his advantage, however, and was forced to flee to Greece. Pompey then lost at the Battle of Pharsalus in 48 BCE and fled to Egypt.

Caesar returned to Rome and the Senate appointed him Dictator. Caesar in turn appointed his loyal sidekick Mark Antony as Master of the Horse (one of those nifty ceremonial titles that really means second-in-command). Ever the shrewd politician, Caesar resigned the dictatorship after twelve days but graciously accepted reelection as Consul, a position that he would hold for the rest of his life. When Caesar went off to chase Pompey to Egypt, Mark Antony stayed in Rome, forgot about actually running the Republic and lived it up instead. Cicero didn't approve and did what he usually did. He made a stirring speech that roused the people and soon rioting degenerated into anarchy.

In Egypt, meanwhile, the fourteen-year-old king Ptolemy XIII Theos Philopator decided to ingratiate himself with Caesar and perhaps halt or at least delay the conquest of his country by Rome. Instead of granting Pompey asylum, the king and his regent, Pothinus, had Pompey beheaded. It was a fatal miscalculation of Roman psychology. When Caesar arrived in Egypt Ptolemy presented him with Pompey's head. Caesar was disgusted and arranged a proper Roman funeral for Pompey.

Ptolemy's 21-year-old co-ruler, his sister *and* wife Cleopatra VII used the situation to seduce Caesar. Her union with the Roman produced a child: Ptolemy XV Philopator Philometor Caesar—also known as Caesarion. Cleopatra convinced Caesar to support her claim to the Egyptian throne and Caesar agreed not to annex her country, yet. Egypt remained independent, but Caesar refused to make Caesarion his heir. Caesar already had an heir: the son of his niece, Atia, his grandnephew Gaius Octavius.

The years 48 to 45 BCE were busy ones for the Roman and Egyptian elite. With Caesar's backing, Cleopatra eliminated her brother's regent, Pothinus. Ptolemy XIII naturally objected to this and allied himself with his other sister, Arsinoe IV. Caesar and Cleopatra waged a war against them and won. In January 47 BCE Ptolemy drowned in the Nile while trying to escape. Cleopatra then made her thirteen-year-old younger brother Ptolemy XIV her co-ruler.

When he returned to Rome in early 47 BCE, Caesar brought Cleopatra and their son, installing them in a luxurious villa. He paraded Arsinoe through the streets of Rome as part of the celebrations of his Triumph, but refrained from executing her. Instead, he imprisoned her in the Temple of Ephesus. She lived another six years before Cleopatra convinced Mark Antony to assassinate her. Arsinoe was stabbed to death by Antony's soldiers on the steps of the Temple, but a least she was given an honourable funeral.

When the Triumph was over, Caesar took stock and was amazed at how quickly Mark Antony had allowed things to go to hell in his absence. He immediately dismissed Mark Antony and they didn't see each other for two years, but by 45 CE they were reconciled. Caesar spent those two years hunting down the last of his opposition, including Pompey's sons. When Caesar returned to Rome in September 45 BCE he filed his will at the Temple of Vesta. He confirmed Octavius as his heir but added that if Octavius died before him then Ceaser's friend Marcus Junius Brutus (85–42 BCE) would inherit everything.

Brutus, an arch conservative, had a talent for making money and was already a rich man, but Caesar was fond of him and his affection demonstrated yet again how blind he was to the foibles of his favourites. Caesar was certainly fond of Brutus' mother, Servilia Caepionis. They'd been having an affair for years although it is unlikely that, as rumoured, Brutus was in fact Caesar's son. Caesar would have only been fifteen at the time of fathering Brutus. Nevertheless the will, and Caesar's possible and enigmatic last words, definitely showed that Caesar felt something paternal towards Brutus.

It's hard to understand Brutus' motives for what happened next. Did he resent Caesar's affair with his mother? Perhaps his reasons were purely political. Perhaps he loved Rome more than he loved Caesar and he may have thought that Caesar's death would be for the good of the Republic. In any event Brutus and his brother-in-law Cassius and several others formed a group called the Liberators who conspired to assassinate Caesar. Certainly a lot of people among the aristocratic classes wanted Caesar dead. Just how many may even have surprised the conspirators.

At the beginning of 44 BCE the Senate had appointed Caesar Dictator Perpetuus—Dictator for Life. And there were not so subtle hints that the people wanted a king. At a public ceremony on 15 February Mark Antony even tried putting a diadem on Caesars head, but the attending crowd didn't approve and Caesar refused. Still, the fact that Mark Antony felt comfortable enough about making the gesture to make Caesar a king at all meant something. Things weren't looking too good for the senatorial aristocracy. They were still living under the illusion that they could hold on to power. Little did they know that their days as the real power in Rome were numbered.

On the night of 14 March 44 BCE Caesar's wife Calpurnia dreamt that Caesar would be assassinated and reminded him of a fortune teller's prophecy that the Ides of March (15 March) would mean his death. Caesar was troubled, but ultimately ignored her.

The next day as Caesar was entering the Senate house someone handed him a parchment detailing the conspiracy. He didn't even look at it and handed it to a servant. Mark Antony learned of the conspiracy, but arrived too late. A large group of senators ushered Caesar into a room to examine a petition—a ruse to put him off guard.

As Caesar sat down to read, Publius Servilius Casca struck at Caesar with a knife, but was so nervous that he only wounded the Dictator slightly in either the breast or the back of the neck. Caesar grabbed Casca by the hand and said, 'Villain, Casca! What are you doing?' Casca then called out to a fellow conspirator, his brother Gaius, and said

'Help, Brother' in Greek. This opened the floodgates. Up to 60 senators rushed in to stab the dictator. In their enthusiasm some even managed to injure each other.

Plutarch says that Caesar was silent during the attack, but also reports that some say that Caesar's last words were muttered to Brutus. In Greek, Caesar said: 'You too, child?' He died with 23 wounds in his body, sprawled before a statue of Pompey. Brutus ran out into the Forum and cried out, 'People of Rome, once again we are free.'

Up to 60 senators rushed in to stab the dictator. In their enthusiasm some even managed to injure each other.

But they were nothing of the sort. A power struggle broke out and Rome descended into civil war, again.

In a spirit of prudence Cleopatra and Caesarion returned to Egypt.

Cicero made a speech in the Senate, denouncing Caesar and condemning Mark Antony's witch-hunt of the dictator's murderers. So convincing were Cicero's arguments that the Senate granted amnesty to the assassins. Cicero went further and began a series of speeches (the Philippics) praising Octavius and urging the Senate to label Mark Antony an enemy of the state. In a letter to Cassius he wrote:

> *I am pleased that you like my motion in the Senate and the speech accompanying it … Antony is a madman, corrupt and much worse than Caesar, who you declared the worst of evil men when you killed him. Antony wants to start a bloodbath.*

Meanwhile the nineteen-year-old Octavius had inherited Caesar's huge fortune and the Caesar name but even more crucially the loyalty of the Roman people. He consolidated his political and military position and formed a second triumvirate with Mark Antony and one of Caesar's oldest supporters, Marcus Aemilius Lepidus. The formation of the Triumvirate effectively marked the end of the Republic. It also marked the failure of Cicero to drive a wedge between the two men closest to Caesar. The Triumvirate used their newfound power to hunt their enemies down. History records that Octavius was against it, but in the end the Senate turned on Cicero and branded him and his supporters 'enemies of the state'. This gave Mark Antony all the excuse he needed. In December 43 BCE, under Antony's orders, soldiers caught up with Cicero at Formia, halfway between Rome and Naples. Cicero's last words were: 'There is nothing proper about what you are doing soldier, but try to kill me properly.' The soldiers decapitated the 63-year-old and the Triumvirate displayed his head and hands in the Forum. Fulvia, Mark Antony's wife, took further revenge by pulling out Cicero's tongue and jabbing it repeatedly with a hairpin.

The next year in 42 BCE, Antony confronted Cassius and Brutus in two engagements at the Battle of Philippi in north-east Greece. Cassius committed suicide after the first battle and Brutus followed his lead soon after Antony's decisive victory in the second.

Antony might have had his revenge, but he had also reached his pinnacle. The Triumvirate's instabilities were about to reveal themselves, although it seemed that initially the three men had done what they could to make it work, Octavius going so far as to marry Mark Antony's stepdaughter, Clodia Pulchra.

Octavius' marriage to Clodia Pulchra was loveless and was never consummated. He returned her to her mother Fulvia, according to him, 'in mint condition'.

Fulvia herself tried to fight Octavius by forming an alliance with her husband's brother Lucius Antonius. Octavius forced them to surrender at Perusia in Etruria (the Etruscan homeland) in early 40 BCE. With typical magnanimity Octavius spared their lives. He sent Lucius to Spain as governor whereupon the fate of Mark Antony's brother is unknown. Fulvia was exiled to Sicyon in Greece, but fell ill there suddenly and died.

The now widowed Mark Antony married Octavius' elder sister, Octavia minor, and moved to Athens. This marriage was designed to sustain the alliance between Antony and Octavious, but became instead the final cause for a breach.

Keen to rule the world through strategic childbearing, Cleopatra seduced Mark Antony while he was visiting Egypt. Their union produced three children: twins Alexander Helios and Cleopatra Selene II and Ptolemy Philadelphus.

Octavius, meanwhile, became infatuated with Livia Drusilla, a young, beautiful, married mother of two. In 39 BCE, he 'forced' her to divorce her husband and he married the nineteen-year-old in January 38 BCE. Livia brought two sons to the union from her previous marriage: Tiberius Claudius Nero who would later become the Emperor Tiberius and his brother Nero Claudius Drusus would be the father of an emperor and the gradfather of another.

Octavius managed to get rid of Lepidus, fellow Triumvirate member, in 36 BCE. The de facto Emperor of Rome exiled him, but Lepidus managed to live for over twenty more years in peace and obscurity before dying in 13 BCE. But Mark Antony's conduct called for stronger measures. In allying himself with Cleopatra, Mark Antony had humiliated both his wife Octavia and her brother.

Despite the immediate consequences of his affair it is interesting to note the future outcome of Mark Antony's and Octavia's marriage. Mark Antony and Octavia had two daughters. The elder daughter, Antonia Major, aka Antonia the Elder, would eventually become the grandmother of the Emperor Nero (through her son, Lucius Domitius). The younger daughter, confusingly named Antonia Minor, aka Antonia the Younger, would eventually marry Tiberius' younger brother Drusus. The union of Drusus and Antonia Minor would produce three children who survived into adulthood: Germanicus Caesar, Claudia Livia Julia (Livilla) and Tiberius Claudius Drusus Nero Germanicus. All three would play pivotal roles in the early empire.

Germanicus Caesar fathered several children, the most important of which were Gaius Julius Caesar Augustus Germanicus, better known to history as the Emperor Caligula and Julia Agrippina, wife to her second cousin Lucius Domitius and the mother of Emperor Nero. Livilla would mother Tiberius Gemellus. 'Gemellus' is Latin for 'twin', but Tiberius' twin Germanicus did not survive infancy. Although Tiberius would later name Caligula and Gemellus joint heirs Caligula would have his cousin Gemellus beheaded as a political inconvenience under the pretext of plotting against him within a few months of his accession.

It is therefore deeply ironic that, while Mark Antony ultimately lost politically and militarily to Octavius, he would win the empire genetically, through his heirs in the decades to come, while *none* of Octavius's blood heirs would survive.

Antony's daughter, Antonia Minor, outlived all her children except Claudius and, when she was 72, she would commit suicide in protest at Caligula's reign, but that was decades in the future. Meanwhile …

Antony and Cleopatra

Initially, in spite of the abominable way that he'd dealt with his wife and brother-in-law, Mark Antony did try to make overtures of reconciliation, but Octavius realised that Mark Antony's character was a destabilising force, and that Rome could really only have one master. Octavius was determined it should be him. He had the support of the army and of the people. Nobody particularly liked Antony's 'whore' Cleopatra and they were increasingly hostile towards Antony himself. The real problem was that Mark Antony's infatuation with Cleopatra had led him to declare that Caesarion, as the natural son of Caesar, was Caesar's *real* heir and so took precedence over an adopted heir, such as Octavius. Adoption was a time-honoured Roman institution. Many of Rome's elite had inherited their wealth and power through adoption and Anthony's implication was insulting. The Senate was outraged and, on the last day of 33 BCE, deprived Antony of his power and placed themselves entirely in Octavius' hands.

The final confrontation at the Battle of Actium in Greece in 31 BCE was somewhat of a rout. In this famous naval battle Octavius had better and fresher crews in smaller and more manoeuvrable ships than Antony's. Cleopatra's ships didn't even engage the Romans. Historians have speculated that even at the end Cleopatra was hedging her bets. If she had been, then she had gravely miscalculated. Actium led to Antony's decisive defeat and the declaration of Octavius as Priceps (First Citizen) Augustus. The 2 September 31 BCE therefore marks the end of the Roman Republic and the beginning of the Roman Empire.

Antony had originally started with a larger army than Octavius, but the behaviour of the Egyptians and the totality of the naval engagement losses caused Antony's armies to desert en masse. Antony ran back to Egypt, but after another army desertion, Mark Antony realised that it was all over for him and he fell on his sword in late July 30 BCE. Octavian officially annexed Egypt into the Roman Empire on 1 August 30 BCE when he marched into Alexandria.

In Alexandria, Theodorus, the tutor of Antyllus, Fulvia and Mark Antony's son, betrayed Antyllus to Octavius. Octavius beheaded the young man, arrested Theodorus on a charge of stealing a jewel from Antyllus and then ordered his crucifixion. Antyllus' younger brother would later become the lover of Julia the Elder, Octavius's daughter. He would be accused of conspiracy to assassinate the Priceps and he would be executed in 2 BCE. Julia would be exiled.

Cleopatra tried to negotiate terms of surrender, but she had nothing to negotiate with and in August 30 BCE she famously committed suicide by poisoning herself with a snake, although the animal of choice was more likely to have been a cobra rather than the asp of legend, for the simple reason that cobras were more common, and their poison less painful.

Before her death, Cleopatra sent seventeen-year-old Caesarion to the port of Berenice on the Red Sea with the plan to send him on to the safety of India. It did no good. Octavian had Caesarion assassinated within days. His pretext was that there were simply 'too many Caesars'. The death of Caesarion marked the end of the Ptolemaic Pharaohs.

Octavius was kinder to Cleopatra's other children. Initially he paraded them in triumph through the streets of Rome bound in gold chains, but having made his political point Octavius sent them to live with his sister, Octavia. There is no record of what Octavia thought about having to bring up her husband's 'bastards'. While in the care of Octavia, Ptolemy Philadelphus died at the age of six, probably from a childhood illness aggravated by the Roman winter. Alexander Helios died no later than 25 BCE at the age of fourteen, possibly for similar reasons to his brother. His twin sister, Cleopatra Selene, would have a very different fate.

In 26 BCE Octavius arranged for her marriage to King Juba II of Numidia. Their rule there didn't last long—a revolution forced them to establish a rule in Caesarea, Mauritania (modern Cherchell, Algeria). They had a son, Ptolemy of Mauritania and a daughter, Drusilla.

Cleopatra Selene died in 7 CE, and her husband and son ruled Mauritania as joint kings until Juba's death.

Ptolemy married Julia Urania and they had a daughter, Drusilla of Mauritania. While Ptolemy was in Rome visiting his second cousin, Caligula, the client king of the Empire made a great impression on the people. Unfortunately he was too popular. Fearing a rival for his people's love Caligula ordered Ptolemy's murder, on the grounds of the common pretext of treason. After her father's assassination Drusilla grew up in Rome and Emperor Claudius later married her off to the Roman Governor of Judea, Antonius Felix. After their divorce she married King Sohameus of Emesa. Their daughter, Iotapi, was an ancestor of Zenobia of Palmyra. Zenobia later held a kingdom independent from Rome before the Emperor Aurelian captured her in 272. Impressed by Zenobia's beauty and bearing, Aurelian let Zenobia live. She later married a Roman senator and historians believe that their children and their descendants lived well into the fourth century

CE. In this sense Mark Antony and Cleopatra's line outlasted the Roman Empire itself.

In the short term, however, Cicero's son, Marcus Tulius Cicero Minor had the last laugh. Upon Mark Antony's defeat he announced the death of his father's murderer to the Senate, tore down his statues and cancelled all the honours the ex-hero had ever been awarded. The works of Cicero survive today only because, long after the Roman Empire was gone, the early Catholic Church declared him a 'righteous pagan' and went to special efforts to preserve his work for posterity.

With the death of his rivals, Octavius, the heir of Caesar, became the undisputed leader of Rome and, although he officially returned to power in 27 BCE, the posturing about him being only a priceps—a first among equals—was all a bit of a sham. In his time his rule was known as a Principate, but history would remember Octavius as the Emperor Augustus.

Cleopatra's Palace, the site of so much intrigue and bloodshed is no longer with us. The eastern harbour of Alexandria subsided in a series of earthquakes in the fourth century CE. In a series of remarkable surveys between 1987 and 2005 underwater archaeologist Frank Goddio uncovered the ruins of Cleopatra's palace and you can see the result of his work at: *www.franckgoddio.org/Default.aspx*.

Imperial Rome

History, for the most part, is the study of thugs. The thousands of years of recorded human history is basically one long chronicle of self-aggrandising, ego-driven bullies who manage to con or force hundreds, thousands and millions of people to do things their way—or else.

Some cultural and political systems lend themselves to more brutality than others and the system that Augustus set up in the Roman Empire really wasn't much of an improvement on the Roman Republic's rule of plutocrats. The strength of the Empire depended on the abilities of the people at the top, but there is nothing in a hereditary monarchy that guarantees the quality of ruling offspring. Nor is there anywhere that the populace can return their leaders to for a refund, if found faulty.

Then there are those ever-present cronies and thugs. The cronies are the political types who keep the system running for their own benefit, but what the serious despot needs is the thugs—the gang, the muscle who will do all your dirty work, people like the German Praetorian Guard.

Given the serious shortcomings of the system of hereditary rule, it's hardly surprising that assassination became the primary way of removing the bully-at-the-top. In fact, there's hardly any other way of deposing him. You can't vote him out. If you tell him that you want him to go, he's likely to send the boys around and say, 'Yeah, who's gonna make me? You and whose army?'

This is a fair enough question, but who can afford an army? Who has the time to round one up? It's much easier to find the right moment for a quick stab in the dark or a bit of poison. Assassination is also a good way to get rid of rivals before they become trouble. You'll be forgiven then for thinking that the Roman Empire wasn't so much a government but a huge protection racket run by a bunch of mafia-like families jostling for the job of making offers that no one could refuse.

Then again, aren't all governments protection rackets, to some extent?

A truly exhaustive account of all the assassinations of the Roman Empire would be both exhausting and depressing, so I won't bore you with the full details, so let's just recap on some big names.

The Julio-Claudians

Upon the accession of Augustus it seemed that the killing had stopped but the respite was brief. Although Augustus and Livia married young and had already proven that they could have children with other people, in their entire 51-year marriage they bore no offspring. Livia and Augustus managed only to produce one miscarriage. Augustus had one daughter, Julia, and no direct male heirs. Who might then have inherited the Empire? As a matter of fact, lots of people, all of whom managed to die either in battle or from 'mysterious causes'. You can find the best account of this period of Roman history in Robert Graves's books I Claudius and Claudius the God or renting the superb BBC television adaptation. Although the events of I Claudius are highly fictionalised, one could argue that fiction is really about all we have. The surviving histories of the time were, for the most part, not written at the time of events the record and the historians who wrote them were in the pay of later emperors—who had solid political reasons for tarnishing the reputations of their predecessors.

So we have the account of the Emperor Tiberius and his dalliances with pre-pubescents in the swimming pool of his villa on the island of Capri. As a result of his sexual obsessions, Tiberius left the running of his empire to the Prefect of the Praetorian Guard, Sejanus.

Now, Livilla may have been the older sister of the future emperor Claudius, but she was also the widow of Tiberius's son Julius Caesar Drusus (Drusus the Younger). Sejanus and Livilla had been lovers even before the untimely death of Drusus. Now Sejenus and Livilla virtually ruled Rome for a time until Tiberius paid enough attention to have Sejanus executed in 31 CE. A week later Apicata, Sejanus's former wife, killed herself, but not before denouncing Livilla to Tiberius and revealing that Livilla had assassinated Drusus. In response, Livilla's mother—Antonia the Younger—locked her daughter in her house and starved her to death.

Tiberius spent the last six years of his reign in Capri and it seems he spent nearly all his time molesting children. While the emperor dallied the empire virtually ran on autopilot.

Some say that his successor, Caligula, hastened his death when he either ordered, or stood by, while the Prefect of the Praetorian Guard, Quintus Macro, smothered the 79-year-old Emperor with a pillow.

Caligula

Writers have had a lot to say about Caligula and nearly all of it is bad. History remembers his reign as one long exercise in depravity. Stories include his incestuous relationships with his sisters, his insanity and tyranny. He was certainly ungrateful and had his henchman Macro executed a year into his reign.

As a ruler Caligula was amazingly profligate. He had inherited a treasury from Tiberius that was twenty times larger than the one Tiberius inherited from Augustus, yet Caligula managed to spend it all in a few years on feasts, orgies, public works in his honour and, most importantly, on gladiatorial games—the Romans were big on bloodbaths. As a result he was extremely popular with the people and it helped that he was the son of the much-loved Germanicus.

In fact he was so loved that the ruling classes dared not act against him openly for fear that his assassination would lead to civil war. The other major obstacle was the German Praetorians, who were faithful to Caligula both for being the son of Germanicus and also because the Emperor spent lavishly to keep them happy. So senators and aristocrats died on Caligula's whim while the young Emperor did everything except actually run the Empire.

There are a variety of theories to explain why Caligula was crazy, but it could just be that it's hard to hold onto your sanity when your family seem to spend most of their time killing each other and you never know when you'll be next. Caligula's older brothers Nero Iulius Caesar Germanicus and Drusus Caesar hadn't survived Tiberius's paranoia. Both were arrested for treason and starved to death in prison. His mother Julia Vipsania Agrippina, 'Agrippina the Elder', had died in prison, starved and brutalised. The years of madness all around him may have unhinged Caligula as far back as his childhood. For the most salacious account of Caligula's reign, read Suetonius's *The Twelve Caesars*.

For all his follies among the upper classes Caligula remained extremely popular with the people, who mostly benefited from the Emperor's insanity. But by early January 41 CE even some of the Praetorians had had enough. Cassius Chaerea in particular may have wanted to kill Caligula on both personal and political grounds. Chaerea was the head of the Praetorians and it was customary for the emperor to give him a daily watchword. This was a code to let a guard know that the man who was replacing him on duty was legitimate. Caligula was wont to give Chaerea humiliating watchwords like 'erection' or 'kiss me quick', but it may also be that the Julio-Claudians seemed to be degenerating into madness and Chaerea simply thought that he could do a better job as Emperor with both hands tied behind his back.

Chaerea managed to get quite a few senators and Praetorians in on the conspiracy. On 24 January Caligula was instructing an acting troupe on celebrations in honour of the Divine Augustus when Charea struck. The assassins stabbed Caligula about 30 times. A few minutes later another Praetorian assassin killed Caligula's wife Caesonia, then picked up their daughter, Julia Drusilla. Julia had a reputation for viciousness and she apparently attacked her mother's murderer screaming, biting and clawing, before the soldier grabbed her by the ankles and, swinging the child's body, dashed her head against a wall.

The Senate tried to restore the Republic but couldn't stand up against the Praetorians. The Praetorian Guard mostly comprised men from the tribes of Germania. They liked living in Rome with its culture, good food, fine wine and pleasant climate. They weren't about to end up unemployed and living in some hovel in the Iron Age of the freezing north. The Praetorians knew that the Imperial system was the best arrangement for them and they elevated Caligula's uncle Claudius to the Principate.

They really didn't have much of a choice. The Imperial Family had generally regarded Claudius, with his limp and stammer, as a non-starter. Paradoxically, no one had ever thought that he was worth assassinating. As a result, this intellectual, historian and author of a Latin–Etruscan dictionary (now, alas, lost) was the only member of his family left to assume the crown. In the aftermath of Caligula's assassination Chaerea was arrested. He requested that he be executed with the same sword that had killed Caligula. Claudius granted his request and pardoned nearly all the other assassins.

Legend/history has it that Claudius too was assassinated, eventually succumbing to poisonous mushrooms fed to him by his wife and niece Agrippina the Younger—the only surviving sister of Caligula—in order to ensure the succession of her son, Nero. Nero himself ordered the murder of his mother a few years before being forced to commit suicide. With Nero's death came the end of the Julio Claudians, a transition so chaotic that 69 CE saw the murder of three emperors before Vespasian finally brought things under control in December of that year.

Assassination ended the reign of several more emperors. The usual cause of their murders was infighting among the military. These emperors made the classic mistake of winning a victory then doling out the goodies to favourites, while ignoring those people who felt they warranted a slice of the war-booty pie too. Resentment will get you every time.

The most famous assassination of the later Roman Empire was that of the megalomaniac Commodus who spent more time renaming the months of the year and even the city of Rome after himself than actually running the empire.

After a brief second wind in the third century, the Western Empire entered its slow decline until those pesky German tribes under Odoacer sacked Rome in 476 CE. Unsurprising really, when you consider that as far back as the reign of Caligula the empire had depended on German Praetorians and later, German conscripts to maintain the status quo. Odoacer's main rival was Theodoric of the Ostragoths. In a gesture of civility Odoacer and Theodoric signed a peace treaty. At the banquet to celebrate the treaty, however, Theodoric strangled Odoacer with his bare hands. The new world order was starting off in just the same way as Rome had 1229 years before.

From the Dark Ages to the Enlightenment

For assassinations to count, you really do need organised, centralised power or at least a figurehead whom you can blame for all your troubles and then want to kill. Let's take a look now at a part of the world where people washed regularly and leave the Dark Ages to Europe, where they belong.

It's a little bit Eurocentric to call the years from 500 to 1000 the 'Dark Ages'. The collapse of the Roman Empire and the general barbarity in Europe in that period is only part of the global picture. The ancestors of the future 'Western' nations would be picking lice out of their crotches and living in a climate of superstitious dread for at least 1000 years, while they waited for the Renaissance in around 1500, but other cultures were keeping the flame of civilisation alive and even flourishing. Of particular note is the rise of Islam and its enlightened attitude to scientific enquiry, culture and better hygiene than the Europeans.

Early Muslim assassinations

The foundation of Islam had its fair share of political killings and the Muslim nations would be as prone to assassination as any other. One very early example demonstrates just how far back the Muslim—Jewish enmity goes. In 624 the prophet Muhammad scored a major victory against his pagan enemies, the dominant ruling tribe of Mecca, the Banu Quraish, at the Battle of Badr. Although Muhammad later pardoned many of his enemies, he executed a number of Meccan nobles after the battle.

K'ab ibn al-Ashraf was the chief of a Jewish tribe in Medina, the Banu Nadir. He was disgusted with the Quraish executions and travelled to Mecca to deliver a eulogy in which he encouraged the survivors to continue their struggle. As a poet, K'ab also took his revenge in verse and wrote a number of erotic poems about Muslim women, specifically designed to offend the Prophet.

Muhammad felt that K'ab had slighted the honour of his people and called for the assassination of the Jewish chief. One of the prophet's followers, Muhammad ibn Maslamah led a group to K'ab under the pretext of defecting from Muhammad and wanting to purchase food. On a moonlit night they lured K'ab out of his fortress and killed him. A later, unnamed Muslim historian recounts that, in the aftermath 'there was not one Jew who did not fear for his life.' Soon after the assassination Muhammad drove the Banu Nadir out of Medina.

Muhammad's early victories often came against the odds and they certainly gave the impression that God was on his side, but when the prophet died he had no son to succeed him. Like Alexander the Great almost a thousand years before him, the question of who would be the leader of a people degenerated into a squabble among his followers and the issue remains unresolved to this day.

Shi'a Muslims believed, and still believe, that Muhammad's intention was that his cousin and son-in-law Ali ibn Abi Talib should succeed him. Sunni Muslims, the numerical majority of Muslims, believed that succession should be in accordance with the traditional Arab mandate of the people. In this case, the people's chosen successor was Abu Bakr, and after the prophet's death it was Bakr who became the first Caliph. Although in his two-year rule he won some important military victories, historians credit him for doing something much more important. Abu Bakr and Umar ibn Al-Khattab were instrumental in preserving the Qu'ran in written form. In 634, on Bakr's more-than-likely natural death, but which one tradition ascribes to poison, the Caliphate passed to 53-year-old Umar.

Umar's reign oversaw the lightning expansion of Islam, in particular against Byzantium, the successor of the Roman Empire. After the Battle of Yarmuk, fought near Damascus in 636, the Eastern Romans permanently lost control of the territory south of Anatolia. Another of Umar's successes was the taking of Jerusalem in 637 after a long siege. Upon entering Jerusalem he prayed on a rock in the city. Jewish tradition states that this was the rock on which Abraham almost sacrificed his son Isaac, where Jacob saw the ladder to heaven and where the Ark of the Covenant was placed in the First Temple. Muslim tradition asserts that it was the place where Muhammad was taken to heaven in the company of the Angel Gabriel to receive the wording of Islamic prayers from Moses. The rock is now the site of the Dome of the Rock, built 55 years after Umar's prayers.

For all his successes Umar was a humble man who lived frugally. Perhaps he was too frugal. Abu-Lu'lu'ah—known as Firoz—was a Persian Zoroastrian, or perhaps a Christian (historians aren't sure), and a slave owned by the Governor of Kufa, Mugheera ibn Shu'ba. Umar had given Mugheera permission for Firoz to live in Medina where he earned a living as a carpenter. As a slave he had to give a large portion of his wages to his owner. He sought an audience with Umar begging him to reduce the taxes he was paying to Mugheera. Umar refused, citing that Firoz's skill could earn him much more money than he needed. An infuriated Firoz vowed revenge for the rebuff and he hid in the Medina Mosque to lie in wait. When Umar came into the mosque for his prayers in the early morning in November 644, Firoz came out of hiding and stabbed him several times. Firoz slashed his way out of the mosque, but, as Umar's defenders sought to overpower him, Firoz stabbed himself. There is an elaborate tomb dedicated to Firoz in Kashan, Iran, suggesting that the assassin is a hero to the Shi'a Muslims at least.

Umar lived for two days with a gaping wound around his navel. Upon his death he was buried alongside Muhammad and Abu Bakr in the Al-Masjid an-Nabawi (the Mosque of the Prophet) in Medina.

Umar was by no means the last Muslim leader to die at the hands of an assassin. In late 1121 al-Malik Shahanshah, the Vizier (equivalent to a Prime Minister) of the Fatimid Caliphs of Egypt, died when the new Caliph, 25-year-old al-Amir Bi-Ahkamillah decided that he resented the Vizier's power.

Historical sources lament the passing of an able and astute administrator. Nine years later al-Amir himself would fall to an assassin—a victim of the power struggles between the Nizari faction of the Shi'a and the Mustali tribe.

The Hashashin

The Shi'a Muslims gave rise to various sects, all of whom believed that there were differing numbers of Imams (divinely appointed leaders) in different paths of succession. The largest of these branches is the Twelvers, who comprise 80 per cent of Shi'a and believe that there have been only twelve Imams. The second largest branch are the Nizariyya Ismaili who count 49 Imams to date.

The current Imam is Prince Karim al-Hussayni, the Fourth Agha Khan and a direct descendant of Muhammad through the prophet's daughter Fatima and her husband Ali. To make matters more complicated still, the subgroup of Ismaili Muslims called the Mustaali believe that the succession of Imam's continued through whom they and other sects think of as the ninth Fatimid Caliph, al-Mustaali (who died in 1101), whereas the Nizari Ismaili's believe that the rightful ninth Caliph was al-Mustaali's elder brother, Al-Nizar. It's all very confusing but people have died and the course of history changed over such quibbles.

Whatever the arguments, it's the Nizaris who are of particular interest to the history of assassination. Hasan-I Sabbah was an Iranian Nizari missionary who converted a community in Alamut in the Alborz Mountains in Northern Iran in 1090. Over the next three decades he consolidated the formation of an austere, mystical branch of Islam, the Hashashin, whom even contemporary Muslims regarded with suspicion. Little is known about the Hashashin, but they were politically aligned with the Shi'a Fatimid Caliphs of Egypt, so they were also by definition opposed to the Sunni Abbasid Caliphs of Baghdad and dedicated to their elimination. To this end Hasan trained killers to target rulers.

There is still considerable dispute as to where the term 'Hashashin' came from, but it appears to lead to the English 'assassin' and originates perhaps from 'followers of Hasan' or 'users of hashish'. The latter theory comes from the legend of the indoctrination process into the cult.

Apparently new recruits were exhausted, starved, sleep deprived or isolated to the point that they believed that they were on the verge of death, then given a large quantity of hashish. They would fall asleep, only to wake in a garden being served food and wine by beautiful virgins. The recruit would be told that this was heaven and that the way to reach it was by obeying Hasan (and his later successors, all titled 'Sabbah') in all things—including suicidal assassinations if necessary. Eventually the recruit would sleep again only to awake in the 'real' world, forever pining for his lost paradise and willing to do anything to get it back.

The assassins themselves were known as 'Fedaviyan' from the Arabic 'Fidaiiyiin' or 'Those Who Are Ready To Sacrifice Their Lives For The Cause'. Their dedication was required, as few if any assassins ever survived their attempts, successful or otherwise. As you see there is nothing new about suicidal terrorists dreaming of a 'heavenly reward'.

Over time the Hashashin refined their skills and their mystique and fame grew out of all proportion to their numbers, and eventually one could buy their services to murder anyone for any reason at all regardless of their political affiliation. This might seem mercenary, but it was logical. The Hashashin knew that their best chance of survival lay not in head-on confrontation but in keeping their political enemies so busy at each others' throats that they would be too occupied to go after a small group of Muslim 'heretics'.

The situation was win/win or lose/lose all round—depending on your level of cynicism. Many Muslim leaders made use of the Hashashins' services to kill infidels and their own people, such as the Fatimid Vizier al-Malik Shahanshah, alike. The leaders of the Crusade, Raymond II, Conrad of Montferrat and Philip of Montfort, all died at the hands of Hashashin. In fact Raymond II was the first non-Muslim victim of the Hashashin. Even Jagatai, the son and successor of Genghis Khan supposedly became one of their victims in 1241, and King

Edward I of England, was wounded by a Hashashin's poisoned dagger in 1271, when he was still a prince.

The Great Saladin, Muslim general and conqueror extraordinaire and smiter of the crusaders, so respected the power of the Hashasin that he left them mostly alone.

Aside from their lasting contribution of a single word across many languages to describe politically motivated murder, the Hashashin themselves now provide just a footnote to history. On 15 December 1256 the Mongols, under Hulagu Khan, destroyed the Hashashin base at Alamut and burned the sect's records. What we know of them today comes almost exclusively from outside sources.

Although they lost their political power, they remained a decentralised force for some time before disappearing from history in the 1300s. Hulagu Khan would go on to capture Baghdad and after a siege lasting less than two weeks he took the city on 10 February 1258 and achieved what the Hashashin had set out to do over 150 years before—obliterate the Abbasid Caliphate. In destroying Baghdad, Hulagu also destroyed its great library and the accumulated knowledge of centuries. As many as a million people may have died in the sacking. The city was depopulated and left a ruined shell for hundreds of years. Hulagu, grandson of Genghis and brother of Kublai, died relatively peacefully in 1265.

Muslim Egypt

Over a hundred years after the death of al-Amir the Mameluks were in charge of Egypt. They'd styled themselves 'Sultans' a term that suggests absolute monarchy under Shariah (Muslim religious law) but without the burden of Caliphs, who claimed to be the rightful heirs of Muhammad.

Saif ad-Din Qutuz was born a prince, but had been captured by the Mongols when a teenager and sold as a slave. In Syria he was onsold to an Egyptian slave merchant who sold him to Aybak. For both Aybak and Qutuz it turned out to be the deal of a lifetime.

Back in 1171 Saladin had won the Egyptian throne from the last of the Fatimids and had established the Ayyubid Sultanate. Decades later, in around 1250, a Mameluk general called Aybak would wrest Egypt from the Ayyubids but the fall of Saladin's dynastic legacy had a little help from Shajara al-Dur.

Shajara, whose name means "Tree of Pearls", was one of those fascinating women from the past who is often ignored by conventional histories. Not just another slave-born harem girl, Shajara established a firm powerbase after marrying the Ayyubid Sultan As-Salih Ayyub. When Ayyub died she concealed his death long enough to make sure her own cronies were well-placed and so she was able to hold onto power after his death even though Ayyub was succeeded by his son, Sultan Turanshah. For an Egyptian Sultan, Turanshah committed a very Roman mistake. After a stunning military victory over the Crusader, King Louis IX of France in February 1250, he awarded too many titles to his cronies without respect for the status quo. The Mameluks under Aybak, who had supported Turansha, objected to the division of power and murdered him. Shajara then reigned briefly on her own as Sultana—the only woman in Muslim history to do so—before she and Aybak decided on a marriage of expediency, both consolidating their respective power bases. Although Al-Ashraf II succeeded Turanshah for a few months the Ayyubids were effectively finished, and on his death Aybak became the first Mameluk Sultan.

Over the years Aybak had come to trust his slave Qutuz to the point of making him Regent for his son al-Mansur Ali. At first Aybak was busy fighting wars while Shajara stayed in Egypt and remained the de facto ruler. However, Aybak eventually decided that Shajara had outlived her usefulness and that he wanted to divorce her and get a new wife. When Shajara found out, she took action. In 1257 she lured Aybak to her bath whereupon her eunuchs murdered him. Almost immediately Qutuz assumed control. He arrested Shajara and took her to his mother's house. There her slaves beat Shajara to death before throwing her body over the wall of the Citadel of Cairo.

Qutuz consolidated *his* power, finally eliminating Aybak's son, al-Mansur Ali, in 1259, thus becoming the Sultan of Egypt. His greatest achievement was joining up with the Mameluk general al-Malik al-Zahir Rukn al-Din Baibars al-Bunduqdari—simply known as Baibars—and routing the Mongol invasion of the Middle East under the Christian Mongol warlord Kitbuqa. The victory at the Battle of Ain Jalut in 1260 wasn't just a military triumph; it was hugely important from the point of view of propaganda. It was the first time in history that the Mongols had ever been defeated in battle.

The happy partnership of Qutuz and Baibars didn't last however. Baibars wanted the Governorship of the city of Aleppo, as a reward for helping Qutuz, but instead Qutuz have Aleppo to one Ala al-Din Ali. A month later while on a hunt with the Sultan, Baibars had his revenge and assassinated him.

Baibars became the next Sultan of Egypt. Like Qutuz, he had also been a slave and reigned for seventeen years before dying of natural causes in Syria. Muslim historians remember him fondly for having beaten the Crusaders in three separate crusades.

Al-Malik Al-Ashraf Khalil would be the next Mameluk Sultan to be assassinated—by his Turkish Regent, Baydara. Al-Malik's mistake was to favour Circassian troops from Northwest Caucasus over Turkish Mameluks.

Baydara declared himself Sultan, but his reign lasted for about five minutes before the Circassians assassinated him in turn. Khalil's eight-year-old brother al-Nasir Muhammad then became Sultan. He was overthrown a year later by Baydara's former supporter Katbugha. Forces loyal to al-Nasir managed to reclaim the throne for him in 1298, but he lost it again between 1298 and 1308. When he finally reclaimed the throne at the age of 23, he kept it for life. His traumatic childhood must have affected him somewhat, because he became an aggressive and powerful military leader. One of his wives was even a great-great-granddaughter of Genghis Khan. Upon his death *eight* of his sons would become successive sultans of Egypt. You can imagine what the family dynamics were like.

Europe

Between the years 500 and 1000 Europe wasn't exactly the festering hotbed of intrigue that the Muslim world was, for reasons mentioned above. Political murders in Europe held a little less intrigue, with leaders generally killing each other on the battlefield. Nonetheless the Dark Ages did have a few notable assassinations.

Bohemia

Václav I grew up in a typically dysfunctional aristocratic family and became Duke of Bohemia upon the death of his father Vratislav I in 921. His paternal grandmother, the fervently Christian Saint Ludmila then brought him up for seven months until Václav's pagan mother, Drahomíra, had two Bohemian noblemen strangle the old woman with her own veil. Drahomíra was then effective ruler of Bohemia until her son had her exiled in 925.

Ludmilla's influence on her grandson had stuck and Václav became a fervent Christian, to the ire of much of the Bohemian nobility, in particular his brother and heir Boleslaus. According to legend, Boleslaus invited his brother to the feast of Saint Cosmas and Saint Damian, then hacked Václav to pieces as he was entering the church at Stará Boleslav. Václav was subsequently canonised as a martyr and his name is more familiar to the English speaking world as the 'Good King Wenceslaus' of the Christmas carol fame. Saint Václav remains the patron saint of the Czech Republic. His feast day of 28 September is a public holiday.

Václav seems to have been an unlucky name for the rulers of Bohemia. Václav III Premyslid was king of Bohemia for about a year before he was murdered in Olomouc, Morovia in 1306.

Almost 150 years after Good King Wenceslaus, another Eastern European Saint was assassinated. When he was still alive and Bishop of Kraków, Stanislaus of Szczepanów or 'Stanislaus the Martyr' ran afoul of the Polish King Boleslaw II—also known as 'the Bold', 'the Generous' or 'the Cruel'—depending on your politics.

Stanislaus had been stridently critical of the King's land policies and sex life, but when Boleslaw decided that the Bishop was heading a conspiracy to replace him with his own brother Wladyslaw I Herman, Boleslaw tried to have him executed without trial. When the King's men refused to touch the Bishop, Boleslaw took matters into his own hands. While Stanislaus was performing mass on the Skalka (small rock) outside Kraków, Boleslaw hacked the future saint to pieces and threw the remains into a pool outside a church. The story foreshadows the later assassination of Thomas Beckett.

The murder of Stanislaus disgusted both the church and the nobility and they forced Boleslaw, his wife and his son into exile in Hungary. His brother Wladyslaw I succeeded him.

Pope Innocent IV canonised Stanislaus 174 years later in 1253 and, since 1320, almost all the Kings of Poland have been crowned before Saint Stanislaus's shrine in Wawel Cathedral.

England

Although Thomas Beckett's murder in 1170 was the most famous of English political murders in the Middle Ages, Britain did see a couple of major assassinations worth noting before this.

King Edmund I, 'the Deed Doer', died in the days when kings were much more accessible to the common folk than they were in later centuries. The King was attending a banquet in the town of Pucklechurch in South Gloucestershire. In the crowd around the banquet the King spotted Leofa, a thief who the King had exiled. The king ordered Leofa to leave and when Leofa refused a fight broke out. Leofa killed Edmund just before the King's men killed the assassin. The site of the assassination is located behind what is now the Star Inn.

Thirty-three years later Edmund's grandson, Edward the Martyr, would also die at the hands of an assassin. The King was out hunting when he decided to visit his stepmother Aelfthryth and his ten-year-old half-brother Ethelred. Aelfthryth had long harboured ambitions that her son should inherit the throne and when Edward arrived at her estate alone she seized her opportunity.

While the King was still astride his horse Aelfthryth offered Edward a cup of mead. While he was drinking the Queen dowager's men stabbed him in the back. His body fell to the ground and his horse dragged the body by one foot still caught in a stirrup into a stream at the foot of the hill where Corfe Castle now stands. According to legend the Queen then had the body hidden in a hut where a blind woman lived. In the night a divine light flooded the house and the woman regained her sight. The Queen then removed the body to a marsh. A year later a pillar of fire sprang up at the location of the dead king's bones. When villagers raised the bones, a spring of healing waters rose up. Other miracles followed and both the new stream and the stream at the base of the hill became the centre of pilgrimages for cures for the blind.

In early 980 the King's bones were reburied in the grounds of the church of the Most Holy Mother of God in Wareham, then in 981 they were moved to Shaftesbury Abbey. In 1001 the bishops of the area relocated his bones once more into a reliquary with those of other saints in the abbey.

Aelfthryth didn't live to see all this, as she only survived Edward's murder for a short period, but in the end she may have done her stepson a favour. Edmund was canonised by 1008. Her son Ethelred would go down in history as Ethelred II the Unready—his name derived from the Anglo-Saxon 'unraed' meaning 'without counsel' or 'poorly advised'. Ethelred spent most of his life fighting Vikings only to end up paying them off with bribes. The new king also had to live under the shadow of his half-brother the saint, magnanimously ordering that Edward's three feast days of 13 February, 18 March and 20 June had to be celebrated throughout England. Edward's bones survived the purges of Henry VIII. Recovered in 1931 they were donated to the Russian Orthodox Church Abroad in 1970 and are now housed in St Edward the Martyr Orthodox Church in Brookwood, Surrey.

More a mystery than a confirmed assassination was the death of William II of England'. The Anglo-Saxon Chronicle (an early history of England) maintains that he was 'hated by almost all his people' which made him only slightly more popular than his detested father William the Conqueror who was surely hated by *all* his people. William 'Rufus' II was hunting in the New Forest when he became separated from the rest of his hunting party. According to some accounts it seems that the Lord of Poix, Walter Tirel, accidentally shot the King while aiming for a stag. This is odd, considering that even the King considered Tirel a great shot. Walter tried to save him, but couldn't and fled the scene. The other nobles in the hunting party fled to their estates to secure their power bases, in particular Henry, the King's brother, who ruled as Henry I for the next 35 years.

A local charcoal burner named Purkis found William's body the next day and took it to Winchester Cathedral on his cart. A memorial, the Rufus Stone, erected in 1865, now stands on the spot where William fell.

It may be that Walter Tirel was framed. He fled to France and one chronicler, his friend Abbot Suger of Saint-Denis later recorded that:

> It was laid to the charge of a certain noble, Walter Tirel, that he
> had shot the king with an arrow; but I have often heard him, when
> he had nothing to fear nor to hope, solemnly swear that on the

day in question he was not in the part of the forest where the king was hunting, nor ever saw him in the forest at all.

Suger's testimony seems reliable; he was trusted enough to perform the marriage ceremony of Prince Louis—the future Louis VII of France—and Eleanor of Aquitaine on 22 July 1137.

So if William Rufus was assassinated, it would seem that the most likely suspect was an agent of Henry. Henry is remembered for being clever. He outmanoeuvred his eldest brother Robert III Curthose, Duke of Normandy, for the English throne, although perhaps this was an easy enough task, given that history remembers Robert as somewhat of an incompetent. Of all the brothers, Henry gets the best press even though he did father the war-hungry Empress Matilda (see below). But even in death William's reputation could not be redeemed. The year after he was buried beneath the tower of Winchester Cathedral, the tower fell down.

That meddlesome priest

Thomas Becket had previously enjoyed an excellent relationship with Henry II of England but, to put it mildly, they were both difficult men. Henry had gained the crown from his uncle Stephen after Henry's mother and Stephen's cousin, Empress Matilda plunged the country into a long, bloody and indecisive civil war, now known as the Anarchy.

That wasn't all. At the tender age of eighteen he had fallen madly in love with 30-year-old Eleanor of Aquitaine who was then married to Louis VII. They successfully petitioned to have the wedding annulled on the grounds of consanguity (blood relationship) on 11 March 1152 and Henry and Eleanor married on 18 May, even though they were even more closely related than Eleanor and Louis had been. In short, Henry was used to getting his own way.

Thomas too was used to getting his own way. Born into a wealthy upper-middle class family, his talents eventually attracted the attention of Theobald, Archbishop of Canterbury, who eventually appointed him Archdeacon of Canterbury. In time the Archbishop recommended that Henry appoint Thomas to the office of Lord Chancellor—a sort of senior regal advisor. In a few years Henry trusted Thomas so much that he even sent his eldest son and heir apparent, Henry to live with him. The younger Henry became very attached to his de facto father and subsequent events would leave a breach between the two Henrys that never healed.

When Theobald died Henry chose to appoint Thomas as Archbishop of Canterbury—a job that Thomas begged not to be given on the grounds that it would inevitably create a conflict of interests. Archbishop Thomas knew that if it came to a choice between the King and the Church, Thomas would have to choose the Church and this would make his relationship with the King impossible. When Henry appointed Thomas anyway in 1162, the Archbishop's worst fears were realised. Because he took his job seriously, Thomas turned virtually overnight from a hedonistic courtier into a serious and sober cleric ready to defend the Church at all costs.

His conflict with Henry ultimately came down to a question of money and power, which amounted to the same thing. The Church wanted to remain independent of the Realm, with its own courts, its own properties and its own taxes. Henry wanted to be an absolute ruler, with all his subjects and lands under his rule and nominal ownership.

Thomas turned virtually overnight from a hedonistic courtier into a serious and sober cleric ready to defend the Church at all costs.

Over the next two years the King sought a solution, but at every turn his new archbishop blocked him. Finally Thomas went into voluntary exile on 2 November 1164.

For six more years Henry tried to remove Thomas from his position. Thomas, just as stubborn, tried to have the King excommunicated. In a world where excommunication was a direct passport to hell the King took this as a serious threat. By 1170 he was apoplectic. Chroniclers of the age report that he had quite a lot to say about Thomas. Some of the printable quotes that have come down to us include:

'What a band of loathsome vipers I have nursed in my bosom who will let their lord be insulted by this low-born cleric!'

'Who will rid me of this meddlesome priest?'

'Who will revenge me of the injuries I have sustained from one turbulent priest?'

And most famously…'Will no one rid me of this turbulent priest?'

In the end, four knights took it upon themselves to be the executioners of what they interpreted to be the King's will: Reginald Fitzurse, Richard le Breton, William de Tracy and Hugh de Moreville, Lord of Westmoreland..

The most reliable account of Thomas' assassination comes from an eyewitness, Edward Grim, who was visiting Canterbury Cathedral and who was seriously wounded in the arm trying to protect the Archbishop as the knights fell upon him:

… the impious knight, fearing that [Thomas] would be saved by the people and escape alive, suddenly set upon him and, shaving off the summit of his crown which the sacred chrism consecrated to God, he wounded the sacrificial lamb of God in the head; the lower arm of the writer was cut by the same blow. Indeed [the writer] stood firmly with the holy archbishop, holding him in his arms — while all the clerics and monks fled — until the one he had raised in opposition to the blow was severed … Then, with another blow received on the head, he remained firm. But with the third, the stricken martyr bent his knees and elbows, offering himself as a living sacrifice, saying in a low voice, 'For the name of Jesus and the protection of the church I am ready to embrace death.' But the third knight inflicted a grave wound on the fallen one; with this blow he shattered the sword on the stone and his crown, which was large, separated from his head so that the blood turned white from the brain yet no less did the brain turn red from the blood; it purpled the appearance of the church with the colours of the lily and the rose, the colours of the Virgin and Mother and the life and death of the confessor and martyr. The fourth knight drove away those who were gathering so that the others could finish the murder more freely and boldly. The fifth — not a knight but a cleric who entered with the knights — so that a fifth blow might not be spared him who had imitated Christ in other things, placed his foot on the neck of the holy priest and precious martyr and (it is horrible to say) scattered the brains with the blood across the floor, exclaiming to the rest, 'We can leave this place, knights, he will not get up again.'

The assassination caused a furore among the faithful and nearly destroyed Henry's kingdom. In 1173 Pope Alexander III canonized the martyr and St. Thomas Becket's bones were interred at St. Dunstan's Church in Canterbury, Kent. On 12 July 1174 Henry – who all historians agree did not want Becket literally dead – made a very public demonstration of penitance while barefoot and dressed in sack-cloth and covered in ashes. The tomb of the Saint was one of the most popular places of pilgrimage until Henry VIII destroyed it during the dissolution of the monasteries between 1538 and 1541. The bones were moved in 1220 to a shrine in Trinity Chapel and thought the shrine no longer exists there is a candle on the pavement where it once was.

Henry did not punish the assassins directly but insisted that they atone for their act. It is believed by some that Hugh, Reginald and William might have expiated their sins on crusade in the Holy Land.

The only knight whose fate is known for certain is that of Richard le Breton, who died on the Island of Jersey.

Edward II

King John, the youngest son of Henry II and Eleanor of Aquitaine had twelve illegitimate children that we know of. On his death in 1216 he was succeeded by his first-born legitimate son Henry III who, in turn handed on the thrown to his first-born, Edward I. Edward had seventeen children by his wife Eleanor of Castile (a great-granddaughter of Eleanor of Aquitaine), but for all their efforts their fifteenth child, Edward of Caernarfon, was the only male to survive to adulthood.

Although both Henry III and Edward I have received mixed reviews, historians generally regard Edward of Caernarfon, who became Edward II, as an unmitigated disaster. The first English prince to hold the title of the Prince of Wales, Edward's nature was basically pleasure loving and rather passive. The great controversies of his reign all centred around his homosexual lovers. His first great love, Piers Gaveston, First Earl of Cornwall earned so much enmity that nobles under the leadership of Thomas Plantagenet, second Earl of Lancaster, ganged up on him and the King. Eventually two Welshmen murdered Gaveston under the general orders of Guy de Beauchamp, tenth Earl of Warwick, who died of one of those 'sudden illnesses' three years later in 1315.

Although the Earl of Lancaster won the first round and effectively ruled England for about six years—with Edward as a figurehead—he was unable to hold onto power and in 1318 Hugh le Despenser, first Earl of Winchester and his son Hugh the Younger Despenser seized control. Hugh the Younger soon filled the gap in Edward's heart left by the dead Piers, and the Despensers, with their greed for wealth and power, turned out to be even worse for the nobility than the Edward–Gaveston pairing. Hugh the Younger also effectively cheated his sister-in-laws and their husbands out of their inheritance.

Almost ten years after Gaveston's murder Edward had his revenge on Lancaster and, after another failed coup, he was captured, convicted of treason and beheaded by a court led by the Despensers. Strangely, Lancaster was venerated as a martyr not long after his death, although he was never canonised.

Within months of Lancaster's trial the nobility turned on the Despensers and they were forced into temporary exile, only to return within a year to continue their corruption of the English government.

Through it all, Edward's wife, Isabella of France, sister to King Charles IV of France suffered his affairs in a state of continuous humiliation. By 1324 she had had enough and may have had a hand in helping her husband's enemy, Roger de Mortimer, first Earl of March, escape from the Tower of London.

Isabella then visited her brother in France taking with her the son and heir, Edward III. There, in her brother's court, Isabella found Roger Mortimer and the pair became lovers. This created somewhat of a scandal and the couple retreated to Flanders where they received help to execute a coup. When they landed back in England in September 1326 they met up with Henry Plantagenet, the third Earl of Lancaster, brother to the 'martyred' Thomas who agreed to help them.

The people of London, sick to death of Edward, his lover Hugh the Younger and the older Hugh le Despenser, rallied to the aid of the wronged Queen. Edward and Hugh the Younger fled. Isabella and Roger's forces caught up with the Elder Despenser and he was hanged at Bristol on 27 October 1326. Not long afterwards they captured Hugh the Younger, who tried to starve himself before facing trial, but to no avail. On 24 November 1326 he was convicted of treason.

Four horses dragged him from his cell in Hereford to his place of execution. He was then hanged from a gallows 50 feet high, but cut down before he could choke to death. Officials built a fire. While it burned Hugh was dragged to the top of a ladder. There his executioner sliced off his penis and testicles in full view of a gathered crowd. The severed organs were they thrown into the fire in front of him. The executioner eviscerated Hugh and threw his entrails and heart likewise into the fire. Hugh was then beheaded, his body cut into four pieces and his head mounted on the gates of London.

Edward was also captured and held at Kenilworth and, in January 1327, he was forcibly deposed in favour of his fourteen-year-old son. The former king was imprisoned in Berkeley Castle in Gloucestershire, where contemporary accounts record that he was well treated, but not for long. Sir Thomas More wrote about 200 years later that:

> On the night of 11 October 1327 while lying on a bed [the king] was suddenly seized and, while a great mattress ... weighed him down, a plumber's iron, heated intensely hot, was introduced through a tube into his secret parts so that it burned the inner portions beyond the intestines.

The princes in the Tower

Edward IV died leaving two sons as heirs: Edward V and Richard of Shrewsbury, 1st Duke of York. Edward's brother Richard III became Regent, but within weeks had the boys put in the Tower of London. He was crowned King on 6 July 1483. Richard had Parliament pass a special law, the Titulus Regius, declaring all Edward's children illegitimate. In fact, recent scholarship suggests that Edward IV himself was illegitimate and that Richard was in fact the rightful heir in the first place.

Regardless of the claims and counter claims, the fact is that, after Edward's sons went into the Tower, they never came out again. Richard remained silent on the matter of the fate of the boys although Henry Tudor, Richard's vanquisher on the battlefield and successor who therefore wrote the history, maintained that Richard had assassinated them. Of course, if the boys had survived beyond 1483, they would have been just as politically inconvenient for Henry as for Richard. It's highly likely no one now living knows what really happened, but feel free to explore the issue in more depth at the website of the Richard III Society at *www.richardiii.net.*

In 1674 renovators found the skeletons of two children under the staircase leading into the chapel of the Tower of London. Charles II ordered the skeletons reburied in Westminster Cathedral. In 1933 they were further examined and found to be a mixture of human and animal bones. At the time tests could not confirm the age or gender of the skeletons. Elizabeth II has refused to allow scientists to re-examine the skeletons, so their nature remains a mystery to this day.

Unless you count the judicial predations of Henry VIII, his daughter Elizabeth's execution of Mary Queen of Scots in 158), or Oliver Cromwell's execution of Charles I in 1649, there would not be another assassination of a British monarch to date—though not through lack of trying, as we shall see. After all these de facto assassinations were the result of 'due process' of the law of the day

Assassinations in other parts of Europe weren't particularly popular over the next 600 years. As we've seen, the general chaos of feudalism made it much more likely that VIPs would die on the battlefield rather than as victims of an assassin. And yet there were some places that managed to be 'peaceful' enough for long enough to get in a few important political murders.

Germany

After defeating and slaying his rival Adolf of Nassau-Weilburg , Albert I of Habsburg was elected King of Germany by his aristocratic peers on 27 July 1298. Albert was the founder of the House of Habsburg, whose members would dominate European royalty for more than 500 years. The Habsburgs reigned in Germany as Holy Roman Emperors and were rulers of Austria, Kings of Bohemia, Croatia, Hungary, Portugal and Spain. One was even Emperor of Mexico—from

1864–1867. The guillotined Queen of France, Marie Antoinette, was also a Hapsburg.

For such an illustrious ancestor Albert's death was rather sad. On 1 June 1283 the German nobility forced his twelve-year-old brother, Duke Rudolf II of Austria, to give up his lands and entitlements in favour of Albert. Rudolf died when he was only 20, but not before siring an only son, John.

Albert's nephew grew up resenting being disinherited and asked the King for at least *some* of the family estates. When Albert refused to give him anything, John and three companions formed a conspiracy.

On 1 May 1308 Albert was crossing the Reuss River at Windisch in Switzerland when he became separated from his attendants. The conspirators murdered him and escaped. History records that John lived out his days in a monastery and may have lived beyond the speculated date of his death. Historians refer to him as John the Parricide.

Albert had six sons who grew to adulthood, but they either died without sons or their sons died young and the family line almost became extinct—except for one. Albert II fathered four sons and two daughters, but only the two younger sons: Albert III of Austria and Leopold III were able to keep the family going long enough to create descendants—descendants who would ultimately rule over millions of Europeans for centuries to come.

Portugal

If assassination can ever be considered romantic then the story of Ines de Castro must be one of the few examples.

In 1340 the heir to the Portuguese throne, Pedro I, had only recently married Constance of Penafiel and Castile when he fell in love with his wife's maid, Ines. Pedro's father, Alfonso IV disapproved and hoped that the affair was a passing infatuation. It wasn't. As a result of Pedro's inattention to his wife, Constance only managed to produce two children who survived childhood, Maria, the future Queen of Castile, and the future Ferdinand I. Ines, meanwhile bore Pedro four children, three of whom lived to adulthood: Beatrice, Joao and Denis.

Constance of Castile died in 1349, but Pedro would still not give Ines up and refused to ever think about marrying anyone else. Alfonso, attempted to banish Ines and, when this didn't work, he ordered her assassination, which his agents duly carried out. In response, Pedro initiated a civil war against his father that lasted for two years and although father and son were ultimately reconciled, Alfonso died shortly after the war's end.

Pedro then revealed that he had secretly married Ines after the death of Constance, exhumed Ines' body and had the court acknowledge her officially as Queen of Portugal. The romance of Pedro and Ines has been the subject of plays, poems and over twenty operas, but their story doesn't quite end there.

Pedro never remarried, remaining utterly devoted to the memory of Ines, and they are still buried opposite each other in marble sarcophagi at the Monastery of Alcobaca. Carved in the marble is Pedro's promise that they would be together until the end of the world. Pedro nevertheless found time for one last fling, with Teresa Gille Lourenco, who bore him a son, Joao in 1357.

Ferdinand, son of Constance, succeeded his father but, when he died in 1383 without successors, Portugal fell back into a war of succession. Pedro and Ines's sons lost out, and Teresa's son Joao reigned as Joao I from 1385 until his death 48 years later.

In 1469 the two families were reunited. Ferdinand II of Aragon, the great-great grandson of Pedro and Ines, married Isabella of Castile, the great-great granddaughter of Pedro and Teresa. Ferdinand and Isabella reunited Spain in 1492, and Isabella provided funding for Christopher Columbus's voyage of discovery to the New World.

France

The most controversial and mysterious assassinations involve children. In 1316 Louis X died of heat stroke and dehydration following a game of Jeu de Paume (a sort of medieval handball). His short and completely undistinguished reign had ended after less than two years, leaving as his heir the unborn child of his 23-year-old widow, Clemence d'Anjou. Their son Jean I—John the Posthumous—was therefore born a king, but died at the age of only five days. Many at the time believed that Louis's brother Philippe V murdered the baby to secure his own inheritance.

The death of Jean I was important because it finally settled the question of whether inheritance of the French throne could pass through the female line. The only other claimant to the throne was Jean's four-year-old half sister Jeanne II of Navarre. Philippe V easily outmanoeuvred Jeanne's supporters and invoked the traditional law of the Franks, Salic Law, that barred women from inheriting land. Jeanne therefore lost the French throne; indeed no woman would ever be Queen of France in her own right. But Jeanne's line had the last laugh, although she didn't live to see it. Over two hundred years later her descendant, Henry IV would rule France as the first King of the Bourbon dynasty and the Bourbons continued to rule France until the French Revolution. Henry IV himself was to profit from the assassination of his rival, Henry III.

Henry III had been a controversial king. On 24 August 1572, when he was still Duke of Angouleme, Orleans and Anjou he and his mother Catherine de Medici (daughter of Lorenzo di Medici), were largely responsible for the slaughter of tens of thousands of French Protestant Huguenots in the pogrom that began with the Saint Bartholomew's Day Massacre. In fact Henry's entire reign was marred by religious fighting. What really turned the people against him, however, was when he assassinated a potential heir, the very popular Duke of Guise on 23 December 1588, and the people of Paris drove him out of the city.

In 1584 Henry III had issued an edict suppressing his distant cousin Henry IV's right to succeed him because of his Protestantism. Now Henry III had no friends left and had to turn to Henry IV for help. Together they planned to take back Paris, but their plans were thwarted. A Dominican Friar Jacques Clément gained access to the King claiming he had a secret message. When the King ordered his retainers back for privacy the monk stabbed the King. Guards instantly killed the monk and Henry III, the last of the Valois dynasty, died the next morning, but not before naming Henry IV as his successor.

Henry IV remained a Protestant until his mistress the Duchess Gabrielle d'Estrées convinced him to convert to Catholicism, which he did on 25 July, 1593 although he did issue the Edict of Nantes, officially sanctioning the toleration of the Huguenots.

Gabrielle died shortly after bearing her and Henry's fourth child, a stillborn son, although there were rumours that she might have been assassinated to make way for a less controversial queen. She is the subject of the famous painting 'Gabrielle d'Estrées et Une de Ses Soeurs'. Henry went on to marry Marie de Médicis, the mother of Louis XIII.

In spite of being a great and popular king, the Protestant–Catholic schism that was tearing Europe apart at the time meant that Henry IV became the target of numerous assassination attempts. Eventually, the assassins found their mark. François Ravaillac claimed to have had a vision telling him to convince the King to convert the Huguenots to Catholicism.

When Ravaillac heard that Henry planned to invade the Netherlands he thought that he was planning a war against the Pope, and on 14 May 1610 he managed to stab the King to death when traffic stopped his coach on the Rue de la Ferronnerie. A mob tried to lynch the assassin, but the King's guards apprehended him instead. Under torture, François refused to admit to having any accomplices and finally the authorities took him to the Place de Grève. According to a contemporary source:

'Before being drawn and quartered … he was scalded with burning sulphur, molten lead and boiling oil and resin, his flesh then being torn by pincers.' His parents were exiled and the rest of his family ordered never to use the name 'Ravaillac' again.

Italy

Several other European heavyweights died at the hands of assassins over the next few centuries. Among the more famous were the Medicis.

Even though Giuliano di Piero de' Medici and his older brother Lorenzo the Magnificent were the joint rulers of Florence and the virtual rulers of Tuscany, they became victims of the machinations of their rivals—the Salviati and Pazzi families.

Giuliano and Lorenzo were attending High Mass at the Basilica di Santa Maria del Fiore when a gang of Salviati and Pazzi supporters attacked the brothers. Giuliano was stabbed nineteen times and bled to death on the floor of the cathedral. Lorenzo escaped and the people of Florence, who liked the Medicis, caught the assassins and killed them.

Jacopo de Pazzi was thrown out of a window into a waiting mob who beat him to death and dragged him naked through the streets of the city before throwing his body into the Arno River. Francesco Salviati, the Archbishop of Pisa, was hanged on the walls of the Palazzo della Signoria. Pope Sixtus IV put Florence under an interdict for having killed an archbishop and tried to have his supporter Ferdinand I of Naples attack the city. Ferdinand decided against it when Lorenzo convinced him that if he were successful, the Pope would betray him.

Giulio, the illegitimate son of Giuliano and his mistress Fioretta Gorini, became Pope Clement VII 45 years after his father's death.

Giuliano and Lorenzo are buried in the Medici Chapel of the Church of San Lorenzo di Firenze. Their tomb is adorned with Michelangelo's famous sculpture of the Madonna and Child.

The Netherlands

William I of Orange was the driving force behind the beginning of the Eighty Years War—the Dutch war of independence from the Spanish. Balthasar Gérard assassinated William after Philip II of Spain declared the rebel leader an outlaw and offered the substantial sum of 25,000 Crowns as a reward for his death. Gérard shot William three times in his house in Delft. He attempted to escape, but fell over a pile of rubbish and a servant caught up with him.

William's supporters, the magistrates of Delft, had the assassin tortured. Initially he was hung to a pole and whipped. The torturers then filled his wounds with honey and tried to get a goat lick them, but the goat refused to cooperate. Other punishments recorded included attaching 136 kg (300 pound) weights to each of his big toes. His feet were then put into shoes that crushed his feet into stumps when they shrank upon being exposed to a flame. He had his armpits branded, was dressed in a shirt soaked in alcohol and had burning bacon fat poured over him. His sentence also decreed that his right hand should be burnt off with a red-hot iron and that pincers should tear the flesh from his bones in six different places. Gérard seems to have borne all this so stoically that his torturers urinated on him in frustration. Then his executioners took him to the market place at Delft where four horses tore him apart.

In the end Gérard's family received the reward money for William's death. Phillip II also gave them three estates in the Franche-Comté in France (which includes modern Burgundy).

William I's political descendents eventually won their independence from the Spanish in the Peace of Westphalia in 1648. In 1650 Johan de Witt was elected leader of Holland and, by extension, the newly formed United Provinces as a whole. Many historians now believe that William I's grandson, William III of Orange, was behind the assassination of Johan de Witt. William and his Orangists took advantage of a joint English and French attack on the Dutch Republic in 1672 to seize power.

Reduced to a private citizen, Johan had just visited his brother Cornelis in jail when Orangist and future Commander in Chief of the Dutch and Danish Navy, Cornelis Tromp had Johan shot in the neck. A lynch mob then hanged and mutilated his corpse. Cornelis de Witt was even less fortunate. The mob dragged him from Gevangenpoort prison, shot him, stabbed him, eviscerated him while he was still alive, then hung his body and bashed his brains out.

William III eventually married Mary II of Britain and ruled jointly with her as King and Queen of England and Ireland from 13 February 1689 and of Scotland from 11 April 1689.

New Spain

The Spanish conquest of the New World has a lot to answer for. Ferdinand and Isabella were fanatical Catholics, and most of the latter part of the Spanish Inquisition was orchestrated by Ferdinand. The royal couple's agents then took the theme of religious superiority with them into Central and South America.

The Catholic missionaries sent to the New World considered the civilisations they encountered to be utterly barbaric. The Aztecs liked to make mass human sacrifices on top of their pyramids, so perhaps it's not so outrageous a judgement to make.

What is harder to justify is the way that the missionaries destroyed thousands of records of the pre-Columbian cultures because they were 'works of the devil'. As a result, we know far less about the Aztec, Maya and Inca than we could. Then again these civilisations were in a state of almost continual warfare with one another and did their fair share of looting and pillaging. However, the end result is that the accounts of the Spanish invasion which have survived should be taken with considerable caution. Since we only have the point of view of one side it is worth remembering that one man's 'casualty of war' may well be another's 'assassination'.

The most striking feature of the 'conquest' of the new world was its speed. There were some basic historical accidents that accounted for the sudden, catastrophic collapse of the native civilisations of the Americas.

The first of these was horses. Horses actually evolved in North America. During the last ice age the sea level was much lower than today and the Bering Islands formed a land bridge to Siberia. Horses migrated west into Asia via the land bridge while humans migrated east. When the ancestors of the Native Americans found two continents full of large animals and no other people they had a field day, hunting the native horses to extinction. When the Spanish landed on South American soil with horses, the remote decendants of the horsehunters had forgotten there had ever been such things. Horses were magical beings and the locals thought the Spanish were gods.

The second reason was that in many regions and by many different names—such as Quetzalcoatl or Kukulkan—there were legends of a saviour god who would lead the people to a new golden age. This god was described as a pale-skinned, bearded being. So when Hernan Cortés showed up on the east coast of the empire of the Aztec Emperor Moctezuma, the effect on the Emperor and his people was the Mexican equivalent to the Christian's second coming of Christ.

When Cortés made an alliance with Aztec rivals ... the Spanish were simply taking advantage of a powder keg waiting to go off.

The Aztec religion preached that the world could end at any point, which explained the human sacrifices as a sort of cosmic bribe to appease their gods. But these human sacrifices were prisoners of war—the Aztecs had many enemies. When Cortés made an alliance with Aztec rivals such as the Tlaxcalteca, the Spanish were simply taking advantage of a powder keg waiting to go off. Their saviour god seemed to have sided with the enemy.

The third fact was that the Empire had huge amounts of gold lying around and the Spanish liked gold, a lot, and became obsessed with conquest of these unknown lands.

Finally the South Americans had been isolated from European diseases for thousands of years. When the Spanish introduced illnesses like plague, measles and smallpox, the native populations had no natural immunity and died in huge numbers. The diseases spread rapidly throughout the continent and many communities were effectively crippled long before any Europeans set sight on them.

Moctezuma sought to buy Cortés off with gifts and, when that failed to halt his advance, invited him to his Palace at Tenoctitlan (on the site of present-day Mexico City) where he hoped to intimidate the 'barbarian' with the dazzling power of Aztec civilisation. The guest from hell, Cortés took the Emperor hostage. There are varying stories of what happened to him. One account states that Moctezuma's brother, Cuitláhuac, and his army were successfully attacking the palace so Cortés forced the Emperor to go out on a balcony and appeal to his people to retreat. The people were so disgusted with Moctezuma's cowardice that they stoned him to death. Other sources suggest that Moctezuma had outlived his usefulness and Cortés had him garroted. The Spanish then fled Tenoctitlan. Although Cuitláhuac had one over the conquistadors and their allies by evicting them from Tenoctitlan, he succumbed to smallpox and was dead by October 1520.

Techichpotzin, Montezuma's ten-year-old daughter, had been married briefly to her uncle Cuitláhuac before his death, then married her cousin Cuauhtémoc. Cuauhtémoc continued to fight the Spanish with an ever-shrinking population before the Spanish captured him while crossing Lake Texcoco in disguise. The Emperor presented a knife to Cortés and asked to be killed. Instead, Cortés tortured him in the hope of learning the whereabouts of a non-existent stash of gold. According to one source, Cortés, now the Governor of New Spain, then had Cuauhtémoc decapitated. Another states that Cortés had him hanged in spite of the objections of his men.

Cuauhtémoc was the last true Tlatoani (Emperor) of the Aztec. The Spanish then put a series of puppet rulers in place until 1565.

After the death of her second husband, Techichpotzin, now all of fifteen years old, went into Cortés household, was baptised as Isabel Moctezuma, and later bore Cortés' child. She became a devout Roman Catholic and would be given in marriage to three more conquistadors, from whom she would bear seven children. One of those sons, Ihuitemotzin, baptised Diego Luis de Moctezuma, went to Spain, married Francisca de la Cueva de Valenzuela and in 1627 Philip IV of Spain ennobled their son Pedro Tesifón de Moctezuma as first Count of Moctezuma de Tultengo. The descendents of Moctezuma are still alive today.

Cortés eventually lost the support of the Spanish government and the governorship of New Spain and finally died in Mexico from pleurisy at the age of 62. History judges him as a mass of contradictions—a despot who committed any number of atrocities, but who also looked after the heirs of Moctezuma as if they were his own family, which, in a sense, they were. He is buried in the Templo de Jesús in Mexico City. Cortés was unusual among the conquistadors; hardly any of them died a natural death.

Cortés' second cousin, Francisco Pizarro, played similar havoc with the Inca of Peru. Arriving on the Island of Hispaniola (the modern location of Haiti and the Dominican Republic) in 1502, he helped the Spaniards exploit and destroy the cultures of the various indigenous groups between his exploratory trips. In one jaunt in 1513 he helped Vasco Nunez de Balboa 'discover' and 'take possession' of the Pacific Ocean. Six years later Pizarro arrested Balboa on behalf of Balboa's son-in-law Governor Pedrarias Dávila on trumped up charges of treason. A kangaroo court found Balboa guilty and executioners beheaded him and four 'accomplices' in the town of Acla in north-east Panama. Acla no longer exists; it was abandoned in 1532.

After more adventures Pizarro landed on the coast of modern day Ecuador in 1532 and pillaged until he reached Catahalpa and confronted the Sapa Inca (Inca Emperor) Atahualpa.

Atahualpa had only been Sapa Inca for a short time. At Quito he'd recently won the three-year-long War of the Two Brothers against his brother Inti Cusi Huallpa Huascar, in which an estimated 100,000 Inca died. As part of his victory Atahualpa had Huascar's entire family slaughtered in front of him before imprisoning the ex-Sapa Inca.

Atahualpa was on his way back to the Inca capital of Cusco when Pizarro showed up in Cajamarca. Atahualpa had an army of 80,000 compared to the Spaniard's 106 foot soldiers. The new Sapa Inca must have figured it wouldn't be much of a contest. He told Pizarro in no uncertain terms that the Spaniard wasn't dealing with another coward like Moctezuma, but they agreed to meet the next day, 16 November 1532. Atahualpa showed up at that meeting with a retinue of 8000 unarmed men. A Catholic priest, Vincente de Valverde presented the Emperor with a bible and an ultimatum that he convert to Catholicism or else. The Sapa Inca said he was no one's vassal whereupon Pizarro kidnapped him. This was surprisingly easy to do, as the sounds of gunfire and the sight of Pizarro's few horses terrified the Inca, who were far more easily intimidated than their emperor.

The Spaniards held Atahualpa in a small sandstone building now known as the Ransom Room. Although a captive Atahualpa still exercised some control and it appears he gave orders that his brother be killed to remove any chance of future rivalry. Huascar was assassinated at the hands of his own men, drowned in the river Adamarca. The Spanish, who now considered Atahualpa an unruly vassal who deserved everything he got because he was a godless heathen, decided to put the Sapa Inca on trial on charges including idolatry and fratricide. Naturally they found him guilty and ordered his death by burning, the standard practice for all heretics under the Spanish Inquisition. On hearing of his fate, Atahualpa offered to fill the Ransom Room with gold and two more rooms with silver in exchange for his freedom. Pizarro accepted the offer and the ransom started pouring in, but this wasn't enough to save the Sapa Inca.

The priest Valverde told the Emperor that if he would convert to Catholicism and consent to be baptised, his sentence would be commuted. Shortly after his conversion, the Spanish strangled Atahualpa anyway.

Friar Valverde went on to a long and industrious career of exploiting the natives and treating them like slaves. He later wrote a book, *Account of the Conquest of the Kingdoms of Peru*, which he presented to the King of Spain, the Habsburg Emperor Charles V. Therein he claimed that the natives, lacking souls, could not be considered human. He was living in the town of Oropresa in Peru when the soulless Indians, who had had enough of Valverde's greed and oppression, revolted. Displaying their sense of poetic justice, they assassinated the Friar by pouring molten gold down his throat.

Shortly after his conversion, the Spanish strangled Atahualpa anyway.

As for the Inca Empire, without its God-Emperor, and already teetering from internal divisions, it fell apart. The Spanish installed Atahualpa's brother, Tupac Hualpa as puppet emperor and, after Tupac's suspiciously early death another brother, Manco Inca Yupanqui. Although Manco at first saw the Spaniards as allies, he later turned against them.

Francisco Pizarro in the meantime went off to found the Peruvian capital of Lima in 1535, leaving his half-brothers Gonzalo, Juan and Hernando behind in Cuzco to mess things up. The Pizarro brothers dealt with Cuzco as if it were their own property and used the usual subtle methods of torture and executions to keep the population in line.

They treated Manco like dirt and the Sapa Inca escaped from Cuzco in 1535. By 1536 he had raised an army of 100,000 and in May he laid siege to Cuzco. The ten-month siege ultimately failed because so many of Manco's warriors died of smallpox. His rebellion degenerated into guerrilla warfare and Juan Pizarro was killed during one of the many Incan battles against the Spanish. However Pizarro's long-time cohort, Diego de Almagro, eventually brought the situation under control and imprisoned the remaining Pizarros.

Almagro and Pizarro had benefited from their mutual association for many years and historians credit Almagro with the 'discovery' of Chile even though an exiled Spaniard Gonzalo Calvo Barrientos and a considerable indigenous population were already there. Greed, however, got the better of the two conquistadors.

Almagro figured that Cuzco was now his. Pizarro believed otherwise and set off to liberate' his brothers and Cuzco. On 12 July 1537 Almagro defeated Pizarro's army and captured the commander, Alonso de Alvarado but Alonso and Gonzalo Pizarro later escaped and negotiated for the release of Hernando in exchange for the city. This gambit bought Francisco enough time to raise an army, and he defeated Almagro at the Battle of Las Salinas on 26 April 1538. Pizarro captured Almagro and had him beheaded.

Almagro's son, Diego II, swore to avenge his father's death and eventually succeeded. He stole into Pizarro's palace and shot him, mortally wounding him, before making his escape. Alone at the time, Pizarro used his own blood to draw a cross on the floor before he died. Diego's supporters proclaimed him the true Governor of Peru.

Gonzalo Pizarro sought to avenge the assassination of his brother, Francisco and, a year later, Gonzalo Pizarro had Diego executed in the Great Square in Cuzco. Diego's supporters were still at large, however, and Gonzalo wasn't finished. He raised an army to go to war against the Diego de Almagro faction, but by the time he was ready Peru had a new, pro-Almagro Viceroy, Blasco Nunez Vela. Gonzalo defeated Vela in battle and decapitated him, but his victory was short-lived. Gonzalo's dream of completing the vengeance on his brother's enemies, and maybe even winning Peru for himself, died when his army deserted him. He surrendered to Charles V's new viceroy, Pedro de la Casca and was in turn beheaded.

Hernando Pizarro was sent back to Spain and spent twenty years in jail. He was released in 1560 then largely disappeared from history. He is reported to have died at the age of 100.

Sapa Inca Manco Inca Yupanqui, ever fighting a rearguard action, established a final Inca capital at Vilcabamba in 1539. In that same year the Spanish murdered Manco's sister, wife and empress Cura Ocllo. Supporters of Diego de Almagro murdered Manco in 1544.

The Inca Empire was by now well and truly finished in fact, if not in the imagination and hopes of the remaining Sapa Incas and their few remaining subjects. The Incas found the territory that they could claim and control rapidly shrinking all around them as they continued to die in skirmishes and outbreaks of small pox and they retreated further into the rainforests and further into obscurity. When Titu Cusi died his half-brother and successor Tupac Amaru in turn suspected the Spanish and accused the Spanish priests living in Vilcabamba of poisoning Titu Cusi. Tupac Amaru had the priests executed.

Unaware of the death of Titu Cusi the Spanish sent two ambassadors to Vilcabamba and Tupac allegedly had them murdered too. The Viceroy of Peru, Francisco de Toledo, Count of Oropresa decided to finish what was left of the Inca once and for all. Toledo's troops captured Tupac Amaru and his generals and marched them into Cuzco on 21 September 1572. The Spanish summarily tried and executed the generals. Tupac Amaru, arguably the last Sapa Inca, was convicted of murdering the priests at Vilcabamba. The Spanish hanged him.

His last words, in Quechua, the language of the Inca, were:

Ccollanan Pachacamac ricuy auccacunac yahuarniy hichascancuta.
or: Mother Earth, witness how my enemies shed my blood.

Francisco de Toledo was ultimately charged with embezzlement of imperial funds and recalled to Spain. In 1581 he was jailed and later died there of natural causes.

After the final Spanish defeat of the Inca in 1572 the City of Vilcabamba's location was lost to history until explorer Hiram Bingham III rediscovered it in 1911. Bingham mistakenly thought that the site, now known as Machupicchu, was Vilcabamba and disregarded the ruins of the real Vilcabamba as unimportant. It was only in 1994 that explorer Gene Savoy conclusively established the true location of the last Inca capital—a corpse of a city still veiled in a shroud of Amazon jungle.

It's Bad to be King— or Emperor

The idea of kings ruling by divine right, because they were in some mysterious way better than ordinary people, was dying. For better or worse, people were beginning to think outside of the monarchist box, even if it meant having to box a few monarchs in the process.

Depending on who you talk to, you can trace the beginnings of the modern world to various dates. The dates are almost all Eurocentric, but that's hardly surprising, because historically Europe has dominated the political development of the world that we know today, with certain key nations playing a role in empire building—in particular, the English, French, Spanish, Germans and the Dutch. At the dawn of the 21st century, this looks as if it's about to change. China and India may eventually become superpowers by sheer force of numbers, if their ecologies and economies don't collapse, and South America may be a sleeping giant, but for the moment it's still an Anglo-Euro world.

Some date the start of the modern world as early as the Peace of Westphalia in 1648, which ended the Thirty Years War—which involved most of Europe—and the Eighty Years War between Spain and the Netherlands. Soon after followed the Treaty of the Pyrenees in 1659, which marked the peace between France and Spain. Others date the beginning of the modern era to the French Revolution in 1789.

Whichever date you choose, it was still a world of kings and emperors, and would remain so in many countries well into the twentieth century. In a monarchy, if you wanted to change who was in power, for the most part you had to resort to regicide. With few exceptions, these murders failed to change the course of history in any significant way. The murder of kings in the 1800s still had the general flavour of a dogfight among the aristocracy and the elite and these assassinations generally meant little more than the same old show with a new cast.

However, by the 1900s the nature of assassination changed with the rise of individuals and revolutionary groups grasping the political weapon. More than ever, assassination wasn't something that elites were doing to other elites, but something that the people were doing to elites.

Tsar Paul I

Paul I of Russia was the son of Catherine II of Russia—Catherine the Great—and was widely rumoured to be the son of Catherine's lover Sergei Saltykov rather than of Catherine's husband Tsar Peter III.

Catherine came to power in her own right when Tsar Peter III's personal bodyguard, the Leib Guard, revolted against the unpopular monarch and forced his abdication. Catherine took over the throne with the support of the Russian nobility. Shortly after his abdication Peter was assassinated. Catherine never punished the assassins; historians believe that she and her lover Grigori Orlov were behind the orders to kill the Tsar.

Catherine herself started the rumours of Paul's paternity towards the end of her life and her motivation was probably to hurt her son, whom she despised, and who in turn despised her. Catherine was an astute political animal—a control freak who managed to hold onto power for 34 years.

In spite of the rumour, Paul physically and temperamentally resembled the Romanovs so he was probably his father's son after all. On his mother's death he set about reforming his kingdom. A child of the Enlightenment, Paul sought to improve the lives of Russia's vast serf population. He tended to favour his own supporters while ignoring or insulting those of his mother's supporters still in positions of power and influence. Like so many before him, he was alienating the rich and powerful—virtually begging to be assassinated.

A conspiracy led by the Chief of Police, Count Petr Alekseyevich Pahlen, finally did away with the Emperor. A group of officers who Paul had dismissed made their way to the Tsar's bedroom and tried to compel him to sign a notice of abdication. When Paul refused a soldier struck him with a sword then others strangled and trampled him to death.

Paul's widow, Maria Feodorovna, knew of Pahlen's role in her husband's death and wielded considerable influence over her sons, Tsar Alexander I and Tsar Nicholas I. She ensured that Pahlen was virtually exiled to his estates in damp, foggy and remote Courland, where he later died.

Alexander II

Eighty years after his grandfather Paul's death, Alexander, son of Nicholas I, also died by assassination. History remembers Alexander as a truly great Tsar, a radical reformer who finally freed the Russian serfs and turned them into a class of independent property owners. This, combined with his military and naval reforms, brought Russia out of the middle ages into something that was much closer to the modern idea of a nation.

However, Alexander made enemies of those whose interests he threatened and those whose interests he failed to support—surprise, surprise—and he was the target of several assassination attempts. On 4 April 1866, Dmitri Karakozov became the first Russian revolutionary in history to attempt to take the life of a Tsar. He failed when, reportedly, Osip Komissarov, a peasant-born, hatter's apprentice knocked Dmitri's elbow just as he was aiming his gun at the Emperor at the gates of the Summer Garden in St Petersburg. Dmitri ran, but was caught and hanged on 3 September 1866. Komissarov was given a title and a stipend as a reward, but embarrassed his fellow aristocrats so much with his lowborn manners that he was later gently removed to a life in the country. Gratitude has its limits, after all.

On 20 April 1879 a former student, Alexander Soloviev also failed to kill the Tsar and was caught after firing his gun five times and missing. He was hanged just over a month later on 28 May.

The attempts on Alexander's life became more serious when a group calling themselves Narodnay Volya—The People's Will—finally got their act together. They failed to blow up the Tsar's train when they exploded a section of the railway between Livadia and Moscow and they failed once again on 5 February 1880 when they exploded a charge under the dining room of the Winter Palace. Fortunately for him, the Tsar arrived late to supper.

Eventually, in early 1881, the assassins succeeded—detonating a bomb beneath the Tsar's carriage while he was riding through the streets of St Petersburg near the Winter Palace. Alexander escaped the wreck, only to encounter a suicide bomber, a Pole called Ignacy Hryniewiecki, who set off an explosion of hand-made grenades, mortally wounding both himself and the Tsar, who died a few hours later. Within three weeks authorities apprehended all the surviving Narodnay Volya conspirators involved in the assassination, and Nikolai Kibalchich, Timofei Mikhailov, Sophia Perovskaya, Nikolai Rysakov Andrei Zhelyabov were all hanged on 3 April 1880.

In a curious sideline, Kibalchich, the explosives expert who designed the missile bomb that destroyed the Tsar's carriage, worked on the design of a manned rocket while in prison. Nothing ever came of the revolutionary's revolutionary idea, and the design was consigned to bureaucratic oblivion. Over a century later though, the International Astronomical Union named a 40 km crater on the far side of the moon Kibalchich, in honour of his scientific foresight. Kibalchich therefore, to the best of my knowledge, is the only assassin to have a crater on the moon named after him.

The People's Will failed to spark the revolution that the assassination was intended to provoke, but the event did create a precedent for the Russian Revolution a generation later.

Jean-Paul Marat

Life under the French Revolution wasn't much of an improvement on the corrupt French monarchy that had brought it about. If anything, the

Revolution was one long bloodbath of assassination in which hundreds of the aristocracy died as their heads were prematurely separated from their bodies. Since executions by a government don't normally count as assassinations—even if the due process of law is a farce—the Revolution itself only provides us with one famous 'official' assassination.

Jean-Paul Marat was a Swiss-born physician who spent most of his professional career in England, and was always interested in politics and in writing. When the French Revolution broke out, he wrote extensive essays on politics that gained wide circulation.

In September 1789 he began his own private newspaper *L'Ami du Peuple*—meaning 'The Friend of the People'—in which he devoted most of his column inches to defining 'enemies of the people', who were mostly people who didn't agree with his philosophies. His views met with considerable opposition in the first three years of the Revolution and for that matter even after his election to the National Convention of 1792 (the French revolutionary government).

Independently minded, Marat didn't seem to care who he alienated, but he did gain considerable popular support and acquired considerable clout on the matter of who would or would not be guillotined. In fact his arguments fed considerable fuel to a wave of mob violence that gripped Paris in early September 1792. For two days, from 2 September, crowds of Parisians stormed the city, looting and attacking seemingly at random. Half the incarcerated population of the city, some 1200—mostly political—prisoners, died in the chaos.

Four days before Marat's death a young woman from Caen called Charlotte Corday took a room in Paris, bought a knife and wrote an address to the French explaining what she was about to do and why. She would kill Marat because of his involvement in the September Massacre and because of his persecution of his political enemies, the Girondists.

Marat suffered from a debilitating skin disease that forced him to seek relief in long hot baths—in which still managed to write. Charlotte was able to con her way into Marat's bathroom by pretending to be an informant to a Girondist uprising in Caen. She named names and was generally convincing. When she asked what would happen to the Girondists, Marat replied that they would all be guillotined. Charlotte then stabbed Marat with her new knife, severing his aorta.

On 3 December 1792 at the trial of Louis XVI, The Architect of The Terror, Maximilien Robespierre said: 'It is with regret that I pronounce the fatal truth. Louis ought to perish rather than a hundred thousand virtuous citizens. Louis must die, so that the country may live.'

At her own trial Charlotte echoed these sentiments: 'I killed one man to save 100,000.' But nothing could save Charlotte Corday and she was beheaded three months before Marie Antoinette. Immediately after her decapitation, a hired hand named Legro picked up her head and slapped her face. For his rudeness the authorities imprisoned Legros for three months.

Marat became a martyr and Jacques-Louis David immortalised the moment of his death in his 1793 painting *The Death of Marat*, one of the great pieces of assassination art.

Napoleon Bonaparte

Recent forensic investigation has revealed that the former French Emperor might also have been assassinated. After his final defeat at the Battle of Waterloo (18 June 1815) the coalition of European nations that fought against him forced him into exile on the island of Saint Helena. The island is one of the most remote on earth and lies in the South Atlantic, 2800 km south of the Bight of Guinea, about halfway between Angola and the city of Salvador in Brazil. Evidently his exile wasn't enough for some people.

Napoleon's personal physician, Francesco Antonmarchi listed the cause of Napoleon's death as stomach cancer, but in 1955 the diaries of the ex-Emperor's valet, Louis Marchand, came to wide attention.

Louis' observations led many to believe that Napoleon's sickness prior to his death gave every appearance of arsenic poisoning. Since 2001 a number of different analyses of locks of Napoleon's hair have shown that he had levels of arsenic in his body that were 38 times the normal level, although the source of the arsenic may well have been a hair tonic. A question mark still hangs over the whole subject.

If it was arsenic poisoning, the most likely assassin was the courtier Charles Tristan Marquis de Montholon, who had two possible motives for hastening Napoleon's death. Napoleon had become the lover of Montholon's wife; but the poisoning might also have been a favour for his friend and Louis XVIII's brother, the Duke d'Artois.

The Duke had attempted to assassinate Napoleon in 1800. Montholon had embezzled army funds and d'Artois had rescued Montholon from punishment. The courtier thus owed the Duke a favour. Montholon may have poisoned Napoleon over a period of months. It's also possible, however, that Napoleon was dying of stomach cancer while Montholon, oblivious, simultaneously poisoned the ex-emperor's wine. What's left of Napoleon is now in the Crypt under the Église du Dome at Les Invalides Military Memorial in Paris.

Napoleon, of course, was able to rise to power in the first place because of the French Revolution and the numerous assassinations of that bloody time. The French monarchy had been under considerable pressure ever since the death of Louis XIV. Louis XV succeeded his great-grandfather at the age of five after a disastrous four years in which four males in line to the French throne had died, mostly from smallpox. Although he would reign for 58 years Louis was ill equipped to be king. Timid and indecisive, he relied on his regent and ministers in his early years. By the time he was 33 his official advisors had left him and he increasingly sought guidance from his common-born mistress, Jeanne-Antoinette Poisson, the Marquise de Pompadour—an influence that both the aristocracy and the masses ill-favoured. The perception at the time was that the King and his mistress were doing nothing much but spending public money on their own luxuries.

On 5 January 1757, the mildly insane domestic Robert Damiens attacked Louis on the grounds of Versailles and stabbed him with a penknife. The King was wearing thick clothing at the time and the blade only penetrated about a centimetre between the King's fourth and fifth ribs. Nevertheless it was the first attempt on a French king's life since the death of Henry IV almost 147 years before.

Damiens became the last person executed in France by drawing and quartering, but not before undergoing tortures that included burning off his hand using sulphur, being stabbed with red-hot pincers and having molten wax, molten lead and boiling oil poured into his wounds. The records account that although horses attempted to pull him apart his joints were so strong that after several hours his executioners had to cut his limbs. Apparently, he was still alive when his head and trunk were burnt at the stake. The execution was such a spectacle that balconies overlooking the sight at the Place de Grève were rented out at 5000 francs, the equivalent of $700. The execution did nothing for the King's popularity and, though its brutality was not under his direct control, considerable numbers of people thought it barbaric and held him accountable. Incidents like this and the perception of profligate spending that only continued with the reign of Louis' grandson, Louis XVI and his Austrian-born wife Marie Antoinette, only added more fuel to the fire that would burn as the French Revolution.

After the National Convention beheaded Louis XVI and Marie Antoinette the new French authorities imprisoned their son, the seven-year-old Louis-Charles. The boy was regularly beaten and generally abused until the non-reigning Louis XVII died from tuberculosis at barely ten years old.

You could think of his death as assassination by neglect.

Shaka Zulu

King Shaka Zulu is the man who can be credited with turning a once obscure African tribe into a major military force and full-blown nation. After the death of his father, Senzangakona, Shaka became the a man of his time and place. When Zwide, Chief of the Ndwandwe, assassinated Shaka's mentor Dingiswayo, chief of the Mthethwa, the young king's revenge was protracted and gruesome. Shaka murdered Zwide's mother by locking her in a house full of hungry jackals. The animals tore her to pieces and ate her. He then burned the house to the ground. History does not record what happened to the jackals.

In 1820 Shaka defeated Zwide in battle during the Zulu civil war. Although Zwide escaped, Shaka's ally Chieftainess Mjanji of the baPedi murdered Zwide soon afterwards.

Shaka continued his program of conquest of and alliances with the southern African tribes and might even have become an emperor, but he became increasingly autocratic and alienated too many of his own people. In the end his half-brothers Dingane and Umthlangana murdered him, threw his body into an empty grain pit and filled it with stones. Dingane became King and assassinated Umthlangana shortly afterwards, just to keep things simple.

Dingane later tried to have his general Ndela kaSompisi assassinate another half-brother and rival, Mpande. Ndela delayed overlong, and Dingane ordered his death by slow strangulation with a cowhide thong. Ndela's squeamishness was ultimately to no avail. Dingane himself fell to an assassin, Zulu Nyawo, in the Hlatikhulu Forest, while he was fighting Mpande. Mpande ruled over the Zulu for 32 years and all subsequent kings of the Zulu are descended from Mpande, since neither Shaka or Digane had children of their own. The Zulu bloodline is quite safe now. The current Zulu King, Goodwill Zwelithini kaBhekuzulu has about 27 children from five wives and several concubines.

Eurocentric history might have ignored the Zulue altogether, except that under Dingane the tribe became so powerful that they posed a serious challenge to British imperialism. It was a battle that the Zulu, with their prehistoric weapons, would never win, but they put up a good fight and gave the British a bloody nose or two.

Empress Myeongseong of Korea

The last Empress of Korea was murdered at her residence in the Gyeongbokgung Palace in Seoul. She was a long-standing opponent of expansionist Japanese interests at the time and historians generally consider the Japanese Minister to Korea, Muira Goroo, to have been behind her murder. Muira hadn't wasted any time; he'd only been in his job 37 days when the Empress died.

The assassination created considerable international outrage and Goroo was recalled to Japan and stood trial along with 55 other people charged in connection to the Empress's death—an event now known as the 'Elumi Incident'. However, the Hiroshima District Court found all 56 accused not guilty on the grounds of insufficient evidence. Goroo went on to become a privy counsellor.

For a long time the Japanese government maintained that Goroo had acted independently of them, but in June 2006 Choy Mun-hyeong, Emirutus Professor of Historical Science at the University of Hanyang, found a letter in the Tribute Archive of the Japanese National Document Archive that seems to confirm that the Japanese Government of the time approved the assassination.

If the Japanese had intended to destabilise Korea with the assassination, the plan certainly worked. In his grief, the Empress' widower, Emperor Gojong, and the rest of the family left the palace. The imperial family never resided there again. In the coming years the Emperor gave concession after concession to the Japanese and made it much easier for them to consolidate their invasion of the region in the build up to the War in the Pacific—better known to Eurocentric history as World War II. Gojong was forced to abdicate in favour of his son Sunjong in 1907, but Korea ceased to be an independent nation with the Japan–Korea annexation treaty of 22 August 1910 which effectively also finished the Joseon Dynasty and the era of Korea's imperial rule.

The Japanese war of expansion continued into China and Mongolia and would ultimately only end with Japan's defeat at the end of World War II on 2 September 1945—fifty years after the assassination of Empress Myeongseong.

Nasser al-Din Shah Qajar: Shah of Iran

Nasser was a Shah of many firsts. He was the first Shah to be photographed, the first Shah to keep a diary and the first Shah to visit Europe. In many ways he was ahead of his time, but he was also behind the times. His persecution of the followers of the Baha'i and Babi faiths led a Babi to a failed assassination attempt in 1852.

Forty-four years later Mizra Reza Kermani, a follower of the political reformer Jamal al-Din al-Afghani, shot the Shah while he was praying at the Shrine of Shah-Abdol-Azim. Mizra was apprehended and didn't live long. When news of the Shah's death reached the Ottoman Sultan, Abd al-Hamid II, the Turkish ruler put Afghani under his protection. Afghani continued to work toward uniting the Islamic world but died of cancer the following year.

Umberto I of Italy

In contrast to the long list of Roman emperors, Umberto I, has the distinction of being the only modern Italian monarch to be assassinated. Umberto was so unpopular that it would have been surprising if he had actually died of natural causes.

Left wing anarchists in particular thought that Umberto's ties to militant powers such as the Austro-Hungarian Empire and Germany were typical of a king who was a fascist before the term was even invented. The anarchist Giovanni Passannante unsuccessfully attacked the King with a knife in 1878 in the first year of his reign. Umberto commuted Giovanni's sentence from death to life imprisonment.

Almost twenty years later, on 22 April 1897, an unemployed ironsmith, Pietro Acciarito also tried to stab the King. He too failed and once again a would-be assassin ended up in jail for the rest of his life.

In 1898 General Fiorenzo Bava Beccaris fired cannons on the citizens of Milan who were protesting the rise of bread prices. As many as 350 people may have died and about 1000 were wounded. When Umberto decorated the General, instead of court martialling him, even the peaceful majority of Italians thought it was an outrage. Gaetano Bresci—an Italian-born weaver who had lived in America—felt that the victims of the Milan protests had to be avenged. On 29 July 1900 Bresci shot the King three times while he was visiting the city of Monza in Lombardy. Umberto died and was buried in the Pantheon in Rome next to his father Victor Emmanuel II.

Gaetano Bresci was caught and sentenced to life imprisonment on Santo Stefano Island, off the Italian coast. The small, circular island houses a facility specifically dedicated to hold political prisoners. The island is now uninhabited and the prison is an occasional tourist attraction. Bresci died in the first year of his imprisonment, probably murdered by prison guards. He is still considered a hero to the anarchist movement.

King Aleksandar Obrenovic: of Serbia

It wasn't only right-wing monarchs that got it. In Serbia, when it became widely believed that King Aleksandar Obrenovic of Serbia, was going to position his wife Draga's brother Nicodiye as heir apparent to the crown, the military balked. On 11 June 1903 military officers broke into the Queen's bedroom and found the royal couple hiding in a wardrobe. They shot Aleksandar and Draga, mutilated their bodies and threw them out of a palace window. This proved, once again, that you only have to make one really bad decision to be marked for death.

The military movement that killed the Serbian Royals placed Peter I of Yugolslavia on the throne. They eventually evolved into the secret society known as the Black Hand, which would have a particularly important role to play in a much more important assassination eleven years later.

Franz Ferdinand: Archduke of Austria-Este

Although technically not a king, or an emperor, Franz Ferdinand's death was probably the most politically significant assassination in history. In a sense the killing of the Archduke didn't start World War I, as is generally claimed—Europe was a house of cards ready to fall at the slightest touch. To cut a very long story short: the first Sultan of the Ottomans, Osman I had established the Ottoman Empire in 1299 as a breakaway state of the Seljuk Sultanate of Anatolia. In a few centuries the Turks under Osman and his successors would create a state that exceeded the Roman Empire in its area and influence. At its height in 1683, the Ottoman Empire, centred on Turkey, stretched from Algiers in the south, to Vienna in the north, Kiev in the east, as well as reaching the Persian Gulf and Arabian Peninsula. The Ottomans were a very big deal, but by 1914 they were at the end of a long decline, their sultans long lapsed into decadent self-gratification. The emerging nationalist movements in what was left of Ottoman territory were smelling their chance at independence.

Germany was young and had secured control of its homeland and much of what is now France and Poland. Kaiser Wilhelm II, however, wanted more, which made Britain, France and Russia nervous so they formed an alliance against the Germans.

South of Germany, Austro-Hungarian Empire was the second largest state in Europe after Russia and its area took up what is now Austria, Hungary, much of southern Poland, the northwest area of the Balkans, a fair part of Romania and Ukraine. The Austro-Hungarian Empire was also beginning to fail from its own internal divisions.

In essence World War I was a disaster waiting to happen—it only needed a triggering event.

As it happened the assassination of Franz Ferdinand was very typical of its day. The previously-mentioned Black Hand had formed in May 1911 to support the Pan-Slavist Nationalist Movement—in particular the Narodna Odbrana (Defence of the People) Movement. In essence, the Black Hand wanted to reunite the Serb populations of Bosnia and Herzegovina with Serbia proper. They felt that, since Greece had already won its independence from the Ottoman Empire, a Pan Slavist Serbia could win theirs from the Austro-Hungarians. At the time the Austro-Hungarian Empire had controlled Bosnia and Herzegovina since 1878. It had taken it from the Ottomans and it wasn't about to let go. The Black Hand therefore had specifically targeted the Archduke as a way of provoking a war of independence.

The assassination of the 50-year-old heir to the Austro-Hungarian crown was supposed to start a purely *local* war with Austria that the Serbs could win. So Colonel Dragutin Dimitrijevic—Apis—of the Black Hand, the mastermind behind the assassination of Aleksandar and Draga of Serbia in 1903, paid about fifteen people to kill Franz Ferdinand. The assassins struck while he was riding in an open car with General Oskar Potiorek, the Governor of Bosnia-Herzegovina, through the streets of the provincial capital of Sarajevo. As it happened, only about nine were directly involved.

Danilo Ilic recruited Nedjelko Cabrinovic, Trifko Grabez and Gavrilo Princip. The choice was rather cynical, as Danilo's recruits were all suffering from tuberculosis, then incurable, and knew that they would not live long. They were thus young, idealistic and expendable.

Tragically, Nikola Pasic, Prime Minister of Serbia, heard about the plot, but failed to apprehend the group before they left the country for Sarajevo. Subsequent events suggest that Pasic may not have tried too hard, or that he was frustrated by a military with a mind of its own.

Cvijetko Popovic, a captain with the Serbian Border Guard, helped the three enter Bosnia-Herzogovina. Other recruits then joined the conspirators: Veljko Cubrilovic, Vaso Cubrilovic, Misko Jovanovic and Muhamed Mehmedbasic.

On the appointed day, Mehmedbasic found it impossible to act because he claimed that a policeman was standing next to him. So he did nothing that might alert the authorities and left the scene. When another realised that Franz Ferdinand's wife, Archduchess Sophie, would also be in the car, he decided that he didn't want anything to do with killing a woman. Nedjelko Cabrinovic threw a bomb at the royal couple, but the driver saw the bomb and accelerated. The bomb bounced off the car—or according to some accounts, off the Archduke's arm—and exploded under the following car, seriously injuring the occupants and many of the crowd.

When the bomb went off the panicked crowd overwhelmed several of the conspirators and they were unable to do anything further. In the confusion Gavrilo Princip tried to shoot the pair, but couldn't make the car out. Nedjelko then took cyanide and jumped into the nearby River Miljaka. The cyanide, however, was past its use-by date and weak and the Miljacka only 10 cm deep, so instead of ending up poisoned and drowned Nedjelko ended up just sick and wet. A furious mob soon seized him and beat him up before the police took him into custody. Gavrilo meanwhile took refuge in Moritz Schiller's delicatessen on Franz Joseph Street.

The Archduke and Archduchess were rushed to safety. They then insisted on visiting the victims of the bombing in hospital. The driver took a direct route to Sarajevo hospital, but General Potiorek countermanded the driver halfway, ordering him to take another route.

While the driver was backing up along Franz Joseph Street Gavrilo Princip saw the car, recognised this golden opportunity and fired twice from his Belgian Fabrique Nationale M 1910 semi-automatic pistol. The first shot penetrated the side of the car and hit Sophie in the abdomen. The second shot hit Franz Ferdinand in the jugular. Franz died within minutes, Sophie within the hour. They were later buried in the crypt of their country home of Schloss Artstetten.

Princep immediately took the cyanide that Ilic had given him, but it was no more effective than Nedjelko's and he was soon vomiting. Onlookers and the police quickly apprehended him.

The first shot … hit Sophie in the abdomen. The second shot hit Franz Ferdinand in the jugular.

The Austro-Hungarians seized the murder as a pretext to demand concessions from Serbia in a letter called the July Ultimatum. Although Serbia agreed to most of the demands, cutting off supplies to terrorists, a small border skirmish, on July 28 1914, allowed the Austro-Hungarians a pretext to invade Serbia anyway. Under the Secret Treaty of 1892 France and Russia were then forced into war with the Austro-Hungarians. Germany responded by going to war against France and Russia and also invaded Belgium. Britain and her colonies then joined up against Germany and the resulting mess was the 'Great War'.

As World War I raged and millions died, the conspirators were put on trial. Under Austro-Hungarian law criminals under the age of twenty when they committed a capital offence could not be executed for their crime, so Cabrinovic, Princip and Grabez received a maximum penalty of twenty years imprisonment and Popovic thirteen years. Vaso Cubrilovic received sixteen years, but his elder brother Veljko along with Ilic and Jovanovic were executed by firing squad on 3 February 1915.

As it happened Cabrinovic died in January 1916 from tuberculosis. Popovic and Vaso Cubrilovic were released from prison in November

1918 after the Allies defeated the Central Powers. Popovic eventually became the Curator of the Ethnographic Department of the Sarajevo Museum. Cubrilovic became a University Professor in Belgrade and had a hand in planning the later expulsion of Albanians from Kosovo. He died in 1990.

Gavrilo Princip, the man who many credit with starting World War I, eventually succumbed to the harsh conditions of prison and, like Cabrinovic, to the ravages of tuberculosis. He died on 28 April 1918, aged just 23. The prison where he and two of his fellow conspirators died, the Austrian Fortress of Theresienstadt, later became a Nazi concentration camp.

Muhamed Mehmedbasic managed to escape to Serbia. In 1919 he returned to Sarajevo and was pardoned for his ambiguous role in the assassination. He died in the city during World War II.

The Austro-Hungarians initially demanded the extradition of Apis, but Prime Minister Pasic refused. The point became moot when Austria-Hungary invaded Serbian territory, but the Serbs held their ground. The Austro-Hungarians were busy fighting along other fronts after finding that they'd set off something bigger than they could handle. In fact the Austro Hungarian's wasted efforts in Serbia hobbled their effectiveness to do anything else decisively and the whole campaign turned into one long fiasco.

Nikola Pasic eventually found Apis to be too politically inconvenient to protect. Pasic had Apis and some of his former Black Hand colleagues arrested and, on 23 May 1917, the court found Apis guilty of treason. A firing squad executed him on 24 June 1917, so he never lived to see the collapse of the Ottoman Empire, the destruction of the Austro-Hungarian Empire and the humiliation of Germany. The Black Hand's realisation of the pan-Serbian dream came true in the formation of Yugoslavia on 1 December 1918. Many wars later Boznia-Herzegovina became an independent nation on 6 April 1992. Serbia itself only became an independent nation as recently as 5 June 2006.

The gun that started World War I, the car that the Archduke was riding in and his bloodstained uniform and hat are on permanent display at the Museum of Military History in Vienna. The bullet that started the most terrible conflict in Europe's history to date was recovered from the body of the Archduke and is now an exhibit in the museum in Konopiste Castle near the town of Benesov in the Czech Republic.

As happens so often, the tragedies of ancestors have become the curios of their descendants.

The last days of imperial Russia

The Romanov Dynasty of Russia had a shaky start. As in-laws of the first Tsar Ivan IV—'Ivan the Terrible'—they were persecuted by Ivan's successor and their cousin, Boris Godunov. When the Gudunovs fell from power in 1606, during the Russian civil war, the Romanovs were the only people left who could 'legitimately' inherit the crown. When the Russian aristocracy offered the crown to sixteen-year-old Mikhail Romonov I in 1613, the young man was smart enough and sensitive enough to burst into tears—he thought he was being handed a death sentence. He survived, however, with the help of his father, Fyodor Nikitich Romanov and managed to put his country back together. Russia could never have been an easy empire to manage, but in spite of the troubles that would plague the Romanovs throughout their tenure, they produced or married some powerful rulers, including Peter I—'Peter the Great', Catherine II and Alexander III.

They also produced their fair share of weaklings. Particularly tragic is the story of Ivan VI who reigned for only a year as an infant before being imprisoned by his great aunt Tsarina Elizabeth. He spent the rest of his life in virtual solitary confinement under such secrecy that even his gaolers didn't know his true identity. While in confinement at the Fortress of Shlisseburg near St Petersburg he was finally murdered under the orders of Catherine II, a few weeks short of his 24th birthday.

Ivan's story has some similarities with the curious case of Kasper Hauser almost 70 years later. Kasper was found as a twelve-year-old boy walking the streets of Nuremburg. He was carrying letters saying that he'd been brought up in isolation and the boy confirmed that he'd grown up in a cell. When his strange case later came to international attention people remarked that he bore a resemblance to Karl Ludwig Friedrich, Grand Duke of Baden, who had no known male heirs. When Kasper was murdered by an unknown assassin, many speculated that Kasper was indeed Karl's son and that Karl's uncle and successor, Louis I had removed the mysterious boy as a possible political threat.

But the stories of Ivan and Kaspar are the tragedies of lone men. The story of the last Tsar of Russia is the tragedy of a whole family, and to some extent a nation.

By all accounts Nicholas should never have been Tsar, but there really wasn't much to choose from among the sons of Alexander III. Nicholas' younger brother Alexander died when he was eleven months old. The next younger brother, George, died of tuberculosis when he was 28. Michael, the youngest male Romanov, had a mind of his own, a military, rather than a political one.

Nicholas seemed to have been born under an unlucky star. On 11 May 1891, while Nicholas was on a visit to Japan, one of his Japanese guards Tsuda Sanzoo attacked him, slashing at his face with a sabre. Nicolas's cousin, Prince George of Greece, used his cane to parry a second blow. Tsuda attempted to escape, but two rickshaw drivers, Mukaihata Jizaburo and Kitagaichi Ichitaro, pulled him to the ground. He was sent to prison in Ashikawa Hokkaido where he soon died of one of those mysterious, unspecified illnesses. The Russians richly rewarded the rickshaw drivers and the Japanese government awarded them generous pensions, but when the Japanese and Russians later went to war in 1904 the drivers were accused of spying and their pensions revoked. In the short term, however, Japanese guilt and embarrassment led to unprecedented acts of contrition and apology.

One woman even committed suicide in front of Kyoto palace from the shame of it all.

The Otsu Scandal, as the failed assassination attempt later came to be known, left Nicholas with a scar across his forehead for the rest of his life. The scar was somewhat symbolic. Alexander III had browbeaten his eldest son all his life and considered him overly sensitive and effeminate. Alexander took refuge in his marriage to Alix of Hesse, granddaughter of Britain's Queen Victoria. Unfortunately Alix inherited from her grandmother the gene for haemophilia, a disease that prevents blood clotting and that generally affects only male children, although daughters can carry the disease. This coding error in the Empress Alexandra's DNA would have significant historical consequences. The Tsaritsa would bear the Tsar no fewer than four daughters before finally producing a male heir to the throne. It is possible that other male foetuses the Tsaritsa may have carried had bled to death in her womb.

Nicholas and Alexandra nonetheless enjoyed an extraordinarily happy and close domestic life with their children, but while the Tsar was playing happy families, his empire was falling apart around him. He did nothing to tackle the growing disaffection among the Russian people and the rise of revolutionaries like Leon Davidovich Trotsky, Vladimir Ilyich Ulyanov (Lenin) and the Bolsheviks.

The only shadow in the Tsar's domestic bliss was the delicate health of his heir Tsarevich Alexei. The slightest injury to him caused uncontrollable bleeding and bruising and the child's constitution did not improve with exercise and fresh air. Alexandra was in a continual state of fear that she'd lose her son and turned to anyone who could help including quacks and mystics. In 1912, after Alexei had a fall that left him bedridden for days, the Empress turned to Grigori Rasputin. Rasputin had acquired a reputation for healing through the power of prayer. When he first set eyes on the Prince he forbade doctors to continue their treatment. In the days of primitive medicine it might have been very good advice. Every time Rasputin saw the boy the

Tsarevich got better. Some now speculate that Rasputin used hypnosis to accelerate the healing process. This is plausible, as there is considerable documentation that hypnosis can significantly affect blood flow.

Rasputin's 'miraculous' healing abilities gave him considerable credibility with the Empress and, by proxy, considerable influence over the Emperor. When World War I broke out and Nicholas had to assume military command, for which he was entirely unsuited. He left control of the government in the hands of Alexandra, who was no more adept, relying on Rasputin's advice. His recommendations were completely self-serving and only destabilised the government further. The Tsarista's German family connections meant that the whole nation distrusted her. None of this escaped the attention of the court observers, who not only reported to the Tsar, but leaked reports to the press. The government's credibility was crumbling as the revolutionary movement grew.

Finally, a group of nobles, led by Prince Felix Yusupov and his friend—and possible lover—the Tsar's cousin Dmitri Pavlovich, had had enough. Felix also asked his very attractive wife, Irina Alexandrovna to get involved. Irina was the daughter of Tsar Nicholas's sister Grand Duchess Xenia Alexandrovna and the surviving correspondence between Irina and Felix is highly illuminating, not only for what it reveals about the plot, but also for the light it sheds on the personalities of the protagonists.

In a letter to Irina, referring to the plot to kill Rasputin, Felix wrote:

> You too must take part in it … Dm(itri) Pavl(ovich) knows all about it and is helping. It will all take place in the middle of December, when Dm(itri) comes back.

Irina wrote to Felix in November 1916:

> Thanks for your insane letter. I didn't understand the half of it. I see that you're planning to do something wild. Please take

care and do not get mixed up in any shady business. The dirtiest thing is that you have decided to do it all without me. I don't see how I can take part in it now, since it's all arranged … In a word, be careful. I see from your letter that you're in a state of wild enthusiasm and ready to climb a wall … I'll be in Petrograd on the 12th or 13th, so don't dare do anything without me, or else I won't come at all.

Felix to Irina, 27 November 1916:

Your presence by the middle of December is essential. The plan I'm writing you about has been worked out in detail and is three quarters done, and only the finale is left, and for that your arrival is awaited. It (the murder) is the only way of saving a situation that is almost hopeless … You will serve as the lure … Of course, not a word to anyone.

Irina to Felix, 3 December 1916:

I know that if I come, I shall certainly get sick … you don't know how things are with me. I want to cry all the time. My mood is terrible. I've never had one like it before … I don't know myself what's happening to me. Don't drag me to Petrograd. Come down here instead. Forgive me, my dear one, for writing such things to you. But I can't go on any more, I don't know what's the matter with me. Neurasthenia, I think. Don't be angry with me, please don't be angry. I love you terribly. I can't live without you.

May the Lord protect you.

Not one to be disheartened by his wife's chickening out, Felix went through with the plan anyway. Felix invited the mystic to his house,

Moika Palace, on the pretext that he could meet his wife. This was obviously a lie, as Irina was still in Crimea at the time.

Rasputin had a reputation as being hard to kill. Some two years earlier, on 29 June 1914, he was coming out of a church when a former prostitute, Khioniya Kozmishna Guseva—one of the many women that Rasputin had seduced and discarded—stabbed the mystic in the stomach and screamed, 'I have killed the Antichrist!' Although Khioniya practically eviscerated Rasputin, physicians managed to push his guts back in and sew him up. Rasputin recovered, thus demonstrating considerable constitutional fortitude.

When Felix and Dmitri had their chance it seemed that Rasputin's legend was true—he took some killing. At least that's the legend that Felix and Dmitri promulgated. They initially served Rasputin wine and cakes laced with enough cyanide to kill ten men. Rasputin's daughter Maria would later claim that because of her father's previous stomach injury he had hyperacidity and wouldn't have touched the wine or the cake. The unpublished 1916 autopsy certainly makes no mention of poison. Felix then shot Rasputin in the back. Rasputin fell, but as Felix knelt down to examine the body, Rasputin seized Felix's neck and choked his attacker before he got up and made his escape. The conspirators chased him and shot him three more times before clubbing him to death. They wrapped Rasputin's body in a sheet and threw him into the ice-covered Neva River. After the body was recovered the Empress buried it on the grounds of the imperial residence of Tsarskoye Selo, near St Petersburg. After the February Revolution, workers from the city now renamed Petrograd, dug up the body and burned it in a nearby wood.

Rasputin's death may have pleased many people, but it seriously demoralised the Romanovs and they became even more ineffectual. As punishment, Nicholas sent Dmitri Pavlovich to the Persian front. Ironically, this exile saved Dmitri's life. When the Bolsheviks later murdered his relatives, Dmitri fled to London, but ended up in Paris, where he had an affair with Coco Chanel. In 1920, through Dmitri's contacts, Chanel made the acquaintance of the Russian Parfumier Ernest Beaux, who created Chanel No. 5. In 1927 Dmitri married Anna Audrey Emery, heiress to an American real estate fortune. They divorced in 1937 and Dmitri became involved with the Fascists, but refused Hitler's invitation to fight against his fellow Russians in World War II. Dmitri died not long after, finally succumbing to the tuberculosis that had plagued him all his life.

His son by Audrey Emery, Paul Ilyinski became an American citizen, served in the US Navy and eventually became the mayor of Palm Beach in 1989. He served for ten years, becoming the only Romanov ever to hold an elected office. When Communist Russia collapsed a delegation of royalists visited him to ask him to assume the title of Tsar. Paul was flattered, but politely refused.

As for Felix Yusupov, he and his family were put under house arrest in one of the Yusupov family farms near St Petersburg, but soon escaped and procured some Rembrandt paintings and jewellery from the family estates before eventually fleeing to Paris, where they bought a house and lived the rest of their lives in relative comfort. Their comfort was subsidised by a successful lawsuit against MGM. In the studio's 1932 film, *Rasputin and the Empress*, the movie inaccurately depicts that Rasputin had raped Felix's wife Irina. The jury decided that Irina had been defamed and the Yusupovs won £25 000 in damages, worth about $10 million today. Incidentally, the court case set the precedent for films carrying the standard disclaimer: 'All characters appearing in this work are fictitious. Any resemblance to real persons, living or dead, is purely coincidental.'

Felix and Irina had a daughter, Princess Irina Felixovna Yusupova, who married Count Nikolai Sheremetiev (1904–1979). They had one daughter, Countess Xenia Sheremeteva Sfyris. Xenia played an important role in her family history decades after the assassination of the Romanovs.

Revolution

Russia actually had two revolutions in 1917.

The February Revolution came about because a harsh winter and the continuing depredations of the Great War had brought about famine and workers began to strike en masse. In late February demonstrators gathered in St Petersburg demanding bread, but matters quickly escalated and soldiers began to desert and join the demonstrations. The Tsar refused to believe the reports of the Chairman of the Duma—the Russian Legislative Assembly—and decided to make his way back to the capital. Revolting troops then diverted the Tsar's train and, on 15 March 1917, as representatives of the new Russian Government, the army forced Nicholas to abdicate in favour of his brother Mikhail. Mikhail in turn was forced to sign a document stating that his assumption of the throne would only be ratified if he were elected by general mandate of the Russian people. Such a mandate never happened. On 12 June 1912 Mikhail and his secretary were removed from their residence in a hotel in the city of Perm, under the orders of the Cheka, the progenitor of the KGB. They were taken to the outskirts of the city, shot and their bodies burned.

The Russian people formed a provisional government under the Constitutional Democratic Party, but it quickly failed, as did a competing government under the Socialist Revolutionary Party. Although the Social Revolutionaries had 57 per cent of the popular vote, they were no match for the much savvier and more brutal Bolsheviks.

Lenin returned from political exile in Switzerland to St Petersburg, now Petrograd, on 3 April and teamed up with Leon Trotsky. Their union and the popular support that they gained culminated in an uprising on 25 October against the Provisional Government. The Bolsheviks took over the capital and stormed the Winter Palace, effectively seizing control of the nation and of the Tsar and his family.

The Provisional government had originally kept the Romanovs in the Alexander Palace at Tsarkoye Selo, but in August had moved them to Toblosk in Siberia. Now the Bolesheviks' military arm, the Red Guard, moved them to Yekaterinberg in Central Russia, where the Bolsheviks had firmer control. There they were held in a house owned by a merchant called Ipatiev. In one of the weirder coincidences of history, it was in the Ipatiev Monastery in Kostroma that the Assembly of the Land of Russian Nobility had asked Mikhail Romanov to assume the Tsarship 304 years before.

With the Romanovs were the family's personal physician Dr Botkin, a lady-in-waiting, Demidova, their cook Kharinotov and their footman Trupp. Their chief gaoler was a former watchmaker from Perm, Yakov Mikhailovich Yurovsky. Units of the Czechoslovak Legion were retreating from Russia and approaching Yekaterinburg. Moscow was concerned that the Czechs would rescue the Tsar and ordered the execution of the whole family. Party leader Yakov Mikhaylovich Sverdlov gave the specific order. The details of the assassination itself remained a closely guarded secret for decades and it was only when the Soviet Union collapsed in 1989 that Yurovski's official account was published. It is mainly from this report that we know what happened next.

Around midnight on 16 July 1918 the guards woke up the Romanovs and their servants. Thinking that they were going to be moved again they dressed. They were instead all led to the cellar and Yurovski read them a letter from the Presidium of the Ural Regional Soviet:

> In view of the fact that your relatives continue their offensive against Soviet Russia, the Presidium of the Ural Regional Soviet has decided to sentence you to death.

Nicholas cried out: 'Lord, oh my God! Oh my God! What is this? I don't understand you.'

Yurovsky shot the Tsar and Tsarevich Alexei himself, killing the man and boy with multiple shots to the head and chest. The servants soon followed. The killing of the Empress and her daughters took longer than anticipated because the guards' bullets bounced off jewels hidden in the dresses the women were wearing. When bayonets also failed the female Romanovs died from close-range shots to their heads. The guards doused the bodies with acid and burned them.

On the night of 17 July the guards took what was left of the Romanov bodies to a mineshaft nearby called the Four Brothers, but Yorovsky ordered their removal to a more secret location. The truck carrying the corpses broke down on the way to the new site and the Romanovs were buried in a pit on a now abandoned cart track called Koptaki Road, 19 kilometres north of Yekaterinburg.

Yorovsky went on to serve as Chief of the Soviet State Treasury and died of a peptic ulcer, aged 50.

In 1977 Boris Yeltsin ordered that the Ipatiev House be demolished. The Church on the Blood now stands on the site.

In 1991 the bodies of the Romanovs and their servants were unearthed and subjected to extensive DNA testing. Blood-spattered relics from the Otsu Scandal retained enough of the Tsar's DNA to definitively cross-identify genetic material recovered from one of the skeletons as Tsar Nicholas. Alexsandra's DNA was linked to that of Queen Victoria's bloodline. Xenia Sheremeteva Sfyris' mitochondrial DNA provided a further match to three of the Imperial daughters. Mitochondrial DNA is only passed along the female line. To date no one has found the remains of Tsarevitch Alexei and his sister Alexandra. Historians generally believe that they were buried in another grave not far from the main pit.

The remains that have been unearthed now lie in a special chapel in the Peter and Paul Fortress in St Petersburg.

Mikhail Romanov and his mistress Natalia Princess Brassova's legitimised son, George Count Brasov, went into exile in England with his mother. George died in a car crash near Auxerre in France while on holiday, two days short of his 21st birthday. With him died the last of the direct male descendants of Alexander III. George's mother survived him by twenty years, dying of cancer in Paris, in poverty.

You can find an extensive list of the members of the Romanov family who managed to survive the Revolution and escape Russia at: *www.angelfire.com/pa/ImperialRussian/royalty/russia/survivor.html.*

The first 'media' assassination: Yugoslavia' s Alexander I

With the rearrangement of reality that occurred in the aftermath of World War I, kings and emperors became an endangered species. With fewer around in the first place there were fewer to assassinate. The decades that followed were a far cry from the bloodthirsty years of the early twentieth century.

The assassination of King Alexander I of Yugoslavia and the simultaneous assassination of the Foreign Minister of France, Louis Barthou, by Vlado Chernozemski received much greater media coverage than historic repercussions.

Although the double assassination is almost entirely forgotten now, it became one of the most publicised events of its day. It was almost certainly the first assassination to be captured on film. The King and Barthou were riding through Marseille, France in a motorcade when Chernozemski jumped onto the running board of the King's car and fired ten shots at its occupants.

The assassination might not even have happened had the Bulgarian legal system not been so dysfunctional. In 1924 Chernozemski assassinated a Bulgarian Communist Party MP and, although he was sentenced to death, he was granted an amnesty in 1932, and went on to assassinate Alexander and Barthou. Shortly after the assassination a French mounted policeman cut him down with a sword and a crowd of onlookers beat him to death.

Jordan: King Abdullah I

With the collapse of the Ottoman Empire after World War I, the British took control of many of its former possessions in the Middle East, but in some cases not for long. Local populaces increasingly demanded autonomy and got it. That certainly didn't mean the new men in charge were necessarily safely ensconced.

When Abdullah I became the first King of Jordan his liberalism worried his Arab allies and his attitude towards Israel was, by local standards, moderate. He was prepared to make peace with the fledgling state when most of his neighbours wanted to destroy it. Three days before Abdullah's death, former Prime Minister of Lebanon Riad as-Solh was assassinated for holding a similarly tolerant attitude towards Israel.

Colonel Abdullah Tell, the Governor of Jerusalem when the city was still under Arab control, was later found to be behind the plot to murder Abdullah. His stooge was a 21-year-old tailor's apprentice, Mustapha Shukri Usho, who on 20 July shot the King three times while he was praying at the Al Aqsa Mosque—the Dome on the Rock. Abdullah died and a bullet also hit Abdullah's grandson Prince Hussein. Hussein was wearing a medal on his chest at his grandfather's bequest and the bullet ricocheted, saving the fifteen year old's life.

Although Abdullah's son Talal formally succeeded his father, he suffered from schizophrenia and was forced to abdicate on 11 August. Hussein began his 45-year reign on his eighteenth birthday and continued the moderate, western approach that his grandfather had established—two of his four wives were westerners and the current King of Jordan, Hussein's son Abdullah II, is half-English.

Abdullah I's brother Faisal had preceded his brother to kingship by becoming the first King of Iraq in August 1921. He died of a heart attack after reigning for twelve years. His son Ghazi ruled until he died in a mysterious car accident, which many suspected was arranged by his Prime Minister Nuri as-Said. Ghazi was well known to have harboured

Nazi sympathies. This and his claim that Kuwait should be annexed to Iraq must have made the King rather an embarrassment. It wouldn't be the last time that an Iraqi leader would set his eyes on Kuwait.

Ghazi was succeeded by his four-year-old son Faisal II. As he grew to adulthood, he and his cousin Hussein enjoyed a close relationship, forming the Arab Federation of Iraq and Jordan on 14 February 1958 as a counterbalance to Egypt and Syria's formation of the United Arab Republic two weeks earlier. The cousins' dream of a continuing alliance fell apart soon afterwards. On 14 July 1958 Iraq's Colonel Abdul Karim Qassim—'az-Zaim'—staged a successful military coup of Iraq. The royal family were ordered to leave their palace in Baghdad, but only reached the courtyard. One of az-Zaim's allies in the coup, Captain Abdus Sattar As Sab'a, shot the entire family. All of them died immediately except for Faisal and his uncle's wife, Princess Hiyam. Faisal died before he could reach a hospital. Hiyam escaped and, unrecognised, managed to be treated in hospital. She successfully escaped to her family in Saudi Arabia, the only living witness to the massacre.

Qassim implemented various populist reforms, such as recognising the equality of all Iraqi citizens regardless of race or religion, but he soon became the target of pan-Arab nationalists, who believed in the unification of all Arab states. He survived an assassination attempt in 1959 and another backed by the British Government and the CIA on 9 February 1963. He died on that day anyway when the Baath Party, led by Ahmed Hassan al-Bakr, staged a successful revolt. Al-Bakr's regime paved the way for that of Saddam Hussein Abd al-Majid al-Tikriti.

Saudi Arabia: King Faisal

At the time of writing, the most recent murder of a king was that of Saudi Arabia's King Faisal in 1975. Faisal was the third son of Ibn Saud, the founder of Saudi Arabia, and succeeded to the throne after he successfully deposed his half-brother and Ibn Saud's second son Saud in 1964. Ibn Saud's first-born and Saud's full brother, Turki, had died aged nineteen in 1919.

Faisal is best remembered today for withdrawing Saudi oil from the world supply in 1973, precipitating the Oil Crisis that quadrupled the price of crude oil and triggered a recession in the ever-energy hungry developed world. This Machiavellian manoeuvre may have played a role in his assassination.

However, in 1965 fundamentalists protested the introduction of television into Saudi Arabia and some protesters died for their cause, shot by Faisal's defence forces. One of them was Khalid bin Musa'id. His younger brother Faisal bin Musa'id bin Abdul Aziz gained his revenge when he assassinated King Faisal. Bin Musa'id was also the son of another of Faisal's half-brothers, Musa'id bin Abdul Aziz, so the motive was more personal than political as the assassin himself later declared. Bin Musa'id also had a history of drug abuse, which may also have played a part.

King Faisal was celebrating the birthday of Muhammad in the Royal Palace at Riyadh when he noticed his nephew in a line, apparently waiting to pay his respects. Faisal bent down to allow bin Musa'id to kiss the royal nose. His nephew instead fired several shots at point-blank range into his face. Faisal collapsed and was rushed to hospital.

Before he died the King requested that his nephew not be executed for his crime. The courts decided otherwise and convicted bin Musa'id of regicide just over three weeks after the assassination. A few hours after the verdict, the authorities beheaded him in the public square in Riyadh. Ironically, considering his family's history with the medium, Saudi Arabian Television recorded the whole assassination.

The Modern World of Assassination

With the decline of monarchies and military empires killing kings and emperors had become old hat and the wave of the future was in killing senior politicians. If you were an ambitious assassin you aimed for prime ministers and presidents.

The twentieth century saw a surge in the popularity of assassination. If you were politically impotent you could at least take a pot shot at the head man (or, more rarely, woman) and grab at least fifteen minutes of fame and publicity for your cause.

Political murder has evolved into the modern image of a lone gunman with a grudge to bear or a fall guy for a conspiracy. In some cases assassination was even a professional job, executed by a hired gun, a trained killer or spy—someone who really knew what he was doing. These are the most glamourous assassinations of all, the ones novelists most like to write about.

I've divided modern assassinations into four broad groups:

• Top-down

These assassinations involve those in power maintaining their powerbase by getting rid of rivals—think of the military targeting 'radicals', acting under orders from an unscrupulous dictatorship. Of course the military often acts on its own and coups d'état can be considered another context for assassination. The Pinochet murder of Salvador Allende is one such example.

• Bottom-up

These are committed or commissioned by those out of power wanting to get in. Think of long-standing 'struggles for freedom' like those of the IRA and the PLO. Please note that while fanatics nowadays also like to target 'ordinary people' they generally have to kill more of them because killing John Smith isn't worth nearly as much as killing Prime Minister John Smith. Murderous acts of terrorism in general therefore don't count as assassinations, but a case like the IRA's killing of Lord Mountbatten does.

• Policy politics

These murders typically cross national borders, when powerful nations want to remove inconvenient political figures without all the trouble and expense of having to go to war. Superpowers tend to favour this sort of activity as part of 'covert operations', but smaller states can get involved too. Sometimes all does not go according to plan, as demonstrated in the infamous Lillehammer Affair where Israeli agents killed an innocent man believing him to be a Palestinian fighter.

• Independents

These are the true lone gunmen who work on the basis that they can't help but succeed, because while their potential victims have to be lucky all the time—they only have to get lucky once. In spite of all the conspiracy theories to the contrary, I believe that Lee Harvey Oswald's assassination of John F Kennedy is such a case.

There are also a smattering of important assassinations that do not involve politicians as such, but people whose murder had political motives, such as that of the gorilla defender Dianne Fossey.

The following brief survey gives you an idea of just how widespread and popular assassinations have been around the world in the twentieth century. The assassinations are grouped according to where they took place.

Africa

Burundi: three Prime Ministers

Three prime ministers of the former Belgian colony of Burundi were assassinated in the 1960s.

The people gave Prince Louis Rwagasore a mandate to lead his people to independence. He had been in power for just two weeks in 1961 and was having dinner at the Hotel Tanganyika when George Kageorgis, allegedly in the pay of the pro-Belgium Christian Democratic Party, shot him dead.

Independent Burundi wasn't any safer. Pierre Ngendandumwe, a native Hutu, was eight days into his second term in 1965 when a Tutsi refugee, allegedly a CIA plant, assassinated him. His successor Joseph Bamina was also assassinated the same year.

Egypt: three more Prime Ministers

Three prime ministers of Egypt have also been assassinated.

Ibrahim Nassif al-Wardani, a pharmacology graduate, assassinated Boutros Ghali in February 1910, because of the Prime Minister's pro-British stance. His grandson, Boutros Boutros-Ghali later served as Secretary General of the United Nations from 1992 to 1996.

Dr Ahmad Mahir Pasha was killed in 1945 while making a speech declaring war on the Axis Powers (Germany's allies in World War II) in a cynical move to get the allies on side, since by 1945 it was obvious who was going to lose anyway. His assassin was 28-year-old Mustafa Issawy, a member of the Fundamentalist Waft Party, who were advocates for Egyptian independence from Britain.

Prime Minister Mahmoud Fahmi an-Nukrashi Pasha was killed by the Fundamentalist Muslim Brotherhood in 1948.

The most famous assassination in Egypt in modern times was that of President Anwar Sadat whom we will look at more closely in Chapter 6.

Nigeria: 'Ken' Saro-Wiwa

The first prime minister of independent Nigeria, Sir Abubakar Tafawa Balewa was elected in 1960 and was two years into his second term when his government succumbed to a military coup d'état in 1966. His body was found by a roadside near Lagos six days after his murder.

Another political murder was that of writer and television producer Kenule 'Ken' Beeson Saro-Wiwa in 1995. Saro-Wiwa spent the last years of his life as a activist, concentrating on defending the interests of the Ogoni people of the Niger Delta against the exploitation of the region at the hands of oil companies. This made him a lot of enemies, and the Nigerian military Abacha Regime kept him intermittently in jail until they arrested him for the last time. He was picked up, long with eight other members of the Movement for the Survival of the Ogoni People in 1994, on trumped up charges for allegedly inciting the deaths of four Ogoni elders. All nine were sentenced to death.

On 10 November Saro-Wiwa watched his eight fellow defendants hang before he too joined them on the gallows. The Commonwealth of Nations suspended Nigeria's membership in protest.

Rwanda: Dianne Fossey

All that American animal behaviour expert Dianne Fossey wanted to do was hang out with gorillas. Her extraordinary ability to gain the trust of the primates led to some interspecies friendships, famously with a young male gorilla, 'Digit'. Usually you wouldn't think that an ethologist (a scientist who studies animal behaviour) would be the target of an assassination, but the gorillas had the misfortune of living in Rwanda where they were the frequent victims of poachers.

Digit became one such victim. Fossey actively interfered with poachers, forming anti-poaching patrols and destroying traps. This and her stand on opposing the capture of gorillas for zoos and the exploitation of gorillas for tourism made her many enemies.

Fossey lived in a cabin at her Karisoke Research Centre in the remote rainforest of the Virunga Mountains in Ruhengi Province of north-west Rwanda. Her assassin cut a hole in her bedroom wall to gain entry, suggesting the killer was familiar with the cabin's layout. On the wall of Fossey's living room next to her bedroom she had mounted a native panga (a knife that poachers often use to kill gorilla) which Fossey had confiscated years before. The killer took the panga, entered Fossey's bedroom and must have surprised her as she was sleeping. The evidence suggests that she woke up and tried to defend herself, but her killer split her skull with the panga before escaping. Fossey's body was found on the floor, two metres from her bed.

Rwandan authorities arrested all of her employees, including a tracker called Rwelenkana, whom Fossey had fired months before. Rwelenka mysteriously 'hanged himself' in prison. The other employees were all released. Several months later the Rwandans accused Fossey's American research assistant of her murder, but the American Embassy warned him in time, and Wayne McGuire was able to make his escape from the country.

Dianne's work was not in vain, but her legacy did have its downside. After years of struggling with limited funding, Dianne Fossey had signed a contract for $1 million for the film rights to her story, based partially on her book, *Gorillas in the Mist*. The 1988 movie remains the most well-known depiction of her life in spite of its factual inaccuracies. Her will stated that proceeds of the film should go to the Digit Fund to continue the poacher patrols, but her mother, Kitty Price, contested the will and won.

Fossey's legacy seems to be losing on other fronts as well. Thousands of tourists visit Virunga every year to see the gorillas. In 2005 eight gorillas out of a population of only around 350 died from tourist-contracted measles.

Dianne Fossey is buried in the grave she set up for her murdered gorillas, near her beloved Digit.

Rwanda: Prelude to Genocide

In 1994, Juvénal Habyarimana, the military dictator and third president of Rwanda, died when his private jet—a gift from French President François Mitterand—crashed in the backyard of his home. With him in the plane was his fellow Hutu, Cyprien Ntaryamir who had been

President of Burundi for only two months. The plane crash was highly suspicious and no investigation ever took place. As it was, the Hutu-dominated Rwandan media immediately claimed that the crash was an assassination and that the Tutsi-dominated Rwandese Patriotic front had shot down the plane.

Extremists among the Hutu majority, seething with years of ethnic hatred towards the Tutsis, began a killing spree that led to the Rwandan Genocide. From 6 April to mid-July 1994 some one million Tutsis and moderate Hutus died, mostly at the hands of two Hutu military groups: Interahamwe and Impuzamugambi. The day after the massacre began, the Tutsi Prime Minister of Rwanda, Agathe Uwilingiyimana, was assassinated. In the face of the growing madness Agathe and her husband had taken refuge in the United Nations volunteer compound at Kigali. Rwandan Presidential troops broke in at 10 a.m. and shot the Prime Minister and her husband. The UN troops who had been sent to guard Agathe were set upon, castrated and gagged with their own genitalia before being shot.

After the genocide Protais Zigiranyirazo, President Habyarimana's brother-in-law and former Governor of Ruhengery Province, escaped to Nairobi and then to Brussels, travelling with a fake French passport. He was arrested on 21 July 2001 and the Belgian authorities handed him over to the UN-established International Criminal Tribunal for Rwanda, who have charged him with genocide. The sheer weight of the genocide charges completely overshadow the other crime that the present Rwandan government now acknowledge—that Protais Zigiranyirazo was the leader of the plot to kill Dianne Fossey.

South Africa: Black and White with Grey Areas

South African Prime Minister Hendrik Frensch Verwoerd trained as a scientist and held a doctorate in psychology, later becoming interested in sociology. He had a particular affinity for social Darwinism, which he read as the idea that societies should select superior specimens of humans at the expense of weaker specimens. Although this logic is full of holes, many cultures throughout history have implicitly or explicitly operated social Darwinism of this type. The caste system in India and the extermination of the Jews and others in Nazi Germany are well-known examples.

When Verwoerd came to power in 1958 he implemented his ideas on a national scale, and history remembers him as the 'Architect of Apartheid'. The creation of apartheid, which called for the separation and marginalisation of the majority black population of South Africa, naturally created enemies. His death, however, had nothing to do with apartheid.

On 16 April 1960, while Verwoerd was opening the Rand Easter Show in Johannesburg, a man named David Pratt shot and injured him. The courts declared Pratt insane and he committed suicide a few months later while incarcerated in a mental hospital in Bloemfontein. In 1966 a parliamentary clerk, Dimitri Tsanfendas believed that a giant tapeworm inside him had told him to kill the Prime Minister. Tsanfendas mortally stabbed the President while he sat at his desk in the House of Assembly. The courts judged him to be insane and he spent nearly 30 years in Weskoppies Psychiatric Hospital before dying there at the age of 81.

Steve Biko is probably the most famous assassinee in South African history. A student at the University of the Natal Medical School (now KwaZulu-Natal) he felt that black, mixed-race and Indian students needed their own university union. He formed the South African Student's Organisation, the seed from which the Black Consciousness Movement formed. His outspoken, but non-violent resistance to apartheid earned him the persecution of the South African government, who blamed him for instigating the Soweto riots of 16 June 1976. On 18 August, two months after the riots, the authorities arrested him. While in the 'care' of the police, he was clubbed so violently that he suffered a massive head injury. He received no medical care and on 11 September the authorities drove him 1200 km to Praetoria Prison where he died shortly afterwards. The police had two stories: that Biko died as a result of a hunger strike or that his head injuries were a 'suicide attempt'.

No one believed them. For oppressed South Africans Steve Biko became a martyr to the cause of freedom to and a poster child for the protest movement. The South African authorities failed to convict the five policemen involved in Biko's arrest. In 2003 the Ministry of Justice refused to consider further prosecution, citing a lack of evidence or witnesses but the Truth and Reconciliation Commission has since reported that some of the policemen involved have acknowledged responsibility and applied for amnesty.

Other notable South African assassinations include Jewish anti-apartheid intellectual, Ruth First in 1982. The South African Bureau of State Security blew her up with a parcel bomb. They sent it to her at the University Eduardo Mondlane in Maputo, Mozambique, where she was living and working in political exile.

Ruth's husband was Joe Slovo, the long-time leader of the South African Communist Party (SACP). He returned to South Africa in 1990 to involve himself with the emerging dialogues between the apartheid government and the African National Congress. When he became ill, he stepped down as SACP leader and Chris Hani replaced him. Hani was just stepping out of his car outside his home in Dawn Park, Boksburg when an anti-Communist Polish immigrant named Janusz Walus killed him with a shot to the head using a gun loaned to him by Conservative Party MP Clive Derby-Lewis.

Joe Slovo took over the SACP again briefly before dying of cancer. Walus and Derby-Lewis were arrested and found guilty of murder and conspiracy, but their sentences were commuted to life imprisonment after the adoption of the new South African constitution in 1995 which forebode the death penalty. Ironically,

Derby-Lewis and his wife, Gaye—who was also in the Conservative Party—had fought against the constitution that spared Clive from execution. Walus and Derby-Lewis are now serving life sentences. Gaye Derby-Lewis was also tried for complicity in the assassination, but was acquitted and emigrated to Australia.

The Middle East

Iran: more prime ministers

Five Iranian prime ministers have died unnatural deaths.

Sayyed Hosein Emami Esfahani assassinated Prime Minister Abdolhossein Hazhir in 1949, but he was only the hit man. The brains behind the operation was terrorist leader Navab Safavi. Safavi's Fadaiyan Islam group were also responsible for killing Prime Minister Sepahbod Haj Ali Razmara in 1951 before the authorities caught up with him and executed him by firing squad. The Islamic Republic of Iran nevertheless considers Safavi a hero. There's even a street in Tehran named after him.

Prime Minister Hassan Ali Mansur died in 1964 when Mohammad Bokhary shot him three times as he was about to present his first State-of-the Union Speech.

The most spectacular assassination in Iran, however, occurred on 28 June 1981. According to the official account, Mujahideen al-Khalq planted a bomb during a conference of the Islamic Republic Party. The bomb killed over 60 people including Prime Minister Ayatollah Mohammad Beheshti. Upon Behesti's death, Mohammad Javad Bahonar assumed the position of Secretary General and Prime Minister, but both he and President Mohammad Ali Rajai were killed when a bomb exploded in Bahomar's office in Tehran in 1981. Rajai had been President for just fourteen days.

Iraq: Hussein and sons

Depending on your viewpoint, the sons of Saddam Hussein—by his first wife Sajida Khairallah Talfah—Uday and Qusay were either casualties of war or victims of political assassinations. By most Western accounts the deaths of Saddam Hussein's sons were no great loss to the world.

A convicted murderer, Uday was installed in his father's regime as the head of the Iraqi Olympic Committee, where his principle duty seemed to be torturing athletes if they lost their competitions. Uday's younger brother, Qusay was the head of his father's Intelligence Service and his claims to fame include the cultural genocide of the Shi'a Marsh Arabs of Iraq and the destruction of their ecosystem. The courses of the Tigris and Euphrates rivers were diverted, leaving the marshes desiccated. Half a million people, whose tribes have lived in the marshes since the beginning of recorded history, were displaced. Although the river flows have since been restored, the marshes will still take a long time to recover, and the majority of the Marsh Arabs have not returned.

When Task Force 20 and the troops of the US Army 101st Airborne Division raided a house in the city of Mosul in 2003, they shot to death Uday, Qusay and Qusay's fourteen-year-old son Mustapha.

Family patriarch Saddam Hussein had ruled Iraq since 1976. He was responsible for the Iran—Iraq war form 1980–1988, the Gulf War in 1990 and any number of other abominations. The Americans used the now famously hollow pretext of 'weapons of mass destruction' to oust a dictator they had played a great part in creating. American forces—acting on a tip off—captured him on 13 December 2003 and a special tribunal found him guilty of crimes against humanity. The new rule of law in Iraq hanged him at 6 a.m. on the second last day of 2006, at Camp Justice army base in north-east Baghdad. Formerly Camp Banzai, the base had been Saddam Hussein's Military Intelligence Headquarters. He was hanged from the same gallows as many of his former victims.

Lebanon and Syria: more dead prime ministers

Lebanon has long had a complicated relationship with neighbouring Syria. In April 1949 Colonel Sami al-Hinnawi and fellow members of the Syrian Social Nationalist Part staged a successful coup to oust the military dictatorship of Syrian President Husni al-Za'im. After Sami was sure of his position he ordered the execution of both al-Za'im and his Prime Minister, Muhsen al-Barazi at Mezze Prison in Damascus. Sami's victory was short-lived. His fellow 'revolutionary' Adib ibn Hasan Shishakli ousted him later that year. In the following year, 1950, Sami was living in exile in Beirut when a cousin of al-Barazi murdered him in revenge.

Eight times Prime Minister of Lebanon, Rashid Abdul Hamid Karami died in June 1987 when, according to the Syrian occupying government, Samir Geagea and ten other members of the right-wing Lebanese Forces political party planted a bomb that exploded in a helicopter carrying Karami to Beirut. Geagea was serving four life sentences for this and other incidents until the Syrian army withdrew from Lebanon in mid-2005. The new Lebanese government pardoned Geagea and friends, releasing them on 26 July 2005. On his release he said:

> I have spent eleven horrific years in solitary confinement in a six-square-metre dungeon three floors underground without sunlight or fresh air. But I endured my hardships because I was merely living my convictions.

The year 2005 a pivotal one in Lebanon. In February explosives of unknown origin took the life of former Prime Minister Rafik Baha ad-Din Hariri. They exploded underneath his motorcade as it travelled along the Rue Minet al Hosn near the St George Hotel in Beirut. The explosives carried a punch equivalent to over 1000 kilos of TNT and killed 21 others. Hariri was buried under the rubble with his bodyguards.

On 20 October 2005 UN-sponsored German Judge Detlev Mehlis announced that he believed that both Lebanese and Syrian military intelligence services were implicated in the assassination of Hariri. Belgian Judge Serge Brammertz is continuing the investigation.

Israel: Prime Minister Yiszhak Rabin

The most widely known assassination in Israel's history is that of two-time Prime Minister Yitzhak Rabin on 4 November 1995. The 1994 joint winner of the Nobel Peace Prize—along with former PM Shimon Peres and the late Palestinian Liberation Organisation leader 'Yasser Arafat'—made considerable headway in creating a lasting temporary ceasefire between Israel, the Palestinians and other Arabs when he signed the Oslo Accords in 1993.

Unexpectedly, he didn't die at the hands of a Palestinian; a fellow Jew killed him. Twenty-five-year-old right-wing Mizrachi radical Yigal Amir objected to the Oslo treaty. On the day of the murder there was a gathering in Kings of Israel Square in Tel Aviv to celebrate the new understanding. Amir intercepted the Prime Minister in a car park near the square and shot him twice with a Beretta 84F semi-automatic pistol. A further shot injured a security guard, Yoram Rubin. Guards apprehended Amir immediately, but Rabin died from massive blood loss soon after the attack. To date he is the only Israeli Prime Minister to have been assassinated. Kings of Israel Square has since been renamed in Yitzhak Rabin's honour.

Subsequent investigation revealed that Amir intended to kill Rabin twice before, but had failed to carry out his plans. His younger brother Hagai and a friend, Dror Adani, were also implicated in the conspiracy to kill Rabin. Yigal Amir *Rabin died from massive blood loss soon after the attack.* was held in isolation at Be'er Sheva Prison, but since 2003 has been in Ayalon Prison serving life for murder.

A determined man, Amir managed to get married while in prison. His wife is a Russian-born teacher of Judaism, Larissa Tremblower. The marriage was conducted under Rabbinical Law by giving his father power-of-attorney to gift a wedding ring. He even attempted to father a child with her by passing a plastic bag full of his semen to her during a visit. After almost three years of applications the authorities finally allowed the couple a ten-hour conjugal visit in 2006.

Amir's brother Hagai is serving sixteen years imprisonment for conspiracy. Dror Adani was released in July 2002 after serving his sentence in full. Apparently, he intends to stay out of politics in the future.

Palestine: 'targetted interception' and 'collateral damage'

If, like the United Nations, you define terrorists as militants who attack civilian targets, then the Palastinian Sunni organisation Harakat al-Muqawama al-Islamiyya (the Islamic Resistance Movement) would seem to qualify. Sheik Ahmed Yassin was nearly blind and a paraplegic as a result of a childhood accident, but these minor factors didn't get in the way of his founding the group better known as Hamas in 1987, with the specific aim of solving the 'Palestinian Question' through Jihad (holy war) against Israel. With its trademark suicide bombings, Hamas has maintained a high profile in the Western media and its leaders and major operatives are in the top ranks of Israeli most wanted lists. Some Israelis like to call their own nation's policy of military assassination 'targetted interception', one of the string of endlessly inventive euphemisms for the violence that humans perpetrate upon one other.

On 6 September 2003 an Israeli Air Force F-16 bombed a building on the Gaza Strip, specifically to 'intercept' Yassin, but the Hamas leader escaped with only superficial injuries.

A few months later, on 22 March 2004, he was leaving his early morning prayers, flanked by two bodyguards and accompanied by two of his sons, when an Israeli helicopter gunship used Hellfire missiles to blow Yassin, his bodyguards and eight other bystanders to pieces. More than twelve others, including his sons, sustained injuries in the attack.

Hamas' co-founder, Abdel Aziz al-Rantissi took over the reigns, but the Israeli Army soon found an opportunity to fire missiles at the car he was riding in. On 17 April 2004 they eliminated Rantissi, his 27-year-old son Mohammed and the bodyguard Akram Nassar. This time they only managed to wound four bystanders—a significant reduction in what the military like to call 'collateral damage' from their previous attempts to destroy Hamas's leadership.

Further deaths followed. A car bomb killed a senior Hamas operative, Izz El-Deen Sheikh Khalil, on 26 September 2004 in Gaza city. Hamas chief explosives expert, Adnan Al Ghoul, and another senior member, Imad Abbas, died when an Apache helicopter fired missiles into their car on 21 October 2004, making it a bumper year for the Israelis.

Being Hamas's explosives expert is clearly a high-risk job. Ghoul's mentor and predecessor Yahya Ayyash had been killed on 5 January 1996 when the Israeli General Security Service planted a bomb in a cell phone. When Ayyash answered it, it blew his head apart.

Asia

India: 'Mahatma' Ghandi

India is famous for the assasinations of three leaders—all with the same surname.

Mohandas Karamchand Gandhi—known as 'Mahatma' which means 'Great Soul'—never held an official position in any government, but by sheer force of personality and his commitment to non-violent civil disobedience he became the only man universally trusted by the various factions of the Indian National Congress after India's independence in 1947. The first government of the Republic of India owed him everything—it was Mahatma Gandhi who gave them their power in the first place.

A lawyer by training, Ghandi was heavily influenced by his mother's Jain philosophy of the sacredness of all life. He first became involved in civil rights issues while living in South Africa and practising as a barrister. He was the frequent target of the racism that white South Africans meted out to Indians. These experiences and his personal values helped him develop his ideals of non-violent revolution. South Africa, ever ungrateful to its Indian population, continued to persecute the minority and Gandhi's struggle for equality provided him with the experience to tackle his 29-year-long fight for Indian independence from the British.

Ghandi's struggle for Indian self-rule involved considerable documentation of the hardships and injustices that ordinary Indians were suffering under colonialism. His methods—in collaboration with the Indian National Congress Party—eventually evolved into a program of peaceful non-cooperation with the British. One of his most famous 'publicity stunts' was making salt to demonstrate symbolically that Indians could free themselves economically from the British.

In the end, after the trauma of World War II and under assault from the assertive Quit India Movement, the British finally caved in and gave India its independence—but at a cost. It partitioned its colonies into the independent states of the predominantly Hindu Republic of India and the predominantly Muslim Republic of Pakistan.

Gandhi had always fought for a united India that transcended class, caste and religion and was unhappy about the partition and, within a couple of months of their independence, India and Pakistan were in conflict with each other in the First Kashmir War (1947–1948).

As it turned out, it clashes over territory and religion were the cause of the three assassinations of the Gandhis. In the case of Mathatma, it began when he insisted that the Indian government pay Pakistan the sum of 55 crores (550 million rupees) as per the British independence agreement. When the Indian government refused to do so, Gandhi went on a hunger strike until the newly elected Congress Party conceded. However, many Hindu extremists thought that Gandhi's stance was a betrayal of Hindu interests and that he was pandering to minority Muslims. Ghandi took this in his stride. He was used to having enemies. By early 1948 Mahatma Gandhi had survived at least five attempts on his life:

- On 25 June 1934, he was on his way to give a speech at the Corporation Auditorium in Pune when someone threw a bomb at the escort car in front of his own. The authorities made no investigations nor arrests in connection with this attempt on Gandhi's life.

- In May 1944 Hindu activist Nathuram Godse felt that Gandhi had betrayed India through his appeasement of minority groups. He made his point clear when he rushed at Gandhi with a dagger during a prayer meeting in Panchangi, but he was overpowered and Gandhi, true to his convictions, declined to press charges.

- On 9 September 1944 Godse was at a demonstration against one of Gandhi's ongoing negotiations with a Muslim leader when a policeman found a dagger on him.

- On 29 June 1946 a train carrying Gandhi between Nerat and Karjat Stations in Bombay crashed into boulders placed on the track.

- On 20 January 1948 Madanlal Pahwa, a refugee from Pakistan whose father had been killed by a Muslim mob, placed a bomb behind a podium at Birla House, Delhi, where Gandhi was due to give another speech. The bomb exploded but no one was hurt. Pahwa was later linked to five other conspirators in Gandhi's eventual assassination.

Gandhi's luck finally ran out on 30 January 1948. He was on his way to another prayer meeting when 'third time lucky' Nathuram Godse finally achieved his long-standing ambition and shot and killed the Mahatma with a Beretta M1934 semi-automatic pistol at Birla House.

Prosecutors later described Godse's accomplice Narayan Dattatraya Apte as the brains of the conspiracy. Both Godse and Apte were convicted of murder and hanged. Madanlal Pahwa served a 'life imprisonment' sentence as a conspirator, but was later released and lived in Dadar, Mumbai until his death. Two others sentenced to life imprisonment and later released were Vishnu Ramkrishna Karkare and Godse's brother Gopal Vinayak Godse.

All the assassins were members of the now long defunct Hindu nationalist political party Hindu Mahasabha, led by Vinayak Damodar Savarkar. Savarkar was arrested and later exonerated in connection with the assassination, but his actual role remains a source of controversy to this day, with many historical sources still regarding him as a conspirator.

Gopal Godse was a back-up shooter who simply lost his nerve at the last minute like many would-be assassins before him. Fifty years after the assassination he was still unrepentant, yet embarrassed at his failure. You can hear an interview with Gopal, in his own words at: *www.dailyherald.com/special/passagefromindia/video/godse.mov*

Gandhi's body was cremated and, according to his wishes, most of his ashes scattered in some of the major rivers of the world including the Nile, the Volga and the Thames. Some ashes are enshrined in the Self-Realisation Fellowship Lake Shrine on Sunset Boulevard, Pacific Palisades, California. His birthday is a national holiday in India.

The Other Ghandis

Pandit Jawaharlal Nehru was a prominent young member of the nascent Congress Party and eventually became the first Prime Minister of India on its independence. He and his wife Kamala Kaul had only one child, a daughter, Indira Priyadarshini. Kamala died of tuberculosis while her husband was in prison for his political activities and became a posthumous national heroine. Nehru would wear a rose in his lapel for the rest of his life in her honour.

In the general elections of 1952 Nehru won overwhelming support and his son-in-law Feroze Ghandi—no relation to Mahatma—also won a seat in the government. Indira and Feroze had married in 1942 and produced two sons, Rajiv Ratna and Sanjay.

As Nehru's daughter grew up, her father became increasingly reliant on her counsel, and she eventually served as her father's chief-of-staff. Indira's closeness to her father created a personal and political rift between her and Feroze. The couple separated in 1952 when Indira moved into her father's house. In spite of his government suffering a series of corruption scandals, Nehru remained in power for the rest of his life and died in office.

A few prime ministers later, on 19 January 1966, Indira too became a prime minister when the Congress Party elected her leader. She won her own massive mandate in 1971, but her tenure was not without controversy. Her colleagues in the party resented the influence that her favoured son Sanjay seemed to wield, but it was her tendency towards authoritarianism that created the most serious problems. She used her majority to change the Indian constitution and strip power from Indian states governed by rival political parties. This effectively made the world's largest democracy a one-party state. Dissenting states protested and opposition parties ganged up on her. She responded by declaring a State of Emergency on 26 June 1975.

In 1977 she was soundly defeated in India's general elections. She and Sanjay were arrested on a number of charges linked to corruption, but she remained a great manipulator and masterfully used her arrest and trial as an opportunity to portray herself as a victim of her opponents' vindictive persecution. The spin-doctoring worked. In addition, the only thing her opponents had in common was their hatred of her and they were unable to maintain a viable government. In the 1980 election Gandhi won a second term.

Indira Gandhi made a lot of enemies but it was her relationships with the state of Punjab and its majority Sikh population that finally outdid her.

As a response to the rise in Sikh militancy, she ordered Operation Bluestar—the storming of the Sikhs' most sacred building—on 3 June 1984. The Harimandir Sahib or 'Golden Temple' in Amritsar had become a fortified base for armed, militant Sikhs. If you can imagine the prime minister of Italy attacking the Sistine Chapel in response to the rise of Catholic militants you get an idea of what this meant. Thousands of pilgrims died in the attack and the Sikhs were outraged. Gandhi caught her militants, but it was a Pyrrhic victory. In a gesture of conciliation, Gandhi chose Sikhs to be among her personal bodyguard, which proved to be a fatally flawed decision.

Gandhi was on her way to an interview with Peter Ustinov for Irish Television on 31 October 1984, when Beant and Satwant Singh turned on their employer and shot her with their semi-automatic machine pistols. Other bodyguards then shot the Singhs. Beant Singh died immediately; Satwant survived his wounds, but was later sentenced to death. Another Sikh, Kehar Singh, was tried and and found guilty of conspiracy. On 6 January 1989 Satwant and Kehar became the last men to be hanged at Tihar Jail in Delhi.

Indira Gandhi died on the way to hospital. In the aftermath of her death anti-Sikh riots erupted throughout New Delhi. In accordance with standard Hindu practice Indira Gandi was cremated near Raj Ghat. The Congress party then convinced Indira's surviving 40-year-old son, Rajiv, to take over the helm. He later gained his own mandate due in large part to the sympathy vote. The Congress Party under Rajiv won enough seats to gain absolute power.

Rajiv, a commercial jet pilot by training, never seemed particularly at ease with politics. His undoing was his policy towards Sri Lanka—

forming the Indian Peace Keeping Force to intervene in Sri Lanka's ongoing de facto civil war. In doing so he alienated hard line Sinhalese and the Liberation Tigers of Tamil Eelam, better known as the Tamil Tigers. The Tamils made numerous accusations that the Indian peace keepers had committed atrocities against their people.

Rajiv resigned as prime minister after a defeat in the general elections of 2 December 1989 and VP Singh succeeded him. Being out of the top job didn't save him, however. In 1991, while Rajiv was campaigning in the town of Sriperumbudur near Madras, a seventeen-year-old Tamil Tiger, Thenmuli Rajaratnam Dhanu presented a garland of flowers to the former prime minister. After she put the flowers around Rajiv's neck she stooped in what seemed like a gesture of respect, detonating a bomb strapped to her lower back. Ten thousand 2 mm steel balls exploded like the discharge from a huge shotgun and tore Rajiv's face apart, also killing the assassin and sixteen others. To date Rajiv remains the youngest person ever to hold the title of Prime Minister of India.

In 1998 an Indian Court convicted 26 individuals for conspiracy in Rajiv Gandhi's death and executed four of them. The Tamil Tigers continue to glorify the memory of the assassin Dhanu to this day.

Japan: five fewer prime ministers, eleven fewer fingers and a translator

In 1878 Shimada Ichiro and six other Satsuma Samurai killed the Japanese Home Minister Okubo Toshimichi while he was en route to Tokyo. The assassins felt that Okubo had betrayed the Samurai by supporting the Imperial Japanese Army during the American-backed restoration of the Meiji emperor in 1867. The murder is famous in Japan, a country whose history of assassination rivals that of Imperial Rome.

In the modern era to date, five prime ministers of Japan have been assassinated.

Ito Hirobumi was the first, fifth, seventh and tenth Prime Minister of Japan, but had finally resigned in 1901. He was one of the main architects of Japan's occupation and annexation of Korea. A Korean nationalist, An Jung-geun, shot him on a railway platform in Harbin, Manchuria on 26 October 1909. The Japanese colonial court sentenced An to death and he was hanged at Chiba prison.

Railway stations seem to be bad news for Japanese prime ministers. The nineteenth, Hara Takashi, was the first non-noble to hold the office—a great achievement in stratified, hierarchical Japan. A right-wing military officer stabbed him to death at Tokyo station in November 1921. Hara left behind an incredibly detailed diary of his life and leadership that remains a primary source of information of his era.

The great Japanese tradition of prime ministerial assassinations at railway stations continued. Just over nine years later, Tomeo Sagoya, a member of the ultra-nationalist secret society, Aikokusha, shot the 27th Prime Minister—there had been eight PMs in nine years—Hamaguchi Osachiat, at—you guessed it—Tokyo Railway Station in November 1930. Although the wounds kept him hospitalised for months he did survive to be re-elected. Unfortunately he only served one month before his continuing ill health forced him to retire in March 1931. A few months later he was dead, so we can count this as a protracted assassination.

Two prime ministers later, Inukai Tsuyoshi was only in power for five months before the Japanese Navy attempted a coup d'état in what historians now call the 15 May incident. Eleven naval cadets, several of whom were just twenty years old, shot Inukai at the Prime Minister's residence on 15 May 1932. His last words were: '*Hanaseba wakaru*', meaning 'If we can talk, we can understand.' One of his assassins replied, '*Mondoo muyoo*'—'dialogue is useless'.

Film legend Charles Spencer Chaplin Jr was visiting Japan at the time and was also a target of the assassination, simply because he had a high profile. At the time of the murder he was out watching sumo wrestling with Inukai's son, Ken, and the assassins didn't manage to kill either of them.

Although the assassins were caught, by now a strange mood had gripped the nation. Years of militarism had resurrected a nostalgia for the 'Samurai Ideal'. The court judging their case received a petition containing 350,000 signatures asking for leniency. This was extraordinary enough, but what made this petition unique was that it was written in blood. Eleven youths in Niigata sent a further petition offering their lives in place of the eleven assassins. To show that they were serious, the youths had also sent eleven of their fingers. The court got the message and the eleven assassins were given light sentences.

Within a year the rule of law collapsed even further with another coup d'état—the February 26 incident of 1936. The navy assassinated Finance Minister Takahashi Korekiyo who had previously served as Japan's twentieth prime minister. Ultimately the military factions of Japan took over the civilian government, leading to Japan's increasing aggression in China and further policies of military expansion including Japan's antagonistic role in World War II.

Seven years later, during the Pacific War, the allies scored a major psychological victory against Japan when American forces ambushed the flight of Fleet Admiral and Commander-in-Chief of the Imperial Japanese Navy, Isoroku Yamamoto, while en route to an inspection tour of the Solomon Islands. Yamamoto had been one of the architects of the attack on Pearl Harbor in 1941. The day after the Americans shot his plane down, Japanese forces found his body in the jungle, near the former Australian patrol post of Buin. Pilot Lieutenant Rex T Barber had shot Yamamoto twice from his P-38 Lightning—once in his left shoulder and once in his lower left jaw, the bullet exiting above his right eye. The US Navy had known where Yamamoto was because for some time they had been able to decode many of Japan's signals. The planning that went into the ambush of Yamamoto marks it as an excellent example of a successful military assassination.

The US Navy later awarded Lieutenant Barber with its second highest award—the Navy Cross.

During it's long peace since World War II, Japan has been free of successful assassinations. One notable exception was the murder of Hitoshi Igarashi. The Japanese translator of Salman Rushdie's Satanic Verses was stabbed to death at his workplace at the University of Tsukuba, Ibaraki, in 1991, in response to the fatwa issued by the Grand Ayatollah Ruhollah Musavi Khomeini against the British–Indian author.

Myanmar/Burma: Generl Aung San

The British Empire annexed Burma in 1886 and General Aung San was born into a family that fought for independence from day one. Even during his university years Aung San's combination of intelligence and charisma made him a natural born leader. When he started working in politics his strategy of organised national strikes proved to be as effective as Gandhi's work in India. Unlike Gandhi though, Aung San also felt that guns had their place. While in exile during the early part of WWII he enlisted the aid of the Japanese, probably on the basis that 'the enemy of my enemy is my friend', but Aung San was no fool. When the Japanese declared Burma an 'independent nation' on 1 August 1943, he made plans to expel them from his country as soon as feasible.

'Unlike Gandhi though, Aung San also felt that guns had their place.'

Ironically, he achieved this with the help of the British on 27 March 1945. Although Winston Churchill didn't think much of Aung San, the Burmese general negotiated the independence of his country from Britain through Churchill's successor, Clement Atlee, initially negotiated to be effective from 19 July 1949.

But Aung San never lived to see the independent Burma. His political opponent Galon U Saw organised a group of paramilitaries to break into a meeting of the interim government-the Executive Council-at the Secretariat Building in Rangoon on 19 July 1947. The Council comprised Aung San and six cabinet ministers. Also present were a cabinet secretary and a bodyguard. The assassins killed everyone at the meeting. Aung San was just 32. The British quickly tried U Saw, sentenced him to death and hanged him at Insein Jail on 8 May 1948. Burma finally became independent on 4 January 1948.

Burma, now Myanmar, hasn't had much luck as a democracy. For much of its independent history it's been under the thumbs of military regimes. Nevertheless Aung San's legacy lives on in his daughter Aung San Suu Kyi, the leader of the National League for Democracy in Myanmar—the pro-democratic, non-violent resistance to the current military dictatorship. She was awarded the Nobel Peace Prize in 1991 for her continuing political struggles. At the time of writing, she remains under house arrest in Rangoon.

Nepal: guess who's coming to dinner?

Nepal made international headlines in mid-2001 when 29-year-old Dipendra Bir Bikram Shah Dev, the drunken eldest son of King Birendra of Nepal opened fire with an assault rifle and a submachine gun on his father, his mother Aiswarya, his younger brother Nirajan, his sister Shruti and nine other members of his family while they were having dinner. His motive was his mother's objection to his proposed marriage to Devyani Rana, a member of the family that ruled Nepal as hereditary prime ministers until 1951. Four family members survived the shooting, but Bodh Kumari Shah, King Birendra's sister's mother-in-law, died of shock when she heard about the massacre.

After the spree, palace guards immediately shot Dipentra, who spent the three days of his kingship in a coma until he died of his wounds.

He was succeeded by his uncle, Birendra's less popular brother Gyanendra who tried to assume absolute control of the country. His people resisted and, on 10 June 2006, the Nepalese Government stripped the Crown of any power, making the Nepalese monarchy a purely ceremonial office. At the time of writing, the fate of the Nepalese monarchy is an open question.

Philippines: Benigno 'Ninoy' Aquino

Senator Benigno 'Ninoy' Simeón Aquino Jr had long been a thorn in the side of the president turned dictator—Ferdinand Marcos. A sort of modern-day Cicero, Senator Aquino's speeches in the Philippine Upper House were designed to cause as much irritation as possible. In a country where a considerable proportion of the population still lives in poverty, his 'Pantheon for Imelda' speech of 10 February 1969 mercilessly attacked the First Lady, Imelda Romualdez Marcos's multi-million Cultural Centre as a 'monument to shame.'

When President Marcos abandoned all pretence at democracy on 21 September 1972, declaring martial law, he arrested Aquino on bogus charges including murder and subversion, punishable by death. The former senator went on a hunger strike that lasted 40 days before his supporters convinced him to save his own life. The Philippine court found Aquino guilty of his charges in 1977, but the execution didn't go ahead, Marcos did not want to create a martyr. Aquino knew however that it would only be a matter of time before he found a way to kill him.

During his years in prison, Aquino's health deteriorated and Imelda struck a deal with him—the administration would send him for medical treatment in America as long as he stopped criticising the Marcos regime and promised to return to the Philippines. He agreed, undergoing successful coronary surgery. However, he eventually chose exile for himself, his wife Corazon—popularly known as Cory—and their family while resuming his attacks on the Marcos regime.

Bobby Kennedy: His murder was the first successful assassination of an American presidential candidate. Candidates now have round-the-clock Secret Service protection.

Above left: Gnaeus Pompeius Magnus, a victim of Ptolemy of Egypt, who thought killing Pompey would earn him Caesar's respect. The Roman decided that the Pharoah was a barbarian and dealt with him accordingly—after bedding Cleopatra—priorities, you know.

Above right: Gaius Julius Caesar ignored a soothsayer's warning to 'beware the ides of March' and his wife's premonition. Perhaps he had a death wish.

Below: The Death of Marat, the most famous piece of assassination art, is considerably prettier than a real forensic photograph.

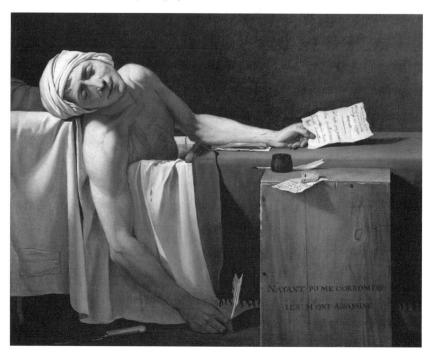

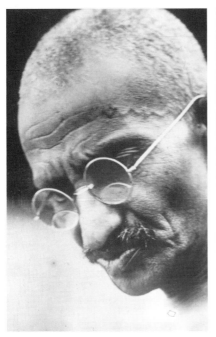 

Ghandi, Ghandi, Ghandi.

Above left: Mohandas K or 'Mahatma' who moved an empire through extreme dieting.

Above right: Indira, daughter of Nehru, who might have lived longer if she'd been more careful with her choice of bodyguards.

Below: Rajiv, son of Indira, who soaked up the family karma like a sponge and paid a heavy price for it.

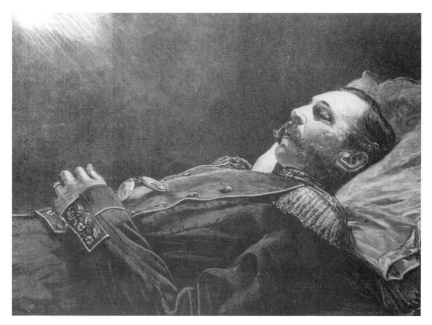

Above: Tsar Alexander II instituted many reforms to drag Russia kicking and screaming out of the middle ages. His reactionary son, Alexander III, undid much of his father's good work, leaving a mess for his own son, Nicholas II. We know how that ended.

Below: If Leon Trotsky had been as politically savvy as he was zealous, Stalin would never have come to power and 20 million Russians would not have died in Joe's purges. Who knows what Russia's role in WWII might have been?

Above: Chechen President, Aslan Maskhadov, the third pro-independence president of the republic to be killed by Russian troops, albeit after he left office.

Right: Anna Stepanovna Politkovskaya may have learned too much about alleged torture by Chechen security forces or died for what she might find out in the future.

Below: Nicolae Ceaucescu, one of the most hated men in the world, now lies in a nondescript grave—a far cry from what his fantasy tomb might have been like, judging from his taste in architecture.

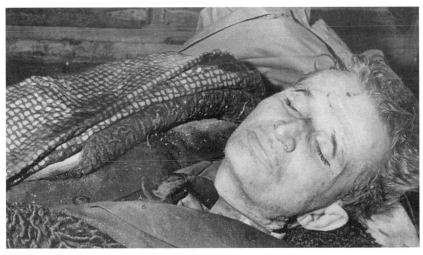

Above: King Umberto I of Italy—the only assassinated Italian head of state. He probably needed the moustache for psychological protection due to his lack of popularity. It kept the cartoonists in pocket money—a pity it wasn't bullet proof.

Below: Archduchess Sophie takes a bullet for her husband Franz Ferdinand. Her human shield failed and Gavrilo Princip's shot set in motion the train of events that lead to the deaths of millions in the 'Great War'.

Above left: Sitting Bull, doing what he did best, when he wasn't losing his homeland to the superior gunfire and the inferior morality of the white man.

Above right: America President, Abraham Lincoln. In another time and place he would have been canonised.

Below left: Malcolm X. God knows what he was thinking.

Below right: Che Guevara, dead with his eyes open and far more successful in death than in life.

Above: Yitzak Rabin during happier times with Bill Clinton (survivor of a lame assassination attempt) and Yasser Arafat (survivor of more attempts than anyone knows), yet it was Rabin who ultimately fell to assassination, from a fellow Jew.

Below left: As a result of dioxin poisoning, Victor Yuschenko is less pretty than he used to be, but at least he's still alive.

Below right: Filipino politician Benigno Aquino—assassinated at Manila airport on his return from exile. His wife, Corazon 'Cory' Aquino, took over the democratic opposition to Ferdinand Marcos and became president herself in 1986.

Due to a deteriorating political situation in the Philippines in early 1983 Aquino returned to see if he could persuade Marcos to step down. Marcos met Aquino's plane with a contingent of over 2000 military and police to 'protect' Aquino—overkill if ever it existed—but as he got off the plane a man called Rolando Galman supposedly shot him dead. Airport security immediately shot Galman—or so goes the official Marcos version. In reality another passenger on Aquino's plane, in military uniform, shot Aquino in the back of the head. Regardless, the Marcos regime had its patsies and a smattering of 'those responsible' for the execution found their way to jail and are still serving time in National Bilibid Prison.

If the ailing Marcos wanted to avoid creating a martyr, he failed miserably. Aquino's assassination fuelled a huge popular movement for revolution and eventually catapulted his widow Cory into power as Marcos' democratically elected successor. She served one term, but she remains an outspoken critic of successive Philippine governments. Manila International Airport is now Ninoy Aquino International Airport.

Ferdinand Marcos fled the Philippines within days of Cory Aquino's election victory and died in exile in Honolulu from multiple organ failure. Although he and associates were indicted for embezzlement, much of the money they siphoned out of the country has yet to be recovered. His remains now lie in refrigeration in Ilocos Norte.

Imelda Marcos was acquitted of her embezzlement charges in America, but is currently involved in a considerable amount of Philippino litigation which may or may not impede her rumoured plans to run as Mayor of Manila in 2007. You can see much of her famous shoe collection at the Marikina City Footwear Museum in Manila.

Australasia

Australia: dirty deeds downunder

By world standards Australia is a backwater for assassinations with only two attempts and three successful political murders to its credit.

Alfred Ernest Albert, Duke of Saxe-Coburg and Gotha, younger brother of the future King Edward VII of England and fifth in line to the British throne at the time, was visiting Sydney on 23 March 1868. The Prince was picnicking in Clontarf when the previous inmate of a mental asylum, and Australia's first would-be assassin, Henry James O'Farrell, shot Alfred in the back, just to the right of his spine. O'Farrell narrowly escaped a lynching and went on trial for attempted murder. In spite of Alfred's intercession on his behalf and his lawyer's arguments of innocence by reason of insanity, O'Farrell was hanged on 21 April 1868, barely a month after the shooting.

The day after the attack 20,000 people attended an 'indignation meeting' in Sydney—one of many held in the following weeks. The first ever visit by a member of the British royal family to Australia had gone off rather badly and an embarrassed public ultimately decided to create a monument to commemorate the Prince's recovery. Donations to the monument exceeded everyone's expectations and the funds were used to found the Royal Prince Alfred Hospital.

Alfred eventually recovered and returned to England. He never visited Australia again, dying at the age of 55 from lung cancer.

The next assassination attempt wouldn't occur for another 98 years. Arthur Augustus Calwell was leader of the Australian Labor Party from 1960 to 1967 and, on 21 June 1966, was giving an anti-conscription speech at a rally in Mosman Town Hall, Sydney. Calwell had just climbed into his car and was about to be driven away when nineteen-year-old student Peter Raymond Kocan approached the passenger window of Calwell's car, aimed a sawn-off rifle at the opposition leader and fired. The window shattered and small shards of glass cut Calwell's face. The glass, however, deflected the rifle bullet, which lodged in the lapel of Calwell's coat.

After his conviction for attempted murder, Kocan spent ten years in a mental asylum. Calwell forgave him and even visited him once.

In jail Kocan discovered poetry and became so good at writing that, after his release in 1976, he penned two autobiographical novellas about life in the asylum: *The Treatment* and *The Cure*. The latter won him the prestigious 1983 NSW Premier's Literary Award for Fiction. He has since continued to win accolades for his work and in 2003 wrote a novel based on his early life: *Fresh Fields*. He now lives in Brisbane, a living testament to redemption and recovery.

Stories such as those of Calwell and Kocan are rare, however.

Liberal Party politician in the rural NSW seat of Riverina and anti-drugs activist Donald Mackay disappeared on 15 July 1977. He was presumed murdered by someone who objected to his anti-drugs campaigning. At the scene of his disappearance Mackay's empty and locked van revealed blood stains and three used .22 calibre shotgun shell casings. The Woodward Royal Commission into Mackay's death mentioned alleged crime boss and drug baron Robert Trimbole as the chief conspirator of Mackay's assassination, but it wasn't until a later inquest had gathered enough evidence that the authorities felt they could successfully make a case. By then Trimbole had left the country, evaded extradition and ultimately died in Spain in 1987. His body was interred in Sydney.

In the early 1990s, NSW State MP John Paul Newman had spent years trying to break up the South-east Asian crime gangs that riddled his electorate and had received numerous death threats for his trouble. On 5 September 1994, he was shot at night outside his home, in front of his fiancée, Lucy Wong. On 13 March 1998 authorities arrested local nightclub owner, Newman's political rival, Fairfield City Councillor and rumoured narcotics drug runner, Phuong Ngo. He was found guilty of murder after two mistrials. Fairfield City Council has named a swimming pool after Newman.

It is Iven Francois 'Toon' Buffett, however, who has the distinction of being the first sitting minister of an Australian government to be assassinated. The Lands Minister and Deputy Chief Minister of Norfolk Island was in his office when his 25-year-old son Leigh, who had a history of psychological problems, shot him dead in the belief that his father was 'the evil prophet'. Leigh Buffett was later acquitted by a forgiving jury.

Central and South America

Bolivia

Argentine-born Marxist Revolutionary, Cuban guerrilla leader, ally of Fidel Castro and poster-boy for left-wing freedom fighters and chardonnay socialists everywhere, Ernesto 'Che' Guevara de la Serna was instrumental in helping Castro create modern Cuba. Victory in the small Caribbean nation wasn't enough for Che. He felt it was his calling to spread guerrilla warfare to other emerging economies struggling to liberate themselves from the yolks of their oppressors. Maybe Fidel found the popular and charismatic Che to be a little too popular and charismatic. Either way Che Guevara disappeared from Cuba in early 1965 and Fidel was rather circumspect on the subject, only later revealing that Che had resigned from his posts in the Cuban government to spread the revolution elsewhere.

Although it would not be generally known for some time, Che was in Africa fighting for the independence of the Congo. The expedition was a disaster, which Che documented in his *Congo Diary* and the Congolese stayed oppressed. Deciding that he couldn't return to Cuba with such a bad track record, Che spent a few months in Dar-es-

Salaam, Tanzania, Prague and Western Europe before heading for Bolivia, where he set up a base camp in the remote region of Nancahuazú. Although there is little evidence that Che was actually making headway with training his guerrillas and it seems his efforts were turning into another Congo fiasco, his mere existence was enough to make Bolivian President René Barrientos Ortuno want to display Che's severed head on a pike in downtown La Paz.

The American government agreed to help Barrientos intercept the revolutionary, which proved to be Che's undoing. An informant betrayed the location of his encampment to the CIA. Bolivian Special Forces captured him on 8 October 1967. The next day Mario Terán, a Sergeant in the Bolivian Army, drew the short straw for the summary execution of Che Guevara. Che's alleged last words were: 'Shoot, coward! You are only going to kill a man.'

His body was flown by helicopter to Vallegrande and displayed to the press lying on top of a laundry tub in the local hospital, where a doctor surgically removed the corpse's hands for later fingerprinting to confirm his identity. The corpse was then buried at an airstrip near Vallegrande. In 1997 his remains were exhumed along with six Cuban fighters for Bolivia and returned to Cuba where they were buried with full military honours and finally placed in a specially-built mausoleum in Santa Clara.

El Salvador: a bishop and several nuns

The fourth Archbishop of San Salvador, Óscar Arnulfo Romero y Galdámez, was an outspoken critic of the Revolutionary Government that had ruled El Salvador since 15 October 1979. The 'Junta' had done nothing to curb the power of the right-wing military death squads who controlled the country and treated it as a warlord fiefdom. In the early eighties and beyond, El Salvador and many nearby countries became playgrounds for assassins.

Someone in power must have tired of the Archbishop's rants against abuses of the people and the government's persecution of the Church, and especially his calls to the military to disobey orders that violated human rights. Someone clearly wanted to shut him up. Salvadoran death squads who the UN later identified as operating under the orders of Major Roberto D'Aubuisson, shot and killed the Archbishop while he was celebrating mass on 24 March 1980, just after the homily.

Fifty thousand mourners from all over the world attended the funeral of Oscar Romero. The Salvadoran government reacted by throwing bombs into the crowd and having sharpshooters fire on the attendees. In the ensuing panic 42 people died. Romero's body is now buried in the Catedral Metropolitana de San Salvador. Many consider him a martyr, and since 1997 the Catholic Church has been considering Romero's case for beatification and canonisation.

Roberto D'Aubuisson later founded the Nationalist Republican Alliance Party, which came to power in El Salvador in 1989 and at the time of writing remains there.

Later in 1980 three American Roman Catholic nuns Ita Ford, Maura Clarke and Dorothy Kazel, and a lay missionary Jean Donovan, were on their way from San Salvador Airport on 2 December 1980, when five soldiers in plain clothes stopped their car and abducted them. The guards beat, raped and killed the women before abandoning the bodies.

The next morning local peasants found the corpses, buried them and told a local priest who informed the American Ambassador, Robert White. The next day the bodies were exhumed. The motive for the atrocity remains obscure, but the political fallout was dire and brought into question the relationship between the American government and its continuing support for military dictatorships, not only in South America, but in other parts of the world. Of course, the media coverage of the nun's murders wasn't the *only* time people had questioned American support for military dictatorships.

Europe

Austria: Friedrich, Adler an assassin reformed

Although Karl von Stürgkh had been elected Prime Minister of Austria in 1911, he ran the country during World War I as a virtual despot. Secretary General of the Social Democratic Party of Austria Friedrich Adler took it upon himself to surprise the Prime Minister while he was dining at the Hotel Meissl & Schadin in Vienna on 21 October 1915 and shouted, 'Down with tyranny! We want peace!' while pumping three bullets into the back of Stürgkh's head, killing him instantly.

Although Adler was condemned to death, the new Emperor of Austria-Hungary, Karl I was so impressed with Adler's defence of himself that he commuted the sentence to eighteen years imprisonment. Two years later, as WWI fragmented the Empire, Adler was pardoned. He resumed his political career and eventually served for fifteen years as Secretary-General to the Second Nationale, the precursor to the Socialist International, the international organisation of left wing political parties of which the Australian Labor Party and the British Labour Party are members.

Like so many other countries during the tumultuous middle years of the twentieth century, Austria went on to become a target of the Nazi regime and eight Nazi agents assassinated the Austrian Chancellor Engelbert Dollfuss on 25 July 1934. The assassins were caught and executed but Austria's days were numbered—Germany annexed Austria in the Anshluss on 12 March 1938.

Italy: Il Duce, the Mafia and the Red Brigades

Benito Mussolini didn't let chronic neurosyphilis get in the way of being elected to the Italian Parliament as a representative of the Fascist

Party. He was able to take advantage of an unstable political situation to rise to the top. On 31 October 1922, at the age of 39, he became the youngest ever prime minister in Italy's history. Like his northern European counterpart Adolf Hitler who came to power a decade later, he was a democratically elected despot and had the support of the rich and the military because, as we all know, fascism is good for business—at least in the short term.

Like any good Fascist—or Communist, or many other 'ists' for that matter—Mussolini wasn't averse to assassination as a tool of statecraft. Historians trace his final consolidation of power to the assassination of socialist leader Giacamo Matteotti, author of *The Fascisti Exposed: A Year of Fascist Domination* (1924) on 10 June 1924. Five Fascist thugs, led by Amerigo Dumini, head of the Ceka, Mussolini's secret police, abducted Matteotti to 'talk to him' and somehow his body, riddled with stab wounds, ended up in a forest. The Fascist-controlled court couldn't find enough evidence to give Dumini more than five years in prison. In fact, he and two of his colleagues ended up serving just eleven months.

Feeling that Mussolini had abandoned him, Dumini confronted 'Il Duce' about his role in the affair, whereupon the Prime Minister arrested the assassin, who spent a further eighteen months in jail. In an effort to get rid of him, Mussolini eventually moved Dumini to Libya and awarded him a substantial pension of 50,000 lire when Dumini made it clear that he had filed a 'tell all' manuscript with notaries in Texas.

During the North African campaign of World War II, from 1940–1943, the British Army captured Dumini and attempted to execute him as a spy. In spite of ending up with seventeen bullets in his body, Dumini escaped and by mid-1941 was back in Italy, where he spent the rest of the war trading in stolen property. After the war the British retried Dumini and sentenced him to 30 years imprisonment. In 1956 the authorities released Dumini on the grounds of ill health. He managed to survive another ten years.

His hapless boss, Il Duce, wasn't so lucky. Although Matteotti's assassination had created a huge scandal for Mussolini, it did consolidate his power and by 1926 he was in full control of Italy. He used his power to establish a personality cult and a police state decorated with public works to revive the glory of the Roman Empire. He backed up successful propaganda with military victories in Ethiopia and his support for Generalísimo Francisco Franco Bahamonde—commonly known as Caudillo or simply Franco—during the 1936–1939 Spanish Civil War. It is, however, his allegiance with Hitler and their 'Pact of Steel' for which he is most famous.

With the general disaster of World War II and the defeat of the Axis powers in North Africa in 1943, King Vittorio Emmanul III of Italy finally wielded sufficient power to remove Mussolini from government. Although the Germans rescued Mussolini and installed him in a short-lived puppet state in northern Italy–called the Italian Social Republic—the former Il Duce managed to accomplish little except write his memoirs, while Allied Forces continued their destruction of the Third Reich. On 27 April 1945, as the Allied armies approached Milan, Italian Communist partisans captured 61-year-old Mussolini and his 33-year-old mistress Clara Petacci. The day after their capture they were shot. Legend has it that Petacci refused to abandon Mussolini and tried to shield him with her body as they were being assassinated. On 29 April their bodies, along with four other ex-members of the 'Republic's' government, were hanged upside down from meat hooks suspended at an Esso petrol station at the Piazzale Loreto in Milan.

Mussolini was survived by his wife, Donna Rachele Mussolini who spent her last years running a restaurant. They had two daughters, Edda and Anna Maria and three sons Vittorio, Bruno and Romano. Romano married actress Sophia Loren's sister Anna Maria Scicolone. They had two daughters, Elisabetta and Alessandra. Alessandra began her career as an actress and topless model for Italian *Playboy*—August 1983, if you want to see a back issue—and is currently a Member of the European Parliament for the Italian Neofascist Movimiento Sociale Italiano.

The late 1970s proved to be high season for Italian assassination. Aldo Moro was about to become Prime Minister for the sixth time, when Marxist terrorists from the Red Brigades abducted him in the Via Fani in Rome on 16 March 1978. Their motive was to ransom Moro's life in exchange for the freedom of several imprisoned terrorists. They held him for 55 days, during which Moro penned several letters asking for the authorities to cooperate with the Red Brigade. Many doubt that the letters expressed Moro's true thoughts. The Italian government refused to negotiate and a founding member of the Red Brigade, Mario Moretti, shot Moro ten times in the back of a car on 9 May 1978. The authorities found his body in the trunk of the car, parked in the Via Caetani exactly half way between the headquarters of the Christian Democratic Party and the Communist Party.

The late 1970s proved to be high season for Italian assassination.

Although philosopher Antonio Negri was originally arrested and charged with the assassination, the charges had to be dropped for lack of evidence. Eventually the authorities tracked down Moretti, but although he was sentenced to six life sentences for the assassination, he served only fifteen years and was paroled and freed in 1998.

On the same day as Moro's death, 9 May 1978, anti-Mafia campaigner Giuseppe Impastato was running in the Cinisi council elections. The Mafia kidnapped him, tied him to the local railway line and exploded a charge of TNT underneath him, blowing him apart. In spite of his death, the people of Cinisi still elected him a councillor.

In June 1996, a former member of the Cinisi Mafia, Salvatore Palazzolo, named Gaetano Badalamenti as the instigator of Impastato's death. On 11 April 2002 Badalamenti received a life sentence for the assassination, 24 years after Impastato's death.

In 1979 the Mafia eliminated several more prominent Italians, including two magistrates, Emilio Alessandrini of Milan and Cesare Terranova of Palermo, councillor Italo Schettini, the manager of Fiat cars Carlo Ghiglieno, and the liquidator of the Banca Privata Italiana Giorgio Ambrosoli.

Although the Italian authorities retained some level of control over the Mafia during the 1980s, the year 1992 saw the death of the Mayor of Palermo Salvatore Lima, Magistrate Giovanni Falcone and Magistrate Paolo Borsellino.

Falcone had been the chief driving force behind the Maxi Trials of 1986–1987, which convicted 360 members of the Mafia for various crimes on the testimony of informants.

Lima was up to his eyeballs in corruption. His job allowed him access to the usual opportunities to receive bribes, hand out favours and act on inside information. He owed his job to the Mafia—aka. *Cosa Nostra*, meaning this thing of ours' or 'our business'—who expected him to turn a blind eye when opportune and make decisions that would keep the world safe for organised crime. When the Maxi trials handed down their judgements the defendants immediately appealed and the Mafia were counting on Lima to appoint High Court Magistrate Corrado Carnevale to the appeal court. Carnevale—also known as 'The Sentence Killer'—had a history of overturning convictions on the flimsiest of technicalities. His decisions made people suspect that he was even more corrupt than Lima.

When the public heard that Carnevale was going to preside over the appellate court the outrage was so intense that he was forced to step down under pressure from Falcone and the rest of the Ministry of Justice. The Mafia felt that Lima had let them down. Cosa Nostra boss Salvatore Riina conspired to have his revenge. On 12 March 1992 one of Riina's assassins, riding a motorbike, intercepted Lima's car while his driver was taking him to Palermo. The assassin shot the car's tyres and the vehicle screeched to a halt. Lima got out of the car and ran, but the gunman jumped off the bike, shot the Mayor in the back, then in the neck before remounting and fleeing the scene.

Two months later Giovanni Falcone, his wife Francesca Morvillo and three policemen, Rocco Di Cillo, Antonio Montinaro and Vito Schifani were in Falcone's car on the motorway between Palermo and Palermo Airport driving at 160 km/h, when Riina's assassins detonated a bomb planted in trenches at the side of the road. The timing of the explosion demonstrated considerable planning and skill, in particular by Riina's associate, Giovanni Brusca. Everyone in the car was killed.

Falcone's best friend, Paolo Borsellino and five policemen, Agostino Catalano, Walter Cosina, Emanuela Loi, Vincenzo Li Muli and Claudio Traina, died two months after Falcone, when a car bomb blew them apart in the Via D'Amelio in Palermo.

Acting on information that an informant had given them, the Italian police arrested Riina on 15 January 1993. Cynics observed that it had taken three decades to track someone down who had been living in the same house in Palermo for all those years. Riina is now serving an array of life sentences in a maximum-security prison, including sentences for the assassinations of Lima, Falcone and Borsellino. The authorities confiscated $125 million of his assets. His mansion in Palermo is now a school for local children. Giovanni Brusca is serving numerous life sentences, but because he turned informant he is allowed out of prison for one week every 45 days in order to visit his family. Palermo Airport is now Falcone-Borsellino Airport in honour of the slain judges.

Norway: Mossad murder in Lillehammer

On 21 July 1973 at least nine agents of Israel's secret service, Mossad, were involved in the murder of an Algerian-Moroccan waiter named Ahmed Bouchiki in Lillehammer, Norway. He was shot several times in front of his pregnant wife in what history now knows as the

Lillehammer Affair. The agents had mistaken Bouchiki's identity for that of Ali Hassan Salameh, chief of operations for Black September, the Palestinian group who organised the Munich Massacre in which twelve Israeli athletes were kidnapped and killed at the 1972 Olympic Games in Munich.

In response to the murder, the Norwegian government gave the Israeli agents a slap on the wrist. Five received short prison terms then a pardon, one was acquitted and three escaped before capture. Mossad finally blew up the real Salameh with a car bomb in Beirut five and a half years later.

Twenty-four years later, in 1992 the Israeli government finally compensated Bouchiki's widow and daughter with the stingy sum of $119,000 and, even then, did not admit responsibility for the fiasco. Mrs Bouchiki was so traumatised that she never remarried. Steven Spielberg's 2006 motion picture *Munich* completely ignores this chapter of the events surrounding the Munich Massacre.

Romania: Nikolai Ceausescu

Romania has done away with four of its prime ministers, the first of these being Barbu Catargiu in 1862. Seventy years later, on 30 December 1933, Ion G. Duca died, like a Japanese prime minister, at a train station in Sinaia . Duca had been trying to control the growing Fascist movement and outlawed their military arm, the Iron Guard. It was an Iron Guard supporter, Radu Constantinescu, who shot him to death.

One of Duca's successors, Armand Calinescu, had only been in office for four months when the Iron Guard got him too. They shot him in his car at least twenty times on 21 September 1939, also killing his driver and Romania's ambassador to Denmark.

The following year the Iron Guard killed former prime minister Nicolae Iorga on 27 November 1940. They abducted Iorga from his house in Bucharest and, in the nearby Strejnicu Forest, they tortured him, shot him in the back and dumped his corpse on the side of a road after stuffing a copy of the 9 September periodical *Neamul Romanesc* in his mouth. It was in this issue that Iorga had publicised a letter in support of the deposed King Carol II of Romania (15 October 1893–4 April 1953). Iorga's real 'crime', however, was that the Iron Guard held him responsible for the arrest of their leader Corneliu Zelea Codreanu who had died during a 'prison breakout' two years earlier.

The Iron Guard—also known as the Legion of the Archangel Michael—later became the chief, and highly enthusiastic, collaborators of the Nazis in the Jewish Holocaust of Romania. They were finally defeated by the Romanian dictator Ion Victor Antonescu on 24 January 1941. Ironically, soon after the end of World War II, Antonescu was tried and executed for war crimes.

In recent times, however, the most high-profile political killing has been that of Nikolai Ceausescu. Immediately after World War II Romania became a satellite state of the Soviet Empire. Its first leader was Gheorghe Gheorghiu-Dej until his death in 1965 from liver cancer. Gheorghe Apostol then took over briefly before Nikolai Ceausescu out-manoeuvred him.

Ceausescu was a textbook Eastern European despot. In the style of Joseph Stalin, as General Secretary of the Romanian Communist Party he constructed a police state buoyed up by an oppressive personality cult built on the foundation of Ceausescu's own paranoia. To his credit Ceausescu did steer a course independent of Moscow, but at the cost of treating Romania like his own private property.

Like a latter-day Commodus he rebuilt Bucharest in his own image, demolishing twenty per cent of the city's downtown area. The People's House, now Parliament House, is the world's second largest building after the Pentagon and ten per cent larger than the Great Pyramid of Giza by volume. Its 1100 rooms, utilising one million cubic metres of Transylvanian marble, 480 chandeliers, 900,000 cubic metres of wood and 200,000 square metres of woollen carpet, remain an enduring testament to his style.

More telling though is his population policy. In 1966 he decreed a ban on contraception and abortion and put in place a special tax on people who remained childless. The population of Romania swelled beyond the economy's capacity to maintain standards of living and there was a huge increase in poverty.

In 1978, Ion Mihai Pacepa of the Romanian Secret Police, became the highest-ranking defector in the history of the Cold War, which gives you an indication of how bad things were becoming. Soon afterwards foreign agents began to infiltrate Romanian internal security en masse. By the late eighties the dictator was living a socialist fantasy that existed only in his head while his people were starving. He even had a royal sceptre made for himself, which led Salvador Dali to send him a congratulatory telegram. Completely unaware of being the butt of Dali's sense of humour, the Great Leader published the telegram in the country's newspapers.

Meanwhile Ceausescu's failure to acknowledge the existence of HIV led to a rampant AIDS epidemic and Romanian orphanages began to burst at the seams. Romanians were going hungry because Ceausescu had sold his country's crops to pay Romania's foreign debt. Ironically, just before his downfall, the debt was actually paid off.

Events reached a head in November 1989 when demonstrations in the city of Timisoara led to open revolt. Because of state suppression of news the rest of Romania only heard about the uprising from Western news sources.

By 22 December major revolts had flared in all the main cities of Romania. Ceausescu and his wife Elena, the Vice-President of Romania, fled Bucharest, but the military caught up with them on Christmas Eve. On Christmas Day 1989 a military kangaroo court condemned the couple to death on charges that included genocide, and officer Ionel Boeru shot them with a sub-machine gun in the city of Targoviste in southern Romania. The Ceausescus are now buried on opposite sides of a path at Ghencea Cemetery in Bucharest.

The Ceausescu's natural children survived but didn't fare very well. Nicu died of cirrhosis of the liver and Zoia died of lung cancer. Their adopted son Valentin still lives, and fought the Romanian government for seventeen years before they agreed to return the art treasures the authorities confiscated from him and his siblings. His parents had originally pilfered them using public money.

Russia: Trotsky and that icepick

Although many remember Lenin and his successor as leader of the Russian people, Joseph Stalin, far fewer remember their comrade Lev Davidovich Bronstein—Leon Trotsky.

Lenin had been no stranger to attempts on his life. Unknown gunmen had shot at him in his car in Petrograd on 14 January 1918 and he escaped unharmed. On 30 August 1918, however, Socialist Revolutionary Party member Faina Yefimovna Kaplan shot him three times just as he was leaving for a meeting, seriously injuring him. Faina was immediately caught, but revealed nothing in interrogation except to state that she acted alone. She was then executed and the Bolsheviks used the assassination attempt as an excuse to rid themselves of a number of political enemies. Wounded in his shoulder and lung, Lenin never quite recovered and he later suffered from strokes, which eventually killed him—another case of protracted assassination.

Upon Lenin's death, Trotsky was heir presumptive, but he hadn't counted on Joseph Stalin's paranoia nor on his powers of manipulation. In a move that Augustus Ceaser would have been proud of, Stalin had himself appointed General Secretary of the Central Committee and formed a troika (triumvirate) with long-standing cronies, Lev Borisovich Kamenev, Trotsky's brother-in-law, and another old

Bolshevik, Grigory Yevseevich Zinoniev. The troika positioned themselves as a moderate stabilising force compared to Trotsky's radical image. They gradually undermined his powerbase to the point where Trotsky lost considerable influence.

It didn't take long for Stalin to turn on Kamenev and Zinoniev, who switched sides, joined Trotsky and formed a United Opposition. By then however Stalin was unassailable and the United Opposition came under increasing attack from Stalin's supporters. On 12 November 1927 Trotsky and Zinoniev were expelled from the Communist Party, with Kamenev following soon after.

Trotksy and his family left Russia and spent four years in Buyukada, near Istanbul. The Trotskys then lived for two years in France until they were no longer welcome and in 1935 they went to Norway.

In 1936, true to form, Stalin, who was now in absolute control, executed his old fellow triumvirs Kamenev and Zinoniev as enemies of the state after the show trials of Stalin's Great Purge. The Purge ultimately also saw the end of anyone who had ever supported Trotsky, and Trotsky himself was condemned to death in absentia.

Under pressure from Moscow, Norway deported the Trotskys who moved Mexico in 1937. The Mexican President Lázaro Cárdenas del Rio welcomed the old Bolshevik as a representative of true 'Marxist-Leninist Socialism.' Some of the people who took them in included the painter Diego Rivera and his wife Frida Kahlo.

In exile Trotsky remained active, writing his version of the events; of the history he had helped make, as well as critiques of Stalinist Russia. The Trotskys moved into their own house in the suburb of Coyoacán, Mexico City in 1939. On 24 May Trotsky survived an attack by Stalinists under the direction of master assassins Iosif Romualdovich Grigulevich and Vittorio Vidali. On 20 August, however, the assassins succeeded in placing Jaume Mercader close to Trotsky under the name and guise of Jaques Mornard, a Canadian Trotsky supporter.

'Mornard' drove an icepick through Trotsky's head and was immediately seized by friends of Trotsky and almost beaten to death. Trotsky was mortally wounded, but ordered that the world needed to know Mornard's story and insisted that the authorities spare his life. Trotsky died the day after.

As it was, Ramon Mercarder kept to his story and no one knew his real name until 1953. Found guilty of murder, Mercarder was imprisoned in Palacio de Lecumberri Prison until 6 May 1960. On his release he moved to Havana and spent the rest of his life moving between the USSR and Cuba. He was awarded the Hero Medal of the Soviet Union, the nation's highest decoration, in 1961. It wasn't until the end of the Soviet Union that the world knew of the details behind the assassination of Leon Trotsky.

In July 2005 the icepick that Mercarder used to kill Trotsky surfaced in the possession of Mexican citizen Ana Alicia Salas. She claimed that the authorities had granted her policeman father, Alfredo Salas, permission to take the icepick into his possession for a 'museum of criminology', but instead he had kept it for himself.

The ownership of the icepick remains in dispute.

Spain: royals, fascists and separatists

Five Spanish prime ministers have fallen to assassins. Indeed, the current royalty of Spain owes its position to an assassination. In the nineteenth century, Don Joan Prim, who was Count of Reus, Viscount del Bruch, Marquis of los Castillejos, played the role of kingmaker and was behind the election of the Duke of Savoy to the Spanish throne on 6 November 1870. The Duke became Amadeo I. Prim's plans fell apart when unknown assassins killed him seven weeks later. Without Prim's backing the political situation in Spain deteriorated. Amadeo abdicated on 11 February 1873 and Spain became the First Republic, which lasted barely two years. Amadeo instead became the ancestor of the modern kings of Italy.

The Italian monarchy ended with Umberto II's 33-day rule before his abdication on 12 June 1946. The current King of Spain, Juan Carlos I is instead descended from Amadeo's distant relation, Alfonso XII, who became King of Spain after a coup d'état restored the monarchy in 1875.

One of the chief backers of Alfonso II was Antonio Cánovas Del Castillo, the principle author of the new Spanish constitution, who even assumed the functions of head of state while Queen Consort Maria Christina was waiting for her infant son, Alfonso XIII, to grow up.

Castillo was no democrat and his constitution deliberately limited the voting power of the working classes. This made him enemies. Italian anarchist Michele Angiolillo Lombardi shot the Prime Minister on 20 August 1897, while he was visiting the thermal baths at Santa Agueda. Anguillo allowed the police to capture him—possibly to avoid giving them an excuse to repress the Spanish even further. They garrotted him in Vergara twelve days later.

When Alfonso XIII assumed the mantel of King, one of his chief backers, Prime Minister José Canalejas was shot by yet another anarchist, Manuel Pardinas, in 1912. Nine years later Prime Minister Eduardo Dato Iradier suffered a similar fate.

The general turmoil in Spain ultimately led to the short-lived dictatorship of Miguel Primo de Rivera, Marqués de Estella, the Spanish Civil War and the decades-long Fascist dictatorship of Franco.

One of the Civil War's early victims was the poet, dramatist and composer Federico Garcia Lorca. Lorca must have had a death wish, because the decidedly left-wing poet chose to move to the decidedly right-wing Granada, where Franco's future allies, the Falange, arrested and summarily executed him on 19 August 1936. During Franco's regime Lorca's work was suppressed for almost 40 years.

In 1973, two years before the dictator's death, Franco's heir apparent, Luis Carrero Blanco, became Prime Minister. Whatever Franco's future plans for Blanco, or whatever Blanco's plans for himself, they came to nothing. Four members of the Basque Homeland and Freedom—the separatist movement known as ETA (Euskadi Ta Askatasuna)—buried almost 100 kg of explosives in an excavation in front of a church under a street in Madrid. ETA detonated the explosives under Blanco's parked Dodge Dart and the resulting explosion vaulted the car over the church and onto the second-floor balcony of another building. The assassination, or Operacion Ogro, had been masterminded by an operative known as 'Argala'. On 21 December 2003 the Spanish paper *El Mundo* published an article in which a retired official, 'Leonidas', admitted to having assassinated Argala in a reprisal in 1978. See *www.elmundo.es/cronica/2003/427/1072098707.html*

Blanco's death was the end of Franco's ideologies and Spain settled into the democratic constitutional monarchy that it remains today.

Sweden: Olof Palme

The normally sedate Swedes were shocked when an assassin shot their 26th prime minister Olof Palme on 28 February 1986 in central Stockholm while he was walking home from the movies with his wife, Lisbet. The gunman killed Palme with a single shot to his back at 11:21 p.m. and Lisbet sustained a shoulder wound from a second shot. The gunman then escaped.

With hardly anything to go on Swedish authorities arrested several people but had to release them through lack of evidence. Drug addict Christer Patterson was arrested and convicted as a result of Lisbet Palme's identification of him during a police line-up almost two years after the assassination, but was later released on appeal because of insufficient evidence. Many people still believe that Patterson was just a scapegoat. He later died of a cerebral haemorrhage from head injuries resulting from a fall or, as some rumours have it, police harassment.

In the absence of a convicted killer, conspiracy theories abound, but the most provocative remains the unsubstantiated claim of former

South African policeman, Colonel Eugene de Kock, who maintained that the racist government of South Africa had successfully conspired to assassinate Palme because of his anti-apartheid stance. Swedish investigators though, were unable to find any evidence when they visited South Africa in October 1996. The case remains officially unsolved in spite of the fact that Swedish authorities have so far spent around $45 million on the investigation and there is still a reward of 50 million kroner ($6.5 million) for solving the crime.

United Kingdom

At one point in his life John Bellingham owned a tin factory, but it failed and led to his bankruptcy. He spent most of his working life in the shipping industry as an agent and broker before moving to Arkhangelsk in northern Russia in 1800. In late 1803 Lloyd's of London insured a Russian ship, the Soleure, which was lost in the White Sea. An anonymous letter told Lloyds that the ship had been sabotaged. The ship's owner, Soloman van Brienen, suspected that Bellingham wrote the letter and started legal proceedings to recover a 4890 rouble debt for which Bellingham was the guarantor. Van Brienen also convinced the Governor General of Arkhangelsk to imprison Bellingham. A year later Bellingham was released, but when the Englishman tried to have the Governor General impeached he was thrown back into prison until October 1808. He was only allowed to leave the country the next year after he had personally petitioned the Tsar.

Bellingham shot him with two half-inch calibre pistols that he had bought a few weeks before.

Back in England, Bellingham tried to persuade the British government to compensate him for his imprisonment, but failed. By 1812 he decided that someone had to pay and it would be the man who represented his 'oppressors'. On 11 May he waited in the vestibule of the Houses of Parliament until Prime Minister Spencer Perceval appeared.

Bellingham shot him with two half-inch calibre pistols that he had bought a few weeks before. After the assassination Bellingham simply sat down and waited for the authorities to arrest him. The court found Bellingham guilty of murder and he was hanged on 18 May 1812.

One hundred and eighty-five years later, during the 1997 elections for the seat of North West Norfolk, a descendent of Bellingham's, Henry Bellingham, was the incumbent Conservative Party MP. Running against him was the Referendum Party's Roger Percival, a descendant of Spencer Perceval. Both candidates lost to New Labour, but Bellingham won his seat back in 2005. Spencer Perceval maintains his unique place in history as the only British Prime Minister to have been assassinated.

The majority of assassinations in the United Kingdom in recent history have in some way been connected to the Irish Republican Army's (IRA) decades-long struggle for a united Ireland, free of British rule. Co-author of the *Guinness Book of Records* Ross McWhirter was equally well known for his right-wing political views and in November 1975 offered a £50,000 reward (US $875,000 in modern terms) for information leading to the arrest of IRA bombers.

This gesture, of course, made him an immediate target and the IRA wasted little time. Members from an IRA cell, the Balcombe Street Gang, staked out McWhirter's house in Enfield, Middlesex and accosted McWhirter's wife when she arrived home on the evening of 27 November 1975. She ran into the house and Ross stepped out at 6:45 p.m. His assassins killed him with two shots and used Mrs McWhirter's car as an escape vehicle, abandoning it in Tottenham.

Two weeks later the authorities apprehended the assassins after a six-day siege at a flat in Balcombe Street, central London, hence the media's dubbing of the group the Balcome Street Gang. In 1977 the courts jailed Eddie Butler, Harry Duggan, Hugh Doherty and Martin O'Connell for life for McWhirter's murder, nine other murders and twenty bombings.

The IRA's most high-profile assassination, however, was that of Louis Mountbatten: First Earl Mountbatten of Burma, last Viceroy and First Governor General of independent India, First Sea Lord and Admiral of the Fleet of the British Royal Navy, uncle of Prince Philip, Duke of Edinburgh and much beloved 'Honorary Grandfather' of Charles, Prince of Wales. As a symbol of the British establishment, short of killing the Queen, the IRA couldn't have picked a better target than the 79-year-old Duke. They planted a bomb in his private boat, moored near his summer home at Mullaghmore, County Sligo, which also happened to be near Bundoran, County Donegal, a holiday destination popular among the members of the IRA. Yes, even terrorists have holidays.

The Duke was taking his eldest daughter Patricia's mother-in-law, the 83-year-old dowager Baroness Brabourne, and Patricia's fourteen-year-old youngest child, the Honourable Nicholas Knatchbull for a spin around Donegal Bay when the IRA set off the 20 kg bomb by remote control. The entire party died in the explosion, along with fifteen-year-old crew member Paul Maxwell from County Fermanagh. After Mountbatten's funeral in Westminster Abbey, he was buried in Romsey Abbey, Hampshire.

The courts sentenced Thomas McMahon to life imprisonment for the assassination in 1979, but he was released in 1998 under the terms of the Good Friday Agreement. The same provision also freed Ross McWhirter's assassins in April 1999. The Good Friday Agreement was a major breakthrough for the Northern Ireland peace process and it ultimately led to the IRA's decommissioning of weapons on 26 September 2005.

The Perils of Presidency

Frequently targets, quite a few presidents have managed to avoid getting killed, even though in some minds not nearly enough have bitten the dust.

To the best of my knowledge there are no insurance policies to cover presidents in the event of assassination. The very word 'president' seems to attract political murder in a way that mere prime ministers can't compete with. Part of the reason could be that the title could mean anything from 'democratically elected leader of a developed nation' to 'military dictator for life of a tin-pot banana republic', so it's hardly surprising that the title carries with it the baggage of absolute solutions.

Central and South America, Africa and, to a lesser extent the Middle East, all have reputations for being in a constant state of revolution and revolving-door presidencies, but proportionally few presidents die in assassinations. Although presidents attract assassins, remarkably few actually succeed in their plots. Most, in fact, survive the attempted coups and, in almost all cases of presidential assassination, hardly anything significant changes.

The sheer number of presidents, however, guarantees a wide playing field, so the entries below are therefore just the tip of the iceberg and even then I've chosen to highlight only what I believe are the most historically important cases.

Central and South America

Argentina

Justo José de Urquiza, former president of Argentina and his sons Justo and Waldino, were murdered by followers of Urquiza's political rival Ricardo Lopez Jordan at Urquiza's residence in Entre Rios, San José Palace on 11 April 1870.

Former military leader, Pedro Eugenio Aramburu Cilveti was in control of Argentina from 1955–1958 in the wake of Juan Domingo Peron's ousting, but continued to be a key player in Argentinean politics. Juan Perón had been one of the most progressive Latin American despots and—to his extremist followers, the Montoneros—Aramburu represented all things anti-Peron. On 29 June 1970 they kidnapped him at midday from the streets of Buenos Aires. They murdered him three days later, but Argentina didn't know about it until his body was discovered a month later on a farm in the town of Timote.

Chile

Salvador Allende had spent nearly four decades as a Socialist Party politician before reaching his zenith as President of Chile in November 1970.

The threat to Allende was that democracy never really took hold in any South American country during the twentieth century. The most powerful interest groups remained the conservative, landed gentry and the right-wing military. The wishes, yearnings and aspirations of South America's ever-shrinking middle classes were at best an irritation and the suffering of the millions of poorly educated peasants was downright dangerous.

Peasants tended to want things like land reform, which to many minds—including that of the American government—meant socialism. This was a hair's breadth from communism, which was never good for business. A democratically elected socialist president who wanted to nationalise key industries like American-owned copper mines, and thereby impoverish plutocrats, was asking for assassination one way or the other. That's exactly what happened. On 29 June 1973 there was an unsuccessful coup attempt, but on 11 September that year the Chilean military, led by General Augusto Pinochet, seized power.

Allende had enough warning to deliver a farewell address to the Chilean people, but he knew he was doomed. In his speech he referred to himself in the past tense. He'd barely finished his speech when he was shot dead in La Moneda, the presidential palace in Santiago. The official cause—we must remember history is written by the winners—

was that he had shot himself with his AK-47 assault rifle, a gift from his friend, Fidel Castro.

It's a historic fact that American President Richard Nixon tried to prevent Allende's election to the presidency. The Nixon administration or the CIA may have had a hand in getting rid of Allende. At the very least they knew about it and did nothing.

Ironically, although Allende nationalised the copper mines, General Pinochet didn't revoke the nationalisation. He turned out to be bad for business anyway and really bad for the Chilean people, who suffered decades of his brutal dictatorship.

Guatemala

President José María Reina 'Reinita' Barrios wanted to rebuild Guatemala City to look like Paris. When he ran out of money, he simply printed more, ruining the economy. Oscar Zollinger was one of thousands of disgruntled Guatemalans. Unlike compatriots he took matters into his own hands and killed the spendthrift president on 8 February 1898.

President Carlos Castillo Armas came to power as a result of a coup that paralleled Pinochet's takeover in Chile, complete with US backing. He did not, however, achieve power immediately. The first post-coup president, Carlos Enrique Diaz de Leon was president for a staggering two days before the military junta abandoned their pretence at civilian rule. Colonel Elfego Aguirre was in power for the only slightly less staggering period of 10 days before the post was handed to Armas. Armas managed to last for three years. Although his motives remain unclear Presidential palace guard, Romeo Vasquez Sanchez, shot Armas dead on 26 July 1957, before turning the gun on himself a short while later. For the next 30 years Guatemala was run by a string of military leaders whose only lasting claim to fame involved graft, corruption and the occasional attempted genocide of the native Mayan population.

Nicaragua

Both Nicaraguan presidential assassinees were called Anastasio Somoza: Anastasio Somoza Garcia and Anastasio 'Tachito' Somoza Debayle, which was hardly surprising since both dictators were father and son. The Somozas, including Tachito's elder brother Luis Somoza Debayle were a dynasty of despots, the very essence of oppressive strongmen that so many American administrations supported as stalwarts against the Cold War bogey of Soviet expansionism. The elder Somoza was the subject of US President Franklin Delano Roosevelt's famous 1939 quote: 'He may be a son of a bitch, but he's our son of a bitch.' At a party in Leon, poet Rigoberto Lopez Perez shot the 'son of a bitch' in the chest before dying in a swarm of bodyguard's bullets—Somoza died a few days later on 29 September 1956.

Almost 24 years later, on 17 September 1980, a commando team led by Argentine guerrilla and revolutionary leader Enrique Merlo killed Tachito in Ascuncion, Paraguay, while he was on a state visit. The 'son of the son of a bitch' died when the guerrillas fired two shots at close range into his car which exploded, instantly incinerating him.

Uruguay

Bernando Berro and Venancio Flores were rival presidents of Uruguay recognised by separate sections of the population. Both died on the same day—19 February 1868—in different parts of the country, shot by unknown assassins. Another Uruguayan President, Juan Idiarte Borda was murdered in 1897.

Africa

Burundi

Melchior Ndadaye was the first democratically elected President of Burundi and an ethnic Hutu. A group of soldiers abducted him on 21 October 1993 during a military coup after Ndadaye had been in power for only three months. The soldiers took him to an army barracks and stabbed him to death with bayonets. Historians generally consider his assassination to have sparked the Burundi Civil War, 1993–2005, that killed around 300,000 people.

Six months and three presidents after Ndaye's death, his successor, Cyprien Ntaryamira, died in a plane crash in Rwanda on 6 April 1994—one of the sparks that set off the Rwanda genocide.

Comoros

The tiny—2235 square km—island nation of Comoros lies north of Madagascar, off the east coast of central Africa. It's one of the world's poorest countries and is almost a textbook case for a banana republic. In fact, that is a little bit harsh. Comoros is actually the world's biggest supplier of the essential oil, ylang ylang, so the nation's 600,000 or so inhabitants do have something to brag about.

You'd think a country where 80 per cent of the population is involved in agriculture would be relatively peaceful, but alas, not so. There have been over twenty coups in the Comoros since its independence.

Ahmed Abdallah Abderemane had come to power for the first time as the first president of an independent Comoros on 6 July 1975, before Said Mohamed Jaffar overthrew him in a coup just over a year later. Ali Solih then overthrew Jaffar before Abdallah overthrew Solih on 13 May 1978. Solih survived the coup, but Abdallah's supporters assassinated him soon afterwards. Solih's elder half-brother and Supreme Court Judge, Said Mohamed Djohar had his revenge in another coup on 26 November 1989, during which his supporters killed Abdallah. Djohar ultimately fell from power due to the machinations of the French-born mercenary, Bob Denard.

However, Denard failed to get French backing for his 1995 coup, he surrendered to intervening French forces and spent ten months in jail. After years of legal wrangling a French court finally found him guilty of "belonging to a gang who conspired to commit a crime." Denard's five-year jail term was suspended on account of his worsening Alzheimer's disease and it is unlikely now that he'll ever stage another coup in the Comorros, except in his own crumbling mind.

Republic of the Congo

Military socialist President of the Republic of the Congo Marien Ngouabi succumbed to the endemic violent rivalries that seem to haunt Africa. The man who had ruled the Congo for seventeen years was assassinated by commandoes on 18 March 1977. Alphonse Massemba-Débat, the man from whom Ngouabi had wrested power on 1 January 1969, was among those accused of the assassination and executed a week later.

Democratic Republic of the Congo

In the neighbouring and confusingly named Democratic Republic of the Congo, Mobuto Sese Seko began his rule in 1965 and would last for 32 years until ousted by Laurent-D'esiré Kabila. Many of his countrymen didn't see Kabila as much of an improvement and during a failed coup attempt on 16 January 2001, Rashidi Kasereka, one of his staff, shot him dead shortly before being shot dead himself. A conspiracy witch-hunt followed and ultimately 135 people were put on trial. The courts sentenced to death the alleged master conspirator of the assassination and a cousin of Kabila, Eddy Kapend, along with 25 others. Sixty-four others received sentences from six months to life. Forty-five were later exonerated.

Egypt

Gamal Abdel Nasserwas President of Egypt from October 1954 until his death in 1970. Although he had been one of the prime movers behind Egypt's independence from the British-controlled King Farouk he didn't assume full power until he had pushed aside his political rivals.

Initially he wasn't universally popular, but a few weeks into his presidency he was making a speech in Manshia Square, Alexandria, when someone tried to shoot him. Instead of taking cover he began shouting defiantly. As a public relations exercise, he couldn't have planned things better. Speculation persists to this day that the attack was staged especially since Nasser also took the opportunity to eliminate further rivals, in particular the Muslim Brotherhood. The image of a leader who refused to cower impressed many and, from that point on, he established a firm powerbase that not even the nationalisation of the Suez Canal in 1956, the building of the Aswan High Dam from 1960–1970 nor the disastrous defeat of the Six-Day War in 1967 could shake.

Nasser's successor was Mohammed Anwar Al Sadat. In the beginning Sadat's colleagues profoundly underestimated him, but he eventually amassed tremendous international respect as a result of his peace initiatives with the Israelis. He remains one of the few Arab leaders who has commanded any measure of respect from the Jewish nation. On 19 November 1977 he became the first Arab leader ever to visit Israel. His relationship with America and Israel led to the Camp David Peace Agreement that garnered Sadat and Israeli Prime Minister Menachem Begin the Nobel Peace Prize in 1978. Sadat's success with Israel, however, provided militant anti-Jewish Arabs with a reason to kill him. General unrest and protests and Sadat's rather extreme suppression of dissidence marred his final years in power and eroded a lot of the good will that he had generated.

Sheikh Omar Abdel-Rahman a blind Muslim cleric, felt that Sadat had become a traitor to the cause and issued a fatwa against him, a mission that members of the Egyptian army aligned to the Islamic Jihad were only too happy to accept.

Sadat's assassination was more spectacular, and bloody, than most. During the 6 October Victory Parade in Cairo, Sadat was standing at the presidential reviewing stand, watching the usual columns of armaments stroll by. At the appointed time the obligatory low level sweep of Mirage jets flew overhead, drawing the attention of Sadat and the tens of thousands of other onlookers. At that moment a truck pulled up in front of the President and his assassins spilled out, throwing grenades and shooting at him with assault rifles. Khalid Ahmed Showky El-Islambouli shouted, 'Death to the Pharaoh' as he shot Sadat in the head, wounding him mortally, and then, 'I have killed the Pharaoh!' In response guards killed two of the assassins, but not before the attackers had injured 28 people and killed seven—the dead included the Cuban Ambassador to Egypt and a bishop of the Coptic Church.

An ambulance rushed Sadat to hospital, but within hours doctors declared him dead. A record number of dignitaries attended his funeral, including ex-US Presidents Jimmy Carter, Gerald Ford and Richard Nixon. Notably absent at the funeral of the first Egyptian head of state to be murdered by his own citizens were any leaders of Arab nations. He is now buried in the Tomb of the Unknown Soldier in Cairo.

Over 300 people were arrested in connection with the killings. In all 23 attackers were tried for Sadat's assassination. Five, including El-Islambouli, were executed on 15 April 1982. Even before his death the Iranian government at the time considered El-Islambouli a martyr and for twenty years a street in Tehran was named after him. In a gesture of diplomacy a later government renamed the street—it is now called Intifada Street—but some Islamic militants still consider El-Islambouli a hero.

Decades later Sadat's assassination is still a cause for controversy. On 4 October 2006, in an interview on Egyptian national television, Sadat's nephew, Taalat Sadat, accused the Egyptian military of complicity in his uncle's death. He was promptly arrested and convicted of defamation on 31 October 2006.

Sheikh Abdel-Rahman was never tried for his role in Sadat's assassination, but he is now serving a life sentence in a maximum security prison hospital in Colorado USA, for seditious conspiracy connected to the 26 February 1993 bombing of the World Trade Centre in New York.

Sadat's successor, Hosni Murabak is still in power. Since his accession Egypt has been under 'emergency rule'.

Liberia

Liberia, the basket-case of Africa, has had, to say the least, more political killings than average, including that of President William Richard Tolber Junior, on 12 April 1980, stabbed fifteen times in only one of many murders in Samuel Kanyon Doe's military coup d'état.

During another rebellion, on 9 September 1990, Doe himself met a gruesome death. Prince Yormie Johnson, then a warlord, now a senator, captured Doe in Monrovia and tortured him before killing him. He captured the whole event on a videotape that the media later screened around the world. Among other highlights it shows Johnson sitting down while one soldier fans him as he watches another slice off Doe's ears. You can still pick up a bootleg copy of the video in Monrovia, if you're interested.

Tanzania and Zanzibar

Sheikh Abeid Amani Karume became the first president of Zanzibar after a popular uprising deposed the reigning sultan. John Gideon Okello a professional revolutionary from the school of Che Guevara had led the coup and invited Karume to be President. Karume accepted and in a move of which Niccolo Machiavelli would have been proud declared Okello to be an enemy of the state at the earliest opportunity. Okello ended up in Uganda and historians have speculated that he was murdered by Idi Amin Dada.

Three months after the revolution Zanzibar and Tanganyika melded to become the United Republic of Tanzania and Karume became its vice president. Four gunmen in Dar Es Salaam assassinated Karume on 7 April 1972. The United Republic still exists, but now Zanzibar continues to appoint its own presidents. In fact the current President of Zanzibar is Karume's democratically elected son, Amani Abeid Karume.

Togo

The first president of independent Togo, Sylvanus Olympio governed for two years before being shot during the coup of General Gnassingbé Eyadéma on 13 January 1963. Eyadéma was actually involved in two coups, in 1963 and 1967. After the first one, he became Chief of Staff. After the second he became President of Togo and ruled as dictator for the next 38 years until his death in 1967.

Eyadéma was known to brag about being the man who shot Olympio. The rivalry continues to the present day in the form of a family feud. Eyadéma was succeeded by his son Faure Essozimna Gnassingbé early in 2005, but within weeks, under domestic and international pressure, he had to step down only to assume the presidency again weeks later when he won 60 per cent of the vote on 24 April 2005.

Olympio's son Gilchrist, who by a bizarre quirk of chance, shares the same birthday as his father's assassin, has himself escaped several assassination attempts and two death sentences under the elder Eyadéma's regime. As head of the Union of Forces for Change Party, Gilchrist Olympio continues to be one of the current Eyadéma's chief political opponents.

The Middle East

Lebanon

Maronite President-elect of Lebanon Bachir Gemayel 14 September 1982 had already paid a price for his involvement in politics. Two years before his election, his eighteen-month-old daughter Maya was blown up in a car bomb intended for him. Gemayel himself died on 14 September 1982, nine days before being due to take office. A bomb exploded at the headquarters of the Kataeb Party in Achrafieh, Beirut that killed him and 25 others. Maronite Habib Tanious Shartuouni of the Syrian Socialist Nationalist Party was convicted of planting the bomb and jailed at Roumieh Prison. The Syrian Army released him in 1990 during their period of control over Lebanon, from 1976–2005.

Gemayel's brother Amine became president and governed under an ever-increasing cloud of unpopularity until the election of René Moawad. Moawad's election had taken place after a year of infighting in which Gemayel governed in name alone.

Moawad's victory was, however, ephemeral. After only seventeen days in power he was travelling in a motorcade returning from Independence Day celebrations on 22 November 1989. A 250 kg (550 lb) car bomb exploded in West Beirut as the motorcade was passing. The blast killed the President and 23 others. No investigation has ever uncovered who was responsible for the bomb, but many suspected Syrian involvement.

Central Asia

Afghanistan

President Sardar Mohammed Daoud Khan seized control of Afghanistan on 17 July 1973 after deposing his cousin and brother-in-law, the last shah of Afghanistan, Mohammed Zahir Shah.

Shah or not, Khan—whose name means 'ruler'—ruled Afghanistan for almost five years until a KGB-backed communist coup shot him and most of his family in the presidential palace 28 April 1978. In true communist style the new government announced that Khan had 'resigned for health reasons'.

Khan's successor, Nur Muhammad Taraki lasted for seventeen months until his intense rivalry with his prime minister, Hafizullah Amin came to a head. Amin had Taraki suffocated with a pillow on 14 September 1979, although the press originally reported that the 'great leader' had succumbed to a 'serious illness from which he had been suffering for some time'.

Amin's takeover so alarmed the Soviets that they sent in the Alpha group of KGB's elite special forces, OSNAZ. Disguised as Afghani military they stormed the presidential palace and killed Amin and his elite guards on 27 December 1979. The Soviet invasion of Afghanistan had effectively begun.

Pakistan

Whether you call the death of Zulfikar Ali Bhutto an assassination depends on whether you recognise the legality of his trial. The politically motivated killing of a president—or ex-president—qualifies in my book.

Long involved in the politics of his country, Bhutto came to power after having founded the Pakistan People's Party (PPP) and eventually winning a war of political attrition against Pakistan's military leader, General Agha Yahya Khan. In the process Bhutto became President, Military Commander in Chief and the civilian Chief Martial Lay Administrator.

Like so many leaders before and since Bhutto started off riding a wave of popularity. This, however, soon eroded as his country's economy stagnated and its politicians seemed to spend all their time bickering rather than actually administrating. In the face of increasing civil unrest and Bhutto's heavy handedness, the military under General Muhammad Zia-ul-Haq declared martial law and arrested Bhutto and members of his cabinet on 5 July 1977. Bhutto was released a few weeks later, only to be re-arrested and ultimately jailed after spending most of his time as a free man touring the country and giving rabble rousing speeches to build up support.

Bhutto was put on trial on charges of conspiracy to murder rival politician Ahmed Raza Kasuri. Bhutto said that the charges were trumped up and the evidence in the case was fabricated. After Bhutto's conviction, failed appeal and almost two years in prison the Zia regime hanged Bhutto early on the morning of 5 April 1979.

Although Bhutto's Kurdish wife Begum Nusrat Ispahani became President of the PPP during the trial, his eldest daughter Benazir was his political successor and became the first-ever female leader of an Islamic nation. She was elected President on 16 November 1988 in the wake of General Zia's suspicious death in a plane accident. Her road has been rather rocky. She was deposed in 1990 under charges of corruption, re-elected in 1993, deposed again in 1996 and is now living in exile in Dubai and barred from contesting elections.

Other assorted presidencies

Bangladesh

President Sheikh Mujibur 'Mujib' Rahma died on 15 August 1975 when a group of junior officers of the Bangladesh army stormed the presidential residence in armoured tanks. They not only killed Mujib, but his household staff and almost his whole family. Mujib's daughters, Sheikh Haisina Wajed and Sheikh Rehano were visiting West Germany at the time, which saved their lives, but they were stranded in exile.

The new president Khondaker Moshtaq Ahmad, Mujib's political rival, virtually condoned the former president's assassination by immunising his killers against prosecution. This was hardly surprising since Ahmad had been one of the principle conspirators. The chief of the army, Khaled Mosharraf, was outraged and staged a coup on 3 November in which Prime Minister Mohammad Mansoor Ali and many other politicians died. Mosharraf himself was killed only four days later, a victim of a counter-coup.

Bangladesh continued to live under a succession of unstable governments plagued by coup attempts. Ziaur 'Zia' Rahman became President in 1977. A group of army officers murdered him, six bodyguards and two aides as part of a failed coup on 30 May 1981, but the government remained in power and instigated a purge of the would-be new regime. Several of the opposition were tried, convicted and executed, including the coup leader, Major General Mohammed Abdul Monjur, who was found hiding in a tea plantation in Chittagong.

Since his death, Zia's widow Kaleda has served twice as Bangladesh's Prime Minister 1991–1996 and 2001–2006—the first woman ever to hold that office.

The exiled daughter of Mujib, Sheikh Hasina Wajed waited a long time for revenge. She became the second woman to hold the prime ministership, from 1996–2001. During her term she repealed the Indemnity Ordinance, the law that had protected her father's assassins from immunity to prosecution. In 1996 the authorities arrested, tried and executed Syed Faruque Rahman for Mujib's murder. Ahmad had already died uncharged and untried for his role in the murder of the 'Father of Bangladesh'.

Greece

Ioannis Antonios Kapodistrias, the first president of Greece, is justly credited for his role in the transition of his country from rule by the Ottoman Empire to independence. He also introduced the potato to Greece with a bit of lateral thinking. Knowing that conservative Greek farmers would snub the potato he ordered that they be 'guarded'. Soon enough the Greeks started stealing the potatoes on the assumption that if they were under guard, they had to be valuable.

This venerable statesman died as a result of a vendetta. Petros Mavromichalis and his brother Tzanis had led a revolt against the governor of Lakonia, a political appointee of Kapodistrias. As a result the President had the rebels arrested. Petros and Tzanis's brother Konstantinos and his son Georgios vowed revenge against this offence to the family honour.

Kapodistrias was about to enter Saint Spiridon Church in Nafplio on 9 October 1831, when Konstantinos fired a pistol at him but missed, the bullet hitting the church, which is scarred to this day. Konstantinos then stabbed the President while Georgios shot their target in the head. A quick-thinking general called Fotomaras witnessed the assassination from a nearby window and shot Konstantinos. The President's bodyguard had also shot Konstantinos, but the gathered crowd were so incensed that the man had failed in his duty to protect the President that they turned on him and beat him to death.

In the confusion Georgios managed to escape and seek asylum in the French embassy, but was forced to give himself up and was later executed by firing squad.

Petros Mavromichalis publicly condemned the assassination. Within a short period of time Greece became a kingdom and King Otto released Petros and Tzanis. Petros later became a senator.

France

Two French presidents have been assassinated. Marie François Sadi Carnot was widely respected for his honesty and integrity, but you can't please all of the people all of the time, especially in politics. While he was making a speech at a public banquet in Lyon on 24 June 1894, an Italian anarchist named Sante Jeronimo Caserio stabbed him to death. Caserio's motive was revenge for the execution of anarchist Auguste Vaillant, executed for the bombing of the Chamber of Deputies, and for that of Emile Henry, executed for bombing the Café Terminus at the Saint-Lazare railway station in Paris, which was itself a reaction to Vaillant's conviction.

Caserio was guillotined after uttering his last words: 'Courage, comrades! Long live Anarchy!'

President Paul Doumer died, not for any political reason, but because a mentally unbalanced Russian émigré named Paul Gorguloff shot him while he was opening a book fair in Paris on 6 May 1932. Doumer died from his wounds the following morning. Gorguloff was guillotined and his last words were 'Russia, my country!'

Palau

Although assassinations generally happen in large countries, small nations are not immune. The Micronesian state of Palau comprises only 459 square kilometres of islands, 800 kilometres east of the Philippines and has a population of just under 20,000. It nevertheless managed to produce three assassins who murdered its first president, Haruo Ignacio Remeliik, on 30 June 1985, with four shots from a .32 calibre pistol shortly after midnight, just as the President was about to enter his house after a day spent fishing.

As far as I know he is the only president to have been assassinated while wearing a T-shirt and shorts. Melwert Tmetuchl, Leslie Tewid and Anghenio Sabino were found guilty of Remeliik's assassination and given mandatory life sentences.

Poland

The first elected president of the Republic of Poland, Gabriel Narutowicz was opening an art exhibition at the Zacheta Gallery in Warsaw on 16 December 1922, when right-wing art critic Professor Eligiusz Niewiadomski assassinated him. It was only five days after his inauguration.

Being a respected art critic at an art exhibition was a perfect cover and Niewiadomski had no trouble coming close enough to the President to shoot him. Although the Professor made his escape the authorities later caught him and he was executed by firing squad at the Citadel of Warsaw. Ten thousand people attended Neiwiadomski's funeral, more than attended the late President's which gives you an idea of the relative popularity of the two men.

South Korea

General Park Chung Hee came to power in that rarest of ways, a bloodless military coup, in the '5.16' revolution on 16 May 1961. He spent the next eighteen years constructing modern capitalist South Korea. He survived two assassination attempts by North Korean agents. The first, conducted by a 31-man team, failed when peasants cutting wood intercepted them. Instead of killing the peasants, the Keystone Cop assassins tried to indoctrinate them into communism then let them go. The peasants reported the cadre to the police and the authorities were waiting for them when they tried to infiltrate the Blue House (the South Korean equivalent to the White House). Two members of the team were killed along with 71 uniformed officers and civilians. A further 69 were wounded. Twenty-nine assassins then escaped, but in the massive manhunt that followed 25 of them were killed and two captured, leaving two ultimately unaccounted for.

The second attempt on the General's life occurred on 15 August 1974, when North Korean secret agent, Mun Se-gwang, fired at Park while he was giving a speech. The bullet missed Park, but fatally wounded his wife, Yuk Yeong-su. Park finished his speech anyway.

Park's successful assassin was Kim Jae-Gyu, the director of the Korean CIA. Although he was one of Park's closest friends, Kim felt that Park was an obstacle to democracy, as dictators usually are. Kim shot Park and the leader of Park's guards on 26 October 1979. Kim's agents killed four more bodyguards before other guards apprehended them. They were all later convicted and executed.

Park' daughter, Park Geun-hye, is currently preparing to run for presidency. She has already survived her own assassination attempt. On 20 May 2006 a 50-year-old man slashed her face with a knife and the ten centimetre wound on her right cheek required remedial plastic surgery.

South Vietnam

Joining the ranks of the first-presidents-of-new-countries-who-don't-survive-their-terms club was the first president of South Vietnam, Ngo Dinh Diem Jean Baptist. It was during Diem's tenure that Buddhist monk Thich Quang Duc famously set himself on fire in Saigon in protest over Catholic Diem's treatment of Buddhists. Several self immolations later, Madame Ngo Dinh Nhu, Diem's sister-in-law and de facto first lady of Vietnam, famously declared that she would 'clap hands at seeing another monk barbecue show'. This sort of comment did nothing to improve the image of Diem's autocratic and nepotistic government and the Army of the Republic of Vietnam led by General Duong Van Minh moved in for the kill.

On 1 November 1963, the army offered Diem and his brother Ngo Dinh Nhu safe passage out of the country if they surrendered, but the brothers chose instead to sneak out of the presidential palace and escape to Cholon. They were captured the next morning, put into the back of an armoured personnel carrier and shot.

Madame Nhu, visiting the United States at the time, blamed the Americans for supporting the coup and held President Kennedy personally responsible for the death of her husband and brother-in-law. With her characteristic lack of diplomacy she later exclaimed that 'Whoever has the Americans as allies does not need enemies.' Many historians now consider Diem's assassination to be the last impediment to Ho Chi Minh's escalation, which triggered the latter phase of the Vietnam War, from 1964–1975.

The rest of Diem's family didn't fare too well. Brother Ngo Dinh Can in 1964 was executed, brother Ngo Dinh Luyen was exiled and brother Ngo Dinh Khoi was buried alive by the Viet Minh for refusing to join them. Brother and Archbishop Pierre Marin Ngo Dinh Thuc survived with the Catholic Church as his shield, in spite of his connections to a minority movement, the Sedevacantists, who don't recognise modern Popes since the reforms of the Second Vatican Council.

Madame Nhu now lives on the French Riviera. One rumour goes that when John F Kennedy was assassinated, twenty days after her husband's death, she told Jacqueline Kennedy 'Now you know what it feels like.'

Presidential survivors

Frequently targets, quite a few presidents have nevertheless managed to avoid being killed, although—in some minds—not nearly enough have bitten the dust. The following presidents have all survived assassination attempts, sometimes spectacularly. Charles De Gaulle, the first president of the 5th Republic of France, was so often a target of assassins that British author Frederick Forsythe was inspired by the attempt of Jean-Marie Bastien-Thiry to write his bestselling novel, *The Day of the Jackal*.

On 22 August 1962, Bastien-Thiry directed his recruits to fire machine guns at De Gaulle's unarmoured Citrôen DS while the president, his wife and entourage were riding through the Parisian suburb of Petit-Clamart. Although the occupants survived uninjured, fourteen bullets hit the car, twenty hit the Café Trianon and 187 hit the pavement. In spite of losing two tyres, the Citrôen escaped at speed.

The would-be killers were arrested and sentenced to death. De Gaulle pardoned all of them, except Bastien-Thiry. De Gualle cited various reasons for this decision, but perhaps the most significant was that the air weaponry engineer had directed the strike, but hadn't had the guts to doing any of the shooting himself. Bastien-Thiry was executed by firing squad at Ivry-sur-Seine while clutching his rosarie.

President Jacques René Chirac survived an assassination attempt more recently. During the 14 July Bastille Day celebrations in Paris in 2002, a lone gunman, Maxime Brunerie, fired at the presidential motorcade from a rifle that he had hidden in a guitar case. Both shots went wide and bystanders overpowered Brunerie.

The would-be assassin wanted to become famous for killing a VIP and then either being shot or shooting himself in front of television cameras. In spite of a judgement of diminished mental capacity, Brunerie was sentenced to ten years imprisonment in 2004. The fact that most people who are reading this haven't heard of him demonstrates how dismally he failed on both counts.

Georgian President Eduard Shevardnadze became de facto ruler of the former Soviet Socialist Republic of Georgia when he ousted Zviad Konstantines dze Gamsakhurdia in a bloody military coup in 1992. Gamsakhurdia had been the first democratically elected President of Georgia since the country's independence from the Soviet Union. He he was found dead almost two years after the coup, in the village of Khibula in western Georgia. There was a single bullet in his head. Shevardnaze himself survived two attempts on his life, in August 1995 and again in February 1998. Both times the Georgian government blamed supporters of Gansakhurdia. Shevardnaze resigned on 23 November 2003 in the midst of near political chaos. Some analysts assert that both Russia and America conspired to bring him down. There is also wide support for the idea that American billionaire financier George Soros used his considerable influence to facilitate matters.

The most famous survivor of a presidential assassination attempt in recent history is Viktor Andriyovych Yushchenko, the third president of Ukraine. Yushchenko's assumption of the presidency came about as a result of a long, nasty and frequently violent campaign between the followers of Yushchenko and those of his opponent, Viktor Fedorovych Yanukovych. In September 2004 Yushchenko became seriously ill with what doctors at Vienna's Rudolfinerhaus Clinic initially diagnosed as acute pancreatitis. His internal symptoms were serious——he suffered from a swollen liver and pancreas and an ulcerated digestive tract. It was the external symptoms that were the most dramatic, however. Yushchenko's face became bloated, pockmarked and greenish. After seeing Yushchenko on television, Dutch toxicologist Bram Brouwer suggested that physicians check him for dioxin poisoning—a diagnosis backed up by British toxicologist John Henry.

It turned out that the pockmarks on Yushchenko's face were chloracne, caused by a dosage of TCDD dioxin that had left a residual concentration 1000 times higher than normal. This is the second highest dioxin level ever recorded in a human. It may have originated in a mycotoxin (fungus killer) called 'T2' that the Soviets are believed to have used as a chemical weapon in Afghanistan. In post-Soviet Russia it seems there are always old weapons lying around.

Yushchenko himself links his poisoning to a dinner he attended with a group of Ukrainian officials the night before he became sick. Although rumours abound that someone in the Yanukovych camp had attempted to poison Yushchenko, authorities and investigators have been able to prove nothing to date. In any case, after considerable arguments over alleged electoral fraud on the part of Yanukovych supporters, Yushchenko was able finally to declare a victory after three rounds of voting, and was inaugurated on 25 January 2005.

Yushchenko remains a man of mixed fortunes. After recovering from his poisoning, he survived a lightning strike while climbing Mount Hoverla on 16 July 2006 and, on 4 August 2006, his rival Yanukovych was voted in as prime minister.

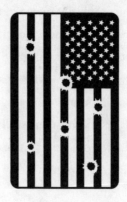

An American Interlude

It's easy to forget that American assassinations, especially American presidential assassinations, make up only a small minority of all political murders throughout history. This doesn't mean that famous and high profile assassinations such as John F Kennedy and Martin Luther King aren't historically important, but one should have some sense of proportion.

Because the media of the United States dominates the media of the English-speaking world—and the world as a whole for that matter—events in that one country tend to attract more attention than anywhere else. It's a classic case of the squeaky wheel getting the grease. Stories originating in America aren't necessarily more special than anywhere else, but as the American media is more than a little parochial, self-obsessed and loud, it tends to drown out other voices. It even affects what the rest of us pay attention to or even consider newsworthy or important.

In fact the glamour of American presidential assassinations is so compelling that writer Charles Gilbert Jr convinced Stephen Sondheim and John Weidman to help him write a musical about it: *Assassins* (1990). It's easy to forget that American assassinations, and especially American presidential assassinations, make up only a small minority of all political murders throughout history, and even in the contemporary world. This doesn't mean that famous and high profile assassinations such as that of John F Kennedy and Martin Luther King aren't historically important, but one should view these events in the context of a bigger picture and have some sense of proportion. You could fill a library with books about the JFK assassination alone, so the following profiles are just an introduction to whet your appetite. If you like you can devote years of your life to reading up on every paranoid conspiracy that grabs your attention, or generate a few dozen of your own. God knows, other people have.

The Wild North

Let's first take a look at America's giant, but frequently neglected northern neighbour.

Little known outside his own country and far less famous than his southern counterparts like George Washington and Thomas Jefferson, Thomas D'Arcy McGee was one of the 36 Fathers of the Canadian

Confederation. In case you ever wondered how something like Canada actually happened and who's responsible for it, look no further than people like McGee. It's interesting to note that both McGee and that other great North American mover and shaker Benjamin Franklin, were both journalists and, in the end, were people who weren't just content to write about history—they had to go make it.

D'Arcy McGee was born in Ireland, migrated to the United States in 1843 when he was seventeen and moved to Canada in 1857. Being Irish, he was naturally predisposed to being anti-British, and channelled his antipathy to helping the cause of Canadian independence. Back then Canada didn't exist, it comprised the six separate colonies of British North America—British Columbia, Prince Edward Island, Newfoundland, New Brunswick, Nova Scotia and the Province of Canada, which is now separated into Ontario and Quebec.

McGee, one of the representatives of the legislative assembly of Quebec, eventually became a participant in two conferences in which the Fathers worked out exactly how to turn the Provinces into a united country. The Charlottesville Conference met in September 1864 and the Quebec City Conference met in October 1864. Bowing to political pressure and no doubt influenced by the American Civil War of 1861 to 1865, which showed how fragile federations could be, Queen Victoria legally created Canada by signing the British North America Act of 29 March 1867. It came into effect on July 1—Canada Day—and the Dominion of Canada was born.

Throughout this paper revolution McGee had advocated non-violent means to achieve the ends of independence. In doing so he alienated his fellow Irishmen, the Fenian Brotherhood, a group of militant radicals who wanted to invade British Canada to bring pressure on Britain to withdraw from Ireland. In helping to create Canada, McGee's assassin must have felt that he was a traitor, and the newly elected representative of Montreal West was shot dead in Ottawa with a bullet from a .32 calibre pistol as he entered his apartment building on 17 April 1868.

Over 40 Fenians or suspected Fenians were arrested and eventually merchant tailor Patrick J Whelan was found guilty. Whelen proclaimed his innocence to the end and he may well have been telling the truth— the evidence against him was entirely circumstantial. Witnesses had seen a man like him at the scene. Authorities found a gun like the one that shot McGee in his possession. Whelan was Irish and therefore likely to be a Fenian. He was hanged during a snowstorm with 5000 people looking on and buried in an unmarked grave in what was the Carleton County Jail, but which is now Ottawa International Youth Hostel.

The case of McGee is almost unique in his country; the history of Canada's much more populous southern neighbour is much more violent.

The Wilder West

Religious leader Joseph Smith Junior has the distinction of founding the only American-grown religion in the modern world, apart from Scientology. His visions and evangelism gave rise to the Church of Jesus Christ of Latter-day Saints, better known as the Mormons. He also founded the less well-known denominations of the Latter-day Saint movement, such as the Community of Christ. Religion tends to inspire fervour, but also antagonism. Smith's religious teachings included Baptism for the dead and a form of polygamy that he called Plural Marriage.

Like all religious leaders and reformers, Joseph Smith made enemies. A group of these, including some ex-followers, came together and formed a newspaper, the *Nauvoo Expositor*, the only issue of which, in 1844, was filled with articles complaining about Smith and his religion. Smith ordered his followers to destroy the paper, which they did on 10 June 1844. Many of the non-Mormons in the area considered the destruction of the paper to be a violation of the freedom of the press and angry citizens forced his arrest. On 27 June 1844, while Smith was in voluntary custody in Carthage Jail, Hancock County, Illinois, an even angrier mob of around 200 men stormed the prison. Smith was armed with a six-shooter and managed to kill two attackers before he ran to an open window in the building's second floor where the mob shot him several times. He fell to the ground and was shot several more times. His elder brother Hyrum Smith, who had also been incarcerated, was already dead, shot in the face.

With the death of their leader and the loss of what little official protection the Mormons had, it was up to Smith's follower Brigham Young to lead the Mormons into the deserts of what was then northern Mexico and found Salt Lake City. Today 60 per cent of Utah's 2.5 million inhabitants are Mormons and the church claims 12.5 million members throughout the world.

I don't know if Oglala Sioux Chief Ta-sunko-witko, better known to Western history as Crazy Horse knew about the Spanish genocides of the indigenous peoples of South America, or whether it would have made any difference to him if he had. Their example showed that against the combination of guns, germs and iron horses his people didn't stand a chance. Nevertheless he put up a good fight.

Best known for killing General George Armstrong Custer, on 25 June 1876, Crazy Horse's outstanding victory and virtual annihilation of the 7th Cavalry at the Battle of Little Big Horn was only the most famous of many military actions against the whites—and only delayed the inevitable. Almost a year later, on 5 May 1877, after the military draw, but psychological defeat of the Battle of Wolf Mountain on 8 January 1877, Crazy Horse led his cold, starving people, including his sick wife, to surrender to American forces at Fort Robinson, near what is now Crawford Nebraska.

Crazy Horse not only had enemies among the whites, but among rival natives as well—in particular two Lakota Sioux, Red Cloud and Spotted Tail, who began circulating rumours that Crazy Horse's surrender was insincere and that he was only buying time until he could grab another chance of annihilating the whites. Crazy Horse was with his wife's parents—Spotted Tail's countrymen—when he heard these rumours and chose to return to Fort Robinson to answer the false allegations. When Crazy Horse arrived at the fort the guards attempted to arrest him. Crazy Horse fought back and Private William Gentiles bayoneted the former Sioux warlord near his left kidney. Crazy Horse died during the night. His family later buried him in the Badlands of what is now Toadstool Geologic Park in the Oglala National Grassland in north-western Nebraska. You can consider the assassination of Crazy Horse as one of the most denigrating of all—a death in custody.

Black Power and Pink Power Struggles

Medgar Evers

In the twentieth century the focus of minority struggle first shifted from Native Americans to the descendents of America's slaves. Civil rights activist Medgar Wiley Evers was the first high-profile casualty of the awakening of black assertiveness after decades, if not centuries, of institutionalised racism.

Evers's main technique against white oppression was the boycott. He would encourage people not to buy from or use the services of people who treated 'negroes' as second-class citizens. He distributed bumper stickers against service stations that read: 'Don't Buy Gas Where You Can't Use the Restroom.' As the Local Field Secretary of the National Association for the Advancement of Coloured People (NAACP) Evers made even more enemies. Two weeks before his death someone threw a Molotov cocktail into his carport. Nine days later, after leaving an NAACP meeting, he was almost run down by a car.

On the night of his death, 12 June 1963, he had just returned home and was in his carport when fertiliser salesman, white supremacist and Ku Klux Klan member Byron De La Beckwith shot him in the back with a .30-06 calibre shotgun fired from a distance of about 60 metres. The bullet went through Evers, into his house and repeatedly ricocheted in the building until finally coming to rest under a watermelon in the kitchen. Evers staggered for about nine meters before collapsing. His neighbour took him to hospital, but Evers died of his wounds and blood loss a few hours later.

Two all-white juries in separate trials in 1964 failed to convict Beckwith and he remained a free man for 31 years, but he couldn't keep his mouth shut and bragged about the assassination at a Ku Klux Klan rally. In 1993 the Mississippi Supreme Court ruled that Beckwith could be tried a third time. After only seven hours of deliberation at Beckwith's 1994 trial the jury found him guilty and he was sentenced to life. He died in prison from heart disease. The 1996 film *Ghosts of Mississippi* recounts the assassination and later trial and won James Woods an Academy Award for his portrayal of Beckwith.

Malcolm X

Malcolm X didn't think of himself as an American so much as a 'victim of Americanism'. The man born Malcolm Little had worked as a shoe shiner, drug dealer and burglar before his cause transformed him into a champion for human rights and dignity, but even early on he demonstrated a reluctance to be the white man's stooge. In the famous book *The Autobiography of Malcolm X* (1965), he described avoiding the draft by telling his interviewing officers that he couldn't wait to get his hands on a gun and 'kill some crackers'.

While serving a prison sentence for burglary, from 1946 to 1952, Malcolm became a Muslim under the auspices of the black Muslim offshoot The Nation of Islam (NOI). On his release he adopted the name 'X' in rejection of 'white slave names'. For the next thirteen years he rose in the Black Freedom Movement and built up an extensive network of powerful friends. He was able to complete his Umrah (pilgrimage to Mecca) because of his connections with the Saudi Royal family. He travelled extensively throughout the world, building up support for the emancipation of African Americans.

Eventually a rift formed between Malcolm and the NOI. Malcolm was a brilliant orator and had been an influential speaker for the Nation. He had even encouraged the boxer, Cassius Clay, to become Muhammad Ali, but Malcolm eventually became fed up with the petty jealousies that his fame attracted as well as the evidence of corruption he saw within the organisation. He was out on his own and he became a target, especially after he formed the Organisation for Afro-American Unity, which only created disunity and split the Black Muslim community right down the middle.

On the 21 February 1965 as Malcolm was giving a speech in the Audubon Ballroom in Manhattan a man entering started shouting at guards 'Get your hand outta my pocket! Don't be messin' with my pockets!' This incident was a decoy and, while Malcolm's bodyguards tried to quiet things down, another man shot him with a sawn off shotgun. Two other men then fired sixteen bullets into the activist's legs, but the shotgun had already killed him.

Three men, all from the NOI, were convicted of the slaying: Thomas Hagan (Talmadge Heyer), Norman 3X Butler (Muhammad Abd Al-Aziz) and Thomas X Johnson (Khalil Islam).

In the confusion of the melee only Hagan was actually apprehended at the scene of the crime, the others not until later. Only Hagan confessed, stating that he'd been given orders, but didn't know who had masterminded the plot or who his fellow assassins were supposed to be. Under questioning Hagan changed his story often but maintained that Butler and Johnson weren't involved. In 1977 Hagan claimed that, in fact, it was other members of the Nation of Islam who were involved: William X Bradley, Leon X Davis, William X Kinley and Benjamin X Thomas. None of these men have ever been charged. The authorities felt that their cases against Butler and Johnson were sound.

Butler, Johnson and Heyer were all paroled in 1985 after serving their full twenty-year sentences. Butler made headlines in 1995 when current NOI leader Louis Farrakhan gave him the job of running the NOI's Number Seven Mosque. Although it wasn't the same building it had the same name as the Mosque that Malcolm had helped build and the *Village Voice* couldn't resist the headline: 'Malcolm X's Killer Appointed to Run Malcolm X's Mosque'. Heyer now goes under the name of Mujabid Abdul Halim and keeps a low profile.

Sixteen hundred people attended Malcolm X's funeral and his legacy lingers on. In 1995 the *New York Post* ran an article claiming that Louis Farrakhan, then only 22, was the mastermind behind the Malcolm X assassination plot. Farrakhan later won a defamation lawsuit against the paper.

The *Post*'s article had come on the heels of the 12 January 1995 indictment of Qubilah Shabazz, one of Malcolm X's six daughters by Hajj Bahiyah Betty Shabazz. The Shabazz family had long felt that Farrakhan was responsible for Malcolm's death and the FBI conducted a seven-month investigation of Qubilah in which they recorded her allegedly planning to hire a hit-man to kill the NOI leader. As far as the FBI were concerned, Farrakhan's guilt was a fantasy, but Qubilah was definitely plotting.

Although she was arrested it became clear that Qubilah's case was one of entrapment. Farrakhan amazed everyone when he spoke in defence of Qubilah and in May 1995 organised a fundraiser for Qubilah's defence, at which he and Betty were very publicly reconciled. The charges against Qubilah were dropped, but the authorities required her to seek treatment for anger management and drug and alcohol abuse.

Another repercussion of this family drama had tragic consequences. Qubilah's twelve-year-old son, Malcolm Shabazz, was sent to live with his grandmother Betty. On 1 June 1997 he set fire to Betty's apartment. Malcolm X's widow suffered from burns to 80 per cent of her body and died in intensive care three weeks later. Malcolm-the-younger spent eighteen months in juvenile detention in Valhalla, New York for manslaughter.

You can find an extensive treatment of the assassination and some of the obligatory conspiracy theories at:
www.thesmokinggun.com/malcolmx/malcolmx.html

George Lincoln Rockwell

Black leaders aren't the only ones who've died in the struggle against racism; 'crackers' could get it too. After serving as a Naval Commander during World War II George Lincoln Rockwell 25 August 1967 became a commercial artist and, in 1959, founded the American Nazi Party on the side. He steadily rose into prominence until he attracted the attention of the mainstream press and the April 1966 issue of *Playboy* magazine featured an interview of him with Alex Haley.

Rockwell was known for his extreme views on 'kikes', 'niggers' and any other 'human scum' but he doesn't appear to have advocated violence; rather he made vague references to 'addressing the issues' or occasionally, mass deportation. His Hatenanny Records label even released a song called 'Ship Those Niggers Back'.

In fact he even admired Malcolm X and aligned himself with the Black Muslim movement because they agreed on the necessity of segregation of the 'races'.

In the climate of America in the sixties, sooner or later someone was going to get at Rockwell—it was only a matter of time. Amazingly his killer wasn't a 'kike' or a 'nigger', but one of his own. On 28 June 1967 he tried to drive into the driveway of the headquarters of his recently renamed National Socialists White People's Party (NSWPP) when he found a felled tree blocking his path. As he tried to remove the tree, two shots were fired at him. He ducked, then ran after his would-be killer, but lost the trail.

It wasn't too long after that someone finally got to Rockwell. The following month, a few minutes before noon on 25 August 1967—his last day on earth—Rockwell was pulling away from the Econowash Laundromat at the Dominion Hills Shopping Centre in Arlington, Virginia when two shots broke through his windshield. Rockwell got out of the car, but collapsed and died face up on the pavement. One bullet had severed major blood vessels just above his heart. The gunman climbed off the roof of the Laundromat and escaped.

A patrolman familiar with the Arlington Nazis arrested John Patler 45 minutes after the shooting when the assassin got off a bus. Patler had been expelled from the American Nazi Party in April that year for having 'Bolshevik leanings', whatever that might mean. In December 1967 he was sentenced to twenty years in prison, but was such a model prisoner that he was paroled on 22 August 1975. Unfortunately for him he violated his parole and served an additional six years at Pulaski Prison.

Even in death, Rockwell was controversial. The Arlington Nazis basically commandeered his body and tried to turn his funeral into a military burial. Although the armed forces gave their approval, the authorities refused to allow anyone wearing a Swastika to attend the ceremony. This, in effect, meant that none of the mourners were allowed into the cemetery, and an all-day stand-off ensued. In the end, the ANP or NSWPP, decided on a cremation and a smaller ceremony.

For several years after his death, Rockwell's supporters would occasionally paint a Swastika on the pavement where he died. Rockwell is still a hero to neo-Nazi skinheads and white supremacists.

Martin Luther King

The most famous of all racially-motivated assassinations remains that of Martin Luther King Jr. The Baptist minister and civil rights activist was justly famous for his powers of rhetoric and ability to inspire loyalty and personal devotion.

At the age of 35 he was and remains the youngest person ever to receive the Nobel Peace Prize because of his message of non-violent resolution to America's endemic racism. In this he freely acknowledged the influence of Mahatma Gandhi and the Indian leader's approach permeated the culture of King's Southern Christian Leadership Conference (SCLC).

King founded this umbrella organisation of a group of black Baptist churches as an organised front of civil disobedience, especially against the southern states' 'Jim Crow' laws, America's very own form of apartheid. King used every form of non-violent protest at his disposal: pickets, protests, marches and rallies. The March on Washington with 250,000 people from a wide range of ethnicities represented the largest protest in Washington's history and wasn't topped until the Vietnam marches of the 1970s. Many still consider it the highpoint of the SCLC's campaign, but not everyone was a fan of Doctor King's approach. Malcolm X thought the March on Washington was too lovey-dovey and called it the 'Farce on Washington'.

Just like Gandhi, King had to face the fact that some people just didn't want to play nice. Violence tended to mar many events despite the intentions of their organisers. On the evening of his death King was schedule—the next day—to try to defuse tensions at a sanitation workers' strike in Memphis, Tennessee. He would never arrive. That night, 4 April 1968, escaped convict James Earl Ray shot King with a .30–06 calibre Remington 760 Gamemaster pump rifle at 6.01 p.m. as the minister was standing on the balcony outside his room at the Lorraine Hotel.

It took only a single bullet to kill King. The bullet entered near his right jaw, fractured his mandible, severed his jugular vein and key arteries and shattered several cervical vertebrae. The force of the blast ripped his necktie off and slammed his body against the wall behind him. He would have died in seconds, but doctors at Memphis Hospital did not pronounce him dead until 7.05 p.m.

The authorities caught up with Ray at Heathrow Airport in London on 8 June 1968, after a manhunt that involved 3500 FBI agents. Ray immediately protested his extradition, but the evidence was either compelling or, if you're a conspiracy theorist, very convincingly planted. There were records that showed that someone named James Earl Ray bought the rifle in question and booked a room at a boarding house opposite the Lorraine Hotel on the day of the assassination. The rifle had been left behind at the scene with Ray's fingerprints on it. James Earl Ray was either the biggest patsy in the world or the dumbest assassin.

Ray himself denied that he killed King, citing that he pleaded guilty in order to receive a 99-year jail sentence rather than the death penalty. He spent the rest of his life trying to withdraw his confession and win a retrial. He even testified to the House Select Committee on Assassinations that he hadn't killed King. Soon afterwards, on 10 June 1977 he and six other prisoners managed to escape Brushy Mountain State Penitentiary, but the police recaptured him three days later. Ray even wrote and published a book *Who Killed Martin Luther King? The True Story of an Alleged Assassination* (1992).

The King family themselves don't believe that Ray murdered Martin Luther and, in 1997, King's son Dexter actually supported Ray's petition for a trial. In 1998 the King family filed a civil 'wrongful death' lawsuit against Loyd Jowers, who was at the time of the assassination the owner of Jim's Grill, near the Lorraine Hotel. Jowers claimed that he was part of a conspiracy to murder King and that late Mafioso Frank Liberto had paid him $100,000 to contract a killer, and that the real shooter was a Memphis policeman named Lieutenant Earl Clark. Eventually, the court found Jowers 'liable' on 8 December 1999. He only had to pay the King family $100 in compensation—that was how they wanted it. Their intention was only to make a point.

The State Department thought the Kings had been duped and in June 2000 tabled a report claiming basically that Jowers' assertions were baloney. Jowers had died a month earlier from a heart attack and Ray had been dead for over two years from kidney disease and Hepatitis C.

King is interred in a marble sarcophagus on the grounds of the King Centre, Sweet Auburn, Atlanta, Georgia. The third Monday of every year is an American national holiday, celebrated on or around Martin Luther King Jr's birthday, but the holiday wasn't observed in all 50 states until 2000. The last county to adopt Martin Luther King Day as a paid holiday was Greenville County, North Carolina.

Being a black civil rights leader is still a risky job. Baptist minister Reverend Jesse Louis Jackson, unsuccessful candidate for the US presidency, was almost the victim of an assassination conspiracy in 1988, but the Franklin County Missouri Sherriff's Department and the Secret Service had been keeping his would-be killers under surveillance. They determined that they were members of the white supremacist militant organisation the Covenant, Sword and the Arm of the Lord (CSA). Neo-Nazi Londell Williams and his wife Tammy were arrested and charged with threatening a presidential candidate before they could even fire a shot. Londel plead guilty. The court fined him $100 and sentenced him to two years' imprisonment. Tammy was sentenced to twenty months' imprisonment a few months later.

Things as a whole may have improved a little for African Americans. Ironically perhaps, the conservative Republican Party administration of George Walker Bush appointed African Americans Colin Powell and Condoleezza Rice as United States Secretary of State, a position fifth in line to the Presidential succession.

Harvey Milk

Things are not necessarily rosy for gays. The most significant politically motivated gay murder was that of Harvey Bernard Milk. He had served in the Navy, worked in finance on Wall Street and even been a producer on *Jesus Christ Superstar* before moving to San Francisco and setting up a camera store with his partner Scott. His involvement in the gay community led him to run, unsuccessfully, for election for the San Francisco Board of Supervisors in 1973 and 1975. On a local scale, the City Supervisors are actually more powerful than the president and can pass and repeal laws and even set local tax rates.

Milk's ambitions weren't unrealistic. In January 1974 outspoken lesbian Kathy Kozachenko had won a seat in Ann Arbor, Michigan. In spite of Milk's initial failures at the ballot, San Francisco's mayor George Richard Moscone recognised Milk's growing popularity and considered him an ally. Finally, in 1977, Milk became the first openly gay male to become an elected official in America. During his eleven months in office he managed to persuade the San Francisco Council to pass a gay rights ordinance and a pooper-scooper ordinance, and he helped defeat the notorious Proposition 6, a proposal to pass a law that would have allowed the State of California to fire teachers on the basis of their sexuality.

Former member of the Board of Supervisors, conservative councillor Daniel James White, was the only Supervisor to have voted against the gay rights ordinance, but had resigned his position on 10 November 1978 because it paid him $12,000 a year less than his job a policeman. White regretted his decision and asked Mayor Moscone to reappoint him. Moscone refused, preferring to appoint a more liberal person to tip the balance of voting power in the council to a more progressive direction.

On 27 November White had arranged an appointment to see Moscone and surreptitiously entered City Hall through a basement window to avoid metal detectors. He was packing a .38 revolver loaded with exploding bullets. The meeting between Moscone and White degenerated into a heated argument and in a private back office the former councillor shot the mayor twice in the trunk and twice in the head, killing him instantly. White then went to the Supervisors' wing and requested a meeting with Harvey Milk. By the time Deputy Mayor

Rudy Nothenberg found Moscone's body and alerted police, it was already too late. White shot Milk three times in the back and twice in the head. Board President Dianne Goldman Berman Feinstein found Milk's body and alerted police, later announcing to the press that White was the principle suspect in the assassinations.

White had by now made his way to St Mary's Cathedral where Moscone's funeral would later take place. There White met with his wife Mary Ann. He confessed to her what he'd done and she convinced him to give himself up, which he did, 45 minutes after the shooting.

Moscone and Milk were laid out together in City Hall and thousands came to pay their respects. Moscone was buried at Holy Cross Cemetery in Colma. Milk was cremated and his ashes scattered in San Francisco Bay.

At his trial, White's lawyers mounted the now infamous 'Twinkie Defence', which argued that White was not in his right mind when he committed the murders because he'd eaten too much junk food, exacerbating a pre-existing clinical depression. Amazingly, the jury bought it and White emerged with a seven-year, eight-month sentence for voluntary manslaughter.

The gay community were understandably outraged and the verdict sparked the White Night Riots of 21 May 1979. An afternoon protest march turned into a riot in which City Hall's glass doors were broken and twelve police cars set on fire, but there were no deaths and few injuries. The police hit back with a riot of there own after things had settled down, when a number of officers took it upon themselves to smash up a few gay bars and bash a few patrons, hardly any of whom had taken part in the earlier riot.

White only served five years and one month of his sentence before he was paroled, but his life was ruined. He committed suicide by carbon monoxide asphyxiation in his car a little over a year after his release.

Upon Moscone's death, Dianne Feinstein became the first and, to date, only female mayor of San Francisco. She was re-elected in her own right in 1979 and again in 1983. She is now the Senior Democratic Senator for California.

The courts abolished the 'Twinkie Defence' in 1982.

Presidential hopefuls

Of all the elected offices in the United States the top job remains the most dangerous—even aspiring to the presidency is dangerous.

Thirty-fifth Governor and later Senator of Louisiana, Huey Pierce Long Junior, was so popular and powerful that his political opponents thought he was a dictator in the making. It didn't help that Long made no secret that he aspired to the presidency. At the height of White's power, conservative eye, ear, nose and throat specialist Doctor Carl Austin Weiss allegedly shot Long at 4:10 in the early hours of 8 September 1935 in a first-floor corridor in the Capitol Building in Baton Rouge with a .32 calibre Browning semi-automatic pistol. Long's bodyguards instantly turned on Weiss and shot him 30 times in the front, 29 times in the back and twice in the head. Not surprisingly, he died instantly, so to this day we have no idea of Weiss's motives. However there is a theory that Weiss was in fact unarmed and merely struck Long in the face. Then, when the guards turned on Weiss, one of them accidentally shot Long in the abdomen and Weiss became the scapegoat for a cover up.

Long died 36 hours after the shooting. His last words were 'God, don't let me die. I have so much to do.' Long's surgeons may have failed to detect a bullet that was still lodged in a kidney and the senator may have died from internal bleeding. We'll never know for sure because his widow, Rose McConnell Long forbade an autopsy. Rose Long won a special election on 21 April 1936 to serve out the rest of her husband's term. Long's eldest son Russell B Long eventually succeeded his father and mother to the Senate. Before he died he and Carl Weiss Junior met and agreed to set aside whatever differences their fathers may have had.

Democrat George Wallace Junior was elected Governor of Alabama in 1962 and was initially well known for his pro-segregation stance. He tried to get the Democratic nomination for the presidential ticket, but in spite of considerable support he couldn't carry the numbers.

At the time Alabama's constitution prevented him from seeking a second consecutive term as Governor. Instead his wife Lurleen Burns Wallace was elected Governor of Alabama in January 1967, but only served seventeen months before dying of uterine cancer in May 1968. During that year George Wallace again tried for the presidency, again unsuccessfully, but this time as a candidate for the American Independent Party. In 1970, however, he managed to win the Governorship again. Two years later he was back with the Democrats, hoping to win another nomination to run for President.

In February 1972, an eccentric if not out-and-out mentally disturbed janitor Arthur Herman Brenner quit his job. In March he wrote in his diary that: 'It is my personal plan to assassinate by pistol either Richard Nixon or George Wallace ... to do SOMETHING BOLD AND DRAMATIC, FORCEFULL & DYNAMIC, A STATEMENT of my manhood for the world to see.'

On 15 May 1972 Wallace was holding a 'Wallace for President—Stand Up for America' rally at the Laurel Shopping Centre in Maryland. The theme of the rally was cruelly ironic in the light of what happened later. At 4 p.m., after Wallace had given his speech and was conducting the usual round of handshaking, Brenner approached him and shot him five times in the abdomen. Some of the bullets went right through him and injured a state trooper, a Secret Service agent and Wallace's personal bodyguard. One bullet ended up lodged in Wallace's spine and although he survived the assassination attempt he was confined to a wheelchair for the rest of his life. The authorities immediately apprehended Brenner who, true to character, asked 'How much do you think I'll get for my autobiography?'

The court found Brenner guilty of attempted murder and sentenced him to 63 years in prison, later reduced on appeal to 53 years.

Examination of his diary, part of which was published in 1973, revealed that Brenner did indeed have nothing political against Wallace, he just wanted to be famous. In this capacity he served as the inspiration for Paul Schrader's character of Travis Bickle, which won Robert De Niro an Academy Award for his role in *Taxi Driver* (1976) the film that played a role in the assassination attempt on Ronald Reagan, as we'll see later.

You can't keep a determined man down and Wallace would eventually fail at a fourth attempt to win a presidential nomination. He did serve a third and a fourth term as Governor of Alabama (1972–1980). He became a born again Christian and changed his position on segregation.

Historians now think that Wallace may not have been the racist that he portrayed himself, but only put on a performance to win votes. If true, it certainly worked. Wallace even wrote to Brenner in jail, forgiving him for what he'd done. Brenner never replied. George Wallace died of a bacterial blood infection on 13 September 1998.

Arthur Brenner will have served out his sentence by the year 2025. If he lives that long, he'll be 75 when he leaves jail.

The Lincoln curse

During the American Civil War, Jefferson Davis had the distinction of being the first and only President of the Confederate States of America from 1861 to 1865.

Union Colonels Ulric Dahlgren and Hugh Judson Kilpatrick had been given orders to carry out a raid on the Confederate capital of Richmond, Virginia, but the Union soldiers bungled the first phase of the raid and Dahlgren was killed near the King and Queen Court House on 2 March 1864. Thirteen-year-old William Littlepage searched Dahlgren's body for a pocket watch. Instead he found papers that he handed over to his teacher, Edward W Halbach, a Confederate home guard. The papers were orders for the assassination of Davis and his cabinet. The Confederate high command planned in turn to kidnap Abraham Lincoln, but later decided not to go through with it.

After it became public knowledge that the South wasn't going to kidnap the President, the idea of kidnapping Lincoln and his cabinet caught the imagination of actor John Wilkes Booth. He also convinced fellow conspirators: carriage repairer George Andreas Atzerodt, pharmacist David Edgar Herold, partisan soldier Lewis 'Payne' Powell, widowed boarding house proprietor Mary Surratt and her son, John Surratt Junior.

From the beginning, the conspiracy was slightly farcical; the conspirators were in over their heads and succeeded through chance and the incompetence of their victims' protectors rather than through any innate skill, ability or planning. The conspirators original plans to kidnap Lincoln on 17 March 1865 were foiled when Lincoln changed his travel plans. Booth then decided on assassination.

At this point John Surratt and some others left the conspiracy. John Surratt was so worried that he ran off to Montreal, Canada and sought out a Catholic priest who offered him sanctuary. He was later arrested anyway. He escaped and ultimately ended up in Egypt where American officials rearrested in November 1866 him and later put him on trial. He was eventually released, the court declaring a mistrial when eight of the twelve jurors found him not guilty on the charge of conspiracy to assassinate. The statute of limitations had run out on his other charges.

On 14 April 1865—the night of Lincoln's assassination— Booth had targeted the President, Vice President Andrew Johnson and US Secretary of State, William Henry Seward Senior. Adzerodt had been assigned to kill Johnson, but he spent the night before getting horribly drunk and on the agreed day never went anywhere near the Vice President. At his later trial his lawyer and witnesses for his defence argued that Adzerodt was a complete coward and that Booth would have been an idiot to give him the task of assassinating Johnson. The legal ploy failed. Adzerodt was found guilty anyway.

The 63-year-old Secretary of State, Seward, ridiculed in his time, but praised by later generations for arranging the purchase of Alaska for a mere $7 million (current value) was in his bedroom on the third floor of his house in Lafayette Park, Washington DC and recovering from a carriage accident.

Herold took advantage of his job as a pharmacist to guide fellow-conspirator Powell to Seward's house and provide him with a pretext for visiting the Secretary of State. Powell gained access by claiming to be delivering some medicine. On his way upstairs Seward's second son, Frederick William, told Powell that his father was asleep. Powell took his gun out and aimed at Frederick's head. The gun misfired so Powell hammered Frederick's skull until he fell to the floor, unconscious. Herold, by now realising that assassination can become messy, decided that he'd had enough and rode off, leaving Powell to finish things on his own. Powell struggled on regardless. He reached Seward and stabbed him repeatedly in the face and neck, leaving the Secretary of State for dead. Because of the carriage accident, however, Seward was wearing a heavy neck bandage and the wounds on his face and neck were disfiguring, but not mortal. As Powel escaped he also managed to injure Seward's eldest son Augustus Henry, his daughter Frances 'Fanny', his nurse Sergeant George Robinson and messenger Emerick Hansell, who arrived while Powell was making his escape.

The consequences of the attack on the Sewards were devastating. Although Seward survived, his wife Frances Adeline and daughter were so traumatised that Frances, even though not present during the attack, died within a few months of a heart attack and Fanny Seward died the following year.

Frederick survived his head lacerations and concussion and would serve twice as Assistant Secretary of State, later editing and publishing his father's memoirs. He would be the longest lived of all the Seward children, outliving his brother Augustus and his adopted sister Olive and dying at the age of 84.

Shortly after the attack on Seward, Abraham Lincoln, his wife Mary Todd Lincoln, friend Clara Harris and her fiancé Major Henry Reed Rathbone were sitting in the presidential box at Ford's Theatre in Washington. It was Good Friday and they were watching the thousandth and final performance in the three-year run of *Our American Cousin.*

The Lincolns had invited General Ulysses S Grant and his wife Julia to accompany them, but the Grants had declined. Julia Grant hated Mary Lincoln, a position that many people sympathised with. Many contemporaries called Lincoln's wife 'Hell-cat' behind her back. The Grants' decision may have saved their lives and Grant would eventually succeed Lincoln as President.

Booth had no trouble getting into the theatre; he was a friend of the owner, John Ford, and he even managed to drill a spy hole to observe the President's party. As a semi-famous actor and younger brother of a more famous actor, his presence didn't arouse any suspicions. Even Lincoln's bodyguard ignored him. Booth wanting to kill the President would have been as unthinkable as say Stephen Baldwin wanting to kill George W Bush.

Booth timed his entrance into the presidential box well. Halfway through Act III, Scene 2, the Asa Trechard character said: 'Don't know the manners of good society, eh? Well, I guess I know enough to turn you inside out, old gal—you sockdologizing old mantrap ...' This apparently side-splittingly funny line threw the audience into paroxysms of laughter, which provided Booth with a well-timed distraction—to read the whole play and understand the line in context, go to: *www.gutenberg.org/etext/3158*

John Frederick Parker was standing in as Lincoln's bodyguard. In an act of negligence that would appal later generations, he left his post to get a better view of the play, then went to a tavern. Later, he was charged with neglect of duty although the charges were dismissed. In 1868 he was eventually fired from the police force for sleeping on duty.

As a result of the general complacency surrounding Lincoln's protection, Booth was able to enter the presidential box undetected and shoot Lincoln in the back of the head with a .44 calibre Philadelphia Derringer single shot pistol. One shot was all it took; the wound was mortal. Henry Rathbone tried to grapple with Booth, but the assassin knifed him, severing a major artery in Rathbone's arm and temporarily disabling him.

Accounts vary as to what happened next. Booth jumped down from the box and landed on the stage. He may have broken his leg in the jump, but this is unlikely in light of subsequent events. He then faced the shocked audience and theatrically shouted: 'Sic semper tyrannis!'—Latin for 'Thus (it is) always with tyrants'—which happens to be the state motto of Virginia. He might also have said 'The South is avenged'. He then managed to run off the stage, an act that would only seem possible with a broken leg if he was extremely high on adrenaline.

Edman Spangler's role was to open the stage door open for Booth so that he could make his way to the alley. Spangler did open the door for Booth, shouting 'Let him by! Let him by!' although Spangler would later swear he knew nothing of the conspiracy.

On the instructions of Dr Charles Leal, attendants took Lincoln and Rathbone across the street into Peterson's Boarding House. Major Rathbone collapsed from blood loss. Lincoln was put in a bed in a room at the rear of the ground floor. The bed wasn't long enough for the President, but doctors made do, removing blood clots, cerebro-spinal fluid and even tissue to relieve pressure on the President's brain. Lincoln had lost so much blood from external and internal bleeding and the lead ball, lodged 15cm into his brain, had caused so much damage that he died the following morning at 7:22 a.m. the first American president to be assassinated.

He was buried in Oak Ridge Cemetery, Springfield, Illinois, but his lasting monument is the Lincoln Memorial in Washington. Long planned, the Memorial wasn't dedicated until 30 May 1922. It remains an iconic building and became the site from which many famous speakers delivered their most memorable oratory, including Martin Luther King's 'I Have a Dream' speech.

Over the years many people tried to steal Lincoln's remains and on 26 September 1901 his body was exhumed so that it could be placed in a new crypt. Just to make sure that someone hadn't stolen the remains, the coffin was opened. Lincoln's embalmed body was almost perfectly preserved. The last living witness of the exhumation, Fleetwood Lindley, died 1 February 1963. Thirteen years old at the time, he remembered the event vividly even many years later.

> Yes, his face was chalky white. His clothes were mildewed and I was allowed to hold one of the leather straps as we lowered the casket for the concrete to be poured. I was not scared at the time, but I slept with Lincoln for the next six months.

It's obviously not such a good idea to let thirteen-year-olds look at presidential corpses, even mummified ones.

Immediately after the assassination Booth escaped and met up with Herold. They went to Dr Samuel A Mudd, as by this time Booth's leg was definitely broken, perhaps in the fall from the box to the stage or he may have fallen from his horse as he made his escape. Mudd set Booth's leg, which was enough to have him charged later as a conspirator. Booth and Herold then met up with a Samuel Cox, who took them to Thomas Jones. Jones hid Booth and Herold for five days near his house before they went on the run again. On 26 April Union soldiers tracked them down to a barn. Herold surrendered, but Booth refused to leave the barn. The soldiers set it on fire and a Union Soldier named Thomas P 'Boston' Corbett, shot Lincoln's assassin dead.

After the end of the war Boston Corbett returned to his trade as a milliner. Like many hat makers of the time he used mercury in his work and, like many of his fellow tradesmen, the mercury poisoned his brain and he went mad. Corbett was always a little on the loopy side— he had previously castrated himself to protect himself from 'sin'. He was sent to the Topeka Asylum for the Insane in 1887, but escaped the year after. Historians presume that he died in the Great Fire in the Forests of Hinckley, Minnesota on 1 September 1894.

By the time authorities caught up with Booth and Herold they had already arrested the other conspirators. A nine-man military tribunal, in which 366 witnesses testified, spent seven weeks trying Atzerodt, Herold, Powell and Mary Surratt. The tribunal found them guilty and sentenced them to death. All were hanged simultaneously at around 1:30 p.m. on the same large scaffold in the grounds of the Old Arsenal Building—now Fort Lesley J McNair—Washington DC. The 180-centimetre drop was too short to break their necks and they died from slow strangulation. They were all declared dead at 2:15 p.m. Over 1000 people gathered to watch the execution. Surratt died relatively quickly—her last words were: 'Please don't let me fall.' Powell jerked and struggled for several minutes.

The bodies were buried within the Fort's walls. Surratt would be the first woman ever to be hanged by the US Government for her part in accommodating the men, buying guns for them and holding them in safekeeping.

The four principle conspirators were later re-interred and the site where they died is today a tennis court. Mary Surratt's remains are now in Mount Olivet Cemetery in Washington DC. The boarding house she ran—where the conspirators met—is still standing as part of Chinatown. It's now a restaurant called 'Wok and Roll'.

David Herold is now buried in the Congressional Cemetery in Washington. George Atzerodt is buried in Old Saint Paul's Cemetery in Baltimore, Maryland. His last words were, 'May we all meet in the other world. God take me now.'

Lewis Powell's last words were 'I thank you. Goodbye.' In 1992 researchers found his skull in storage in the Anthropology Department of the Smithsonian Institute. His bones were reunited and they now lie next to his mother's at the Geneva Cemetery in Seminole County, Florida.

Other conspirators: Samuel Bland Arnold, Dr Samuel Mudd, Michael O'Laughlen and Edman Spangler were sentenced to life in prison and were transported to Fort Jefferson in the Dry Tortugas, 113 kilometres west of Key West, Florida. Fort Jefferson was a prison usually reserved for army deserters and held about 600 prisoners at the time. Edman Spangler received a sentence of six years although the authorities neglected to tell him immediately and Spangler thought he was going to die too right up until the executions.

Booth had assigned Arnold and O'Laughlen the task of turning off the lights in Ford's theatre so that Booth could kill the President in darkness, but like Atzerodt they'd chickened out and had actually left Washington for Baltimore on 20 May—five days after the foiled kidnapping and weeks before the assassination. Arnold later claimed that he had only been involved in the original plan to kidnap the President. He sad he had actually left the conspiracy on 2 April and knew nothing of the assassination plan. O'Laughlen died in a yellow fever epidemic that swept Fort Jefferson in the autumn of 1868 and both the prison authorities and fellow inmates praised Dr Mudd's efforts to help out during this time. When Mudd himself became sick, Spangler nursed him and Mudd always credited him with saving his life.

A few months later, on 8 February 1869, President Andrew Johnson pardoned Arnold, Mudd and Spangler. Mudd returned to a normal life of being a husband and a father to his eight children, practising medicine and growing tobacco, which in those days wasn't as bizarre a contradiction as it seems today. He died of pneumonia in 1883. Spangler went to live and work on the Mudd family farm and died almost eight years before Mudd, probably from the effects of alcoholism. Samuel Arnold lived until 1906 keeping a generally low profile. He is buried at Greenmount Cemetery, Baltimore, Maryland—the same cemetery as Michael O'Laughlen and John Wilkes Booth.

John Surratt was the last of the conspirators to die. After his release he married, fathered seven children, grew tobacco, taught at the Rockville Female Academy and was the treasurer for the Old Bay Line Steamship Company. He died of pneumonia at the age of 72, in 1916.

Major Henry Rathbone recovered from the wounds inflicted by Booth and married Clara on 11 July 1867. They had three children and, in 1882, moved to Hannover, Germany as US Consul. There, the mental instability that Rathbone had shown signs of for some years came to a head. He murdered Clara two days before Christmas 1883 and attempted to stab himself to death, but failed. He spent the rest of his life—28 years—in an asylum for the criminally insane in Hildesheim Germany. He was buried next to his wife in Hannover. In 1952 the cemetery authorities disposed of both their remains in order to make room. No one had visited the graves in years.

He murdered Clara two days before Christmas 1883 and attempted to stab himself to death, but failed.

Mary Lincoln, who had already lost two sons and now her husband, lost another son within a few years. Always careless with money, she began to spend it even more recklessly in her depression and her moods, always difficult, became more intense. Robert Todd Lincoln, the eldest and only surviving son, committed her to an asylum in Batavia, Illinois, in 1875. Later released, she travelled extensively and died aged 63.

The Lincoln curse continues

Robert Lincoln became the 36th US Secretary of War. His father had invited him to the theatre on the night of his death, but he declined and spent the evening at the White House. Having survived that presidential assassination, sixteen years later he was to survive another. At the request of President James Abram Garfield, he was waiting at the platform at the Sixth Street Station of the Baltimore and Potomac Railway when the President was shot and mortally wounded nearby.

Garfield had only been President for six months and fifteen days. The former army general and church minister looked set to be one of the better presidents. He is the only person in history to have been a congressman, senator-elect and president-elect at the same time. A man of unusual talents, he was ambidextrous—he could write Latin with one hand while simultaneously writing Greek with the other. Whatever promise he might have shown was snuffed out at the hands of failed lawyer, preacher, corrupt debt-collector and delusional syphilitic, Charles Julius Guiteau.

Guiteau's scattered work history notwithstanding, he had petitioned Garfield for work, writing him letters expressing a willingness to accept a diplomatic post in Paris or Vienna. Garfield's office soon became accustomed to Guiteau hanging around the corridors of the executive mansion and considered him a crackpot and a nuisance, but not dangerous. Guiteau eventually came to the conclusion that only by killing Garfield could he get a job, because his replacement, Vice-President Chester Alan Arthur, would then hire him.

On July 2 1881 at 9:30 a.m. the President was walking through Sixth Street Station when Guiteau shot him. One bullet entered the shoulder and exited, one bullet went into his chest. Garfield might have lived but the surgeons were unable to find the remaining bullet. The inventor of the telephone, Alexander Graham Bell, even built a special metal detector to find the bullet while the President was hospitalised, but it malfunctioned because Garfield was lying on a metal bed frame. With the bullet still inside him, probably near his lung, Garfield lingered for weeks before finally succumbing to a massive heart attack or ruptured splenic artery, or both, aggravated by bronchial pneumonia and septicaemia. Blood poisoning was common in the days before antibiotics. Modern doctors today would be appalled that Garfield's physicians inserted unclean fingers into their patient and one even punctured the President's liver in the process. Garfield was buried in a mausoleum in Lakeview Cemetery, Cleveland, Ohio.

Nine months later, after a jury rejected his lawyer's insanity defence, Guiteau was hanged in Washington. The lasting political ramification of Garfield's assassination was the passing of the Pendelton Civil Service Reform Act of 1883, which stipulated that most federal government appointments had to be awarded on the basis of merit, rather than at the largess of the President to cronies for services rendered.

Five presidents later, including Grover Cleveland's non-consecutive terms, President William McKinley Junior also made the mistake of inviting Robert Lincoln to what turned out to be his own assassination. McKinley was well into his second term and was known for promoting the local economy with protectionism—placing high tariffs on imports so that people would be encouraged to 'buy American'. His administration also expanded American control to Guam, the Philippines, Cuba, Puerto Rico and Hawaii.

All this imperialism didn't sit well with anarchist Leon Frank Czolgosz who felt that people like McKinley were symbolic of the evils of exploitative capitalism. Inspired by Gaetano Bresci's assassination of King Umberto I of Italy the year before, Czolgosz decided that Americans too needed a 'noble sacrifice'. Czolgosz even bought the same type of gun that Bresci had used, a .32 Iver Johnson safety automatic revolver, for that extra bit of symbolism.

McKinley was in the midst of a session of hand pumping outside the Temple of Music at the Pan-American Exposition in Buffalo, New York on 6 September 1901. Czolgosz pushed to the head of the line and, at 4:07 p.m. he fired. Even at point blank range the assassin managed to miss, the first bullet harmlessly ricocheting off a button. The second was the killer, penetrating the President's abdomen 13 centimetres below the left nipple, tearing through the stomach and the top of the left kidney before lodging in the pancreas. Although the exposition had one of the world's first x-ray machines on site, the invention was still experimental and doctors didn't want to risk using it on the President—they thought his wound wasn't serious enough.

Surgeons removed the bullet, but had to go back in to remove a small piece of clothing they'd left behind. Although the President seemed to improve, gangrene set in and the infection killed him eight days after the shooting.

Czolgosz was apprehended immediately and witnesses to the shooting almost beat him to death. For a while it was uncertain whether or not he would live to stand trial. On 23 September he was found guilty and sentenced to death in a mere formality of a trial. The jury deliberation lasted only eight and a half hours. He was electrocuted in Auburn Prison, New York. His corpse was covered in lime and sulphuric acid to quicken decomposition and his clothes and letters were burned.

The pistol that Czolgosz used is now on display at the Erie County Historical Society in Buffalo, the only presidential assassination weapon not in US Federal custody.

After McKinley's death, Robert Lincoln became wise and declared that he wouldn't be accepting any more invitations from an American president since, every time he did, they ended up dead—in the case of his father, even when he didn't. Even then the Lincoln curse hadn't run its course.

On 9 August 1910 Robert Lincoln was on the deck of the SS Kaiser Wilhelm de Grosse at Hoboken, New Jersey. He was standing behind New York Mayor William J Gaynor when a disgruntled and recently fired city employee, James J Gallagher, shot the Mayor in the throat. By chance New York World photographer William Warnecke captured the moment of the attempted murder. The photo shows the Mayor's blood splattered on his lapels as Lincoln raises his hands to do what he can. Gaynor survived, but doctors chose not to remove the bullet and it remained lodged in the Mayor's throat until his death three years later, a death that the shooting probably hastened.

The last of the Lincolns, Robert Todd Lincoln Beckwith, died in 1985 without producing a single child in three marriages.

The Kennedy curse

So much has been written about the Kennedy assassinations; there have been so many conspiracy theories promulgated and so much speculation and confusion. In the more than forty years since one of the most famous of all assassinations, there have been considerable technological improvements in forensic investigation and it's highly likely that the version below represents the most likely approximation to the truth. It's a remarkably simple story when you strip it of all the mythology, but for those who are committed to conspiracy theories, it's not hard to find really thick books on the subject and gigabytes of information on the internet. For those who don't want to put themselves through all that, here is the straightforward version.

John Fitzgerald Kennedy was one of those rich boys who felt a sense of that quality so rare in the modern world, noblesse oblige—the belief that those who are fortunate should devote some portion of their lives to public service. His election to the Presidency in 1960 was a testament not only to the dedication that he inspired in his supporters, but to the canny manipulation of the media.

Compared to Richard Nixon, who he ran against, Kennedy looked young and energetic. Few people at the time knew that under the brave exterior he was suffering from a slew of health problems, including Addison's disease and osteoporosis of the lower spine, which led him to be addicted to painkillers. On top of this he had to deal with a variety of other issues. His democratic rival, future Vice President and successor—Lyndon Baines Johnson detested him, but Kennedy needed his support in the southern states to win. People questioned Kennedy's true allegiance to America, because of his Catholicism and many considered him too young (43 at the time) to be able to handle the job of the presidency, especially in the light of the Cold War.

As it was the 1960 election was one of the closest in history and Kennedy barely made it in and, as it turned out, the Cold War was his undoing. The misguided invasion of Cuba to oust Fidel Castro turned into the Bay of Pigs Scandal and led to the Cuban Missile Crisis in which Kennedy and Soviet leader Nikita Sergeyevich Khrushchev played 'chicken', bringing the world to the brink of World War III.

This was all a bit too much for Lee Harvey Oswald, who had spent a lifetime feeling alienated. He became interested in communism as an answer to all the worlds evils, even as he was serving in the US Marine Corps, where he scored reasonably well in marksmanship and earned a sharpshooter qualification. He read voraciously on Marxism, although there is strong evidence he was dyslexic. A dedicated truant he mostly educated himself and, as a self-made man, there were serious problems with the job of self-creation he had set himself.

He eventually travelled to Russia, where he attempted to sell the KGB 'secrets' that he had gleaned during his time in the military. The Soviets barely knew what to make of the nineteen-year-old, but the CIA were keeping tabs on him and soon the KGB were too. Both governments seemed to be suffering from 'Emperor's New Clothes Syndrome' when it came to Oswald and he became the subject of attention to one government, simply because he was the subject of the other side's attention.

The Russians let him stay and he married Marina Prusakova after a six-week romance, in April 1959. By 1960 they had a daughter, June, and, by 1962, in spite of the fact that the Oswalds had a very high standard of living by Russian standards, the future assassin had become disenchanted with his life in Russia and took his wife and daughter back home to America, where he worked sporadically while secretly rehearsing how he could single-handedly change the course of history.

On 31 March 1963 Marina took the now famous photo of a black-clad Oswald striking a pose with a Manicher-Carcano assault rifle that he had ordered some days earlier using the alias A Hidell.

On 12 April 1963, after days of surveillance, he attempted to assassinate right-wing political agitator Major General Edwin Anderson Walker. He almost succeeded too. The General was sitting in his dining room, but Oswald's sniper's bullet missed and hit a window frame instead. Walker received shrapnel injuries to his right forearm. Oswald made a clean escape and only later did his role in the assassination attempt come to light.

In September 1963, the Oswalds had a second daughter, Rachel. By now Lee Harvey had become fixated on dreams of his new paradise on earth, Cuba, and achieved some notoriety in the Dallas media for defending Castro's regime. He had even visited the Cuban Embassy in Mexico City to try to get an entry visa. Cuba was even less interested in Oswald than the USSR had been, but Oswald, ever fixated, hadn't given up on Cuba just because Cuba had given up on him.

The Warren Commission, instigated by Lyndon Johnson on 29 November 1963—that august body of investigation that first officially enquired into the JFK assassination—never ascribed a motive to Oswald's act. For what it's worth it seems likely that he wanted to get at Kennedy because of the President's attitude toward Castro and his communist regime. He was also delusional and may have wanted a place in history. He certainly got that.

Oswald had managed to find a job at the Texas School Book Depository Company in front of Dealy Plaza. His job was to fill and mail out school textbook orders for the northern half of Texas. Floors five, six and seven of the Carraway-Byrd building held the book stocks. The lower floors housed the offices of several of the publishers who actually created the textbooks. Kennedy's visit to Dallas was well publicised, including the exact route of his motorcade, which would pass right in front of the building. Oswald brought his rifle to work wrapped in brown paper and disguised as curtain rods. He had created a space on the sixth floor, at the south-east corner window, surrounded by boxes of books to obscure a sniper's den.

The presidential motorcade arrived on Friday 22 November 1963. An open-roofed, convertible stretch limousine carried the driver in the front left seat and a Secret Service agent in the right front. In the middle seat to the left sat the First Lady of Texas, Nellie Connally, with her husband on her right: the Governor of Texas John Connally Jr. First Lady Jacqueline Kennedy sat in the rear left and JFK in the rear right.

As the President's car passed diagonally in front of the Carraway-Byrd building on Dealy Plaza, Nellie Connally turned to JFK and said: 'Mr. President, you can't say Dallas doesn't love you.' Seconds later at 12:30 p.m. Oswald fired. His first shot missed. John, but Jacqueline reacted as if startled. John then turned clockwise to his right as if to make a remark to the President. Oswald's second shot went through the back of the President's neck, shattering several cervical vertebrae and severing vital blood vessels. The bullet continued through to John Connally's right shoulder and stopped in his trunk.

This alone might have been enough to kill the president, but the next shot was the clincher. Shot number three entered the rear of JFK's head and left from the forehead. The bullet virtually blew the right hemisphere of his brain apart. The President slumped forward almost certainly dead. Jacqueline Kennedy started climbing out of the car and onto the rear boot as Secret Service Agent Clifton Hill rushed to her aid.

Doctors made heroic efforts to save JFK's life, but to no avail. If it had been anyone else they wouldn't even have tried. No one survives with half their brain blown away. For the graphic images see: *www.celebritymorgue.com/jfk/jfk-autopsy.html*

Dallas dress manufacturer Abraham Zapruder accidentally captured the whole death scene on his 8 millimetre Bell and Howell Zoomatic Director series camera. The 26 seconds and 486 frames of footage are probably the most heavily scrutinised in history. Zapruder was in shock at what he had seen, but had the presence of mind to call the Secret Service and agreed to hand over the film for investigation. Ninety minutes after the assassination, with the film still in the camera WFAA

TV interviewed Zapruder live and he described what he had seen. WFAA then arranged for Eastman Kodak to make three copies immediately. Zapruder gave two copies to the Secret Service and kept a copy and the original for himself. He sold the rights to the film's use to Life magazine for $125,000 (equivalent to about $1.5 million in today's terms). One of Zapruder's stipulations was that Life would not publish frame 313, which showed JFK's head exploding. You can see Zapruder's film at *homepage.ntlworld.com/neal.mccarthy/jfkvideos.htm*

After the assassination of JFK, Oswald left his rifle behind thinking that he had wiped it clean of fingerprints. In the confusion after the murder Oswald made his way out of the book depository. He was the only depository employee unaccounted for and he instantly became a suspect.

At 12:40 p.m. Oswald caught a bus that quickly became stuck in a traffic jam. He got off and caught a cab to within two blocks of his boarding house. Marina and their daughters were living with friends at the time. By 1:00 p.m. Oswald had retrieved his revolver and a beige jacket, then he started walking. Forty-five minutes after the assassination, Officer JD Tippet was driving on his own, working his usual beat in South Oak Cliff, when he spotted a man answering the description of the President's killer. He drove up to the man and asked him to stop. The man did so. They spoke briefly through the patrol car driver's vent window. Tippett got out and the man shot him four times with a .38 calibre revolver before running away. Four witnesses saw Oswald kill Tippett.

The man who captured Kennedy's assassination on film, Abraham Zapruder, later donated the first installment of his rights payment— $25,000—to Marie Frances Gasaway, Tippett's widow. Zapruder's donation to Tippett's widow was one of many. The sympathetic public eventually gave Frances Gasaway Tippet the equivalent of almost $4 million in today's terms.

Oswald made his way into the Texas Theatre in Oak Cliff without paying, but the ticket vendor spotted him and phoned the police.

Minutes later the police attempted to arrest him, but Oswald fought back. The police dragged him out of the theatre while he screamed that he was the victim of police brutality.

For the next two days Oswald played dumb, denying that he had anything to do with the deaths of Kennedy and Tippet. He alternated between saying that he didn't know what his arrest was all about with implying that he was the victim of a conspiracy. At a press conference he said 'I didn't shoot anyone … They're taking me in because of the fact that I lived in the Soviet Union. I'm just a patsy!'

In the audience of the press conference was Jack Leon Ruby, a Dallas nightclub owner with acquaintances in the Mafia and a history of violent temper and erratic behaviour. The man born Jacob Rubenstein always carried a gun. He later claimed that he loved the Kennedys and he only wanted revenge on their behalf—and to show the world that 'Jews have guts'. He stalked Oswald—and in those days of lax security—managed to make his way into Dallas Police Headquarters, intercepting Oswald and his cadre of police just as the authorities were preparing to transfer him to a county jail.

At 11:21 a.m. on 24 November, as television cameras monitored the event, millions of people saw Jack Ruby shoot the 24-year-old assassin while yelling, 'You killed my president, you rat!'

Doctors attempted to operate on Oswald, but the trauma to his abdominal region was irreparable and he died of massive internal bleeding 48 hours and 7 minutes after President Kennedy.

Ruby was judged legally sane at the time of the killing and received a death sentence, but his mind rapidly deteriorated. Many of the Kennedy conspiracy theories arose because of Ruby's random pronouncements. He wanted to talk to the Warren Commission because 'a whole new form of government is going to take over this country and I know I won't live to see you another time.' While he was awaiting trial he also claimed that a second holocaust was going on and Jews were being killed in the building where he was staying, so you can read his quotes any way that you like. See for example: *homepage.ntlworld.com/neal.mccarthy/jfkvideos.htm*

By 1966 Ruby was dying of lung cancer, but the final cause of his death was a pulmonary embolism. He died at Parkland Hospital where both Kennedy and Oswald had been pronounced dead. He is buried at Westlawn Cemetery in Chicago.

Computer animator Dale Myers spent ten years reconstructing the actual assassination and the finished piece won him an Emmy for outstanding individual achievement in graphic and artistic design. The background to this monumental task is certainly worth a look at: *www.jfkfiles.com/jfk/html/anim.htm*

For a panoramic view of Dealey Plaza see:

www.virtualvisitor.com/dealey/dealey.html

The Dallas Municipal Archives has a collection of photos:

http://jfk.ci.dallas.tx.us/

Three other commissions since the Warren Commission: the Ramsey Clark panel in 1968, the Rockefeller Commission in 1975 and the House Select Committee on Assassinations (HSCA) 1978 and 1979 have examined the evidence and each justify their existence by putting their own spin on events. The HSCA in particular added fuel to the conspiracy file by adding a fictitious fourth bullet to the mix based on acoustic evidence that many now consider flawed. You can read the reports for yourself at: *www.archives.gov/research/jfk*.

If you have a high-speed internet connection I highly recommend that you watch PBS's excellent Frontline Report 'Who Was Lee Harvey Oswald?' *www.pbs.org/wgbh/pages/frontline/shows/oswald*

Bobby Kennedy

Less than five years after JFK's murder, his brother Robert Francis Kennedy also fell to an assassin's bullet. The 65th Attorney General of the United States, under his brother's administration and during the first term of Lyndon Johnson, had made huge inroads in fighting organised crime, often confronting the head of FBI, John Edgar Hoover, over matters of strategy and jurisdiction. Bobby's attacks on the corrupt Teamsters Union of James 'Jimmy' Hoffa were legendary and he had also worked tirelessly for civil rights. In short, he had made lots of enemies and his death would also be fertile ground in which to grow more Kennedy conspiracy theories.

By mid-1968 Kennedy was running for the presidential nomination and with his pedigree he was almost sure to get it. Johnson had tried to run for a second elected term but, even though he and Kennedy were often at odds, Johnson was realistic enough to see that his own popularity was seriously on the wane and put himself behind Kennedy's bid. With Kennedy's consistently good performance in the primaries it seemed as though there was going to be another member of the Kennedy dynasty in the White House.

It all came unstuck shortly after midnight on 5 June. Kennedy had just celebrated his victory in the Californian primary elections. As he was leaving through the kitchen pantry of the Ambassador Hotel in Los Angeles, a 24-year-old mentally ill Palestinian named Sirhan Bishara Sirhan fired a .22 calibre Iver Johnson revolver eight times into the crowd in the cluttered room. His bullets managed to hit Kennedy three times and one grazed him. Kennedy didn't die immediately but soon fell into a coma and died the next day. Six others were injured.

Sirhan fired a .22 calibre Iver Johnson revolver eight times into the crowd.

Kennedy's bodyguard Rosey Grier and Olympic Gold Medal decathlete Rafer Lewis Johnson immediately overpowered Sirhan.

At his later trial Sirhan confessed to having killed Kennedy 'with 20 years of malice aforethought', probably on account of Kennedy's favouring of Israel over Palestine. Sirhan was twelve when he came to

America, so it's highly likely that his hatred was fuelled to some degree by his upbringing. Although even today he maintains that he has no memory of the crime, the record of his statements has a sort of Jack Rubyesque quality of contradiction about them. Later discoveries of his diaries revealed rambling, incoherent and repetitive passages, but a single entry was an obsessive account of wanting to kill Kennedy.

For a long time there were questions pertaining to anomalies about the number of shots fired and why, if Sirhan had shot Kennedy from the front, did Kennedy have a bullet hole in the back of his head surrounded by close range gunpowder residue. Author Dan Moldea seems to have answered these questions, revealing in his 1995 book *The Killing of Robert F Kennedy* that Sirhan had intended to shoot Kennedy at point blank range between the eyes, but in Sirhan's words: 'that son of a bitch turned his head at the last second'.

Sirhan was found guilty of murder and sentenced to death, but before the authorities could execute him, California repealed the death penalty. He has been in prison for almost 40 years now and has been denied parole thirteen times. His next chance will be in 2011.

With Kennedy's death, the Democratic wave collapsed. The next Democrat in line, Hubert Humphrey, simply wasn't Bobby Kennedy. Richard Nixon won the Presidency by a landslide and we all know where that led.

JFK's widow, Jacqueline, left America with her children in 1968. She had told a friend: 'I hate this country. I despise America and I don't want my children to live here anymore. If they're killing Kennedys, my children are number one targets ... I want to get out of this country.'

American presidential survivors

Andrew Jackson

American presidents don't always die when someone wants to kill them. The first person to attempt the assassination of a President of the United States was Richard Lawrence, a mentally unbalanced, unemployed house painter. He was convinced that he was really King Richard III of England, rightful heir to the British throne. He believed that Congress owed him a huge sum of money, that President Andrew Jackson was stopping him from getting it and that the President had also killed Lawrence's father. The fact that Lawrence's father had died in 1823 and had never even been to America didn't seem relevant, but when you're completely loony tunes you don't let facts confuse the issue.

After stalking Jackson for several months, Lawrence finally struck late in the morning of 30 January 1835. He lunged at the President in the rotunda of the Capitol Building in Washington DC and attempted to shoot him at almost point blank range, but both of his Derringer duelling pistols misfired. Lawrence had picked a muggy day for murder and the moisture interfered with the operation of the pistols. Humidity saved Jackson's life—and madness saved Lawrence's. Jackson's guards quickly apprehended the would-be assassin as Jackson tried to hit him with his walking stick. Lawrence was found not guilty by reason of insanity and spent the rest of his 26 years of life in the newly-built Government Hospital for the Insane in Washington DC. Over a century and a name change later, the institution, now St Elizabeth's Hospital, currently houses John Hinckley Jr—Ronald Reagan's failed assassin.

'Teddy' Roosevelt

Three years after retiring as 26th American president, Theodore Roosevelt Jr was the victim of an assassination attempt. In the early evening of 14 October 1912, Teddy Roosevelt was in Milwaukee, Wisconsin as part of a re-election campaign. He was climbing into his car when John Flammang Shrank shot him in the chest with a .38 calibre bullet. The bullet would have been fatal, but it had first struck a steel spectacle case and a 50-page speech. Long windedness and myopia saved the President's life. The bullet still penetrated his chest and lodged near his heart. Amazingly, Roosevelt refused to be taken to hospital and delivered his 90-minute speech at the Milwaukee Auditorium anyway. When he reached hospital the doctors refused to remove the bullet and it stayed there for seven years—the rest of Roosevelt's life. He eventually died from a coronary embolism. Whether the bullet had anything to do with his death is debatable—he had been overweight for most of his life.

Shrank told police that the ghost of William McKinley had come to him in a dream and told him to kill Roosevelt, who was a traitor who had to die. Public sentiment wanted Shrank dead, but the courts found him insane and he spent the last 31 years of his life as a patient at the Central State Mental Hospital in Waupun. When he heard that Teddy Roosevelt's cousin, Franklin Delano Roosevelt was running for a third presidential term Shrank's health deteriorated. The news that FDR had been elected to a fourth term would certainly have killed Shrank, had he not already died.

FDR

FDR himself almost did not make it to the White House. When he was still President Elect, a newly immigrated Italian, the mentally unstable, misanthropic, anarchist bricklayer, Giuseppe Zangara tried to kill him.

At around 9 p.m. on 15 February 1933 FDR was giving a speech in Bayfront Park, Miami, Florida. The 150 cm tall Zangara had to stand on a wobbly chair to get a clear shot with his .32 calibre pistol. His first shot missed. A woman next to the would be assassin pushed him and his next five shots fired wildly. Zangara wounded several people, including Chicago Mayor Anton 'Tony' Joseph Cermak, who was sitting next to Roosevelt. Poignantly, Cernak told Roosevelt, 'I'm glad it was me and not you.' The Mayor became the only casualty of the assassination attempt. He died nineteen days later from complications arising from his abdominal wound.

The authorities immediately apprehended Zangara. They learned that he had originally wanted to kill Herbert Hoover, but had given up on the idea after FDR's election. Two weeks after Cernak's death, Zangara died in Old Sparky, Florida State Penitentiary's famous electric chair. Zangara's last words were dramatic:

> You give me electric chair. I no afraid of that chair! You one of capitalists. You is crook man too. Put me in electric chair. I no care! Get to hell out of here, you sonofabitch (spoken to the attending minister) ... I go sit down all by myself ... Viva Italia! Goodbye to all poor peoples everywhere! ... Lousy capitalists! No picture! Capitalists! No one here to take my picture. All capitalists lousy bunch of crooks. Go ahead. Pusha da button!

Physicians later determined that constant pain from chronic gall bladder adhesions and stomach ulcers had driven Zangara mad.

Harry S Truman

Puerto Rican national terrorists, Griselio Torresola and Oscar Collazo, wanted independence for Puerto Rico and felt that it wasn't going to happen unless President Harry S Truman was dead.

The Blanca Canales group's Jayuya Uprising for Puerto Rican independence had failed on 28 October 1950. Torresola's sister had been wounded and Collazo's brother had been arrested: it was now time to act. Truman's death would draw the attention of the world to their cause.

Truman resided for most of his presidency at Blair House—the official state guesthouse for American presidents on Pennsyvania Avenue. The White House was undergoing extensive renovations at the time. At 2:20 p.m. on 1 November 1950, Torresola and Collazo tried to enter Blair House. The attempt failed and a dramatic 40-second gunfight broke out between guards and the would-be assassins. Gunfire wounded three White House policemen, one mortally—Private Leslie William Coffelt was shot three times. As he died Coffelt fatally shot Torresola, the policeman's bullet entering one of Torresola's ears and exiting from the other.

The news of Coffelt's death upset the President much more than the threat to his own life. He later said of the attempt: 'A president has to expect such things.'

Oscar Collazo was sentenced to death. Truman commuted the sentence to life imprisonment and, in 1979, Jimmy Carter pardoned Collazo who returned to Puerto Rico, where he died in 1994.

Leslie Coffelt lies buried in Arlington Cemetery. The day room for the uniformed division of the Secret Service at Blair House is named after him.

Truman turned out to be one of the most unpopular presidents in history, his administration marred by corruption scandals. It's ironic that the attempt on his life should have come about because of a cause that hardly anyone felt passionate enough to kill for. At the time of writing the Commonwealth of Puerto Rico is still an unincorporated territory of the United States, or an unincorporated organised territory, depending on whom you talk to.

Tricky Dicky

Richard Milhous Nixon was the target of one of history's more bizarre assassination attempts. Mentally ill tyre salesman, Samuel Byck planned to hijack a plane with a borrowed .22 calibre revolver and a home-made two-gallon gasoline bomb hidden in a briefcase. He intended to crash the plane into the White House. During the planning, he made audio recordings explaining his plans and motives. His motive was that the Small Business Administration had turned down his application for a loan. He sent the tapes to Jonas Salk—the researcher who discovered the vaccine to prevent polio—and Stephen Sondheim for reasons that only he knew. Perhaps these weird recordings partially influenced Sondheim's later writing of the *Assassins* musical.

In any event Byck drove to Baltimore-Washington International Airport, fatally shot aviation administration police officer George Neal Ramsburg and proceeded to storm onto Delta Air Lines Flight 523 to Atlanta. Pilots, Fred Jones and Reese Lofton, told Byck that they couldn't take off until the wheel chocks were removed. Byck shot both men. Jones later died of his injuries. Byck then grabbed a female passenger, forced her into the cockpit and told her to fly the plane. Airport security and police had surrounded the aircraft by this time and Officer Charles Troyer started shooting through the plane's closed front door with his .357 Magnum revolver, hitting Byck in the chest and stomach. Byck collapsed then shot himself. He lived just long enough to say 'Help me' to the police after cabin crew let them in.

Gerald Ford

There were two attempts, both in 1975, on the life of Gerald Rudolf Ford—the only American president who nobody voted for. Purported ecology nut and former member of Charles Manson's 'Family', Lynette

Alice 'Squeaky' Fromme wanted to 'talk' to Ford about the plight of California's Redwoods. On the morning of 5 September, at Capitol Park in Sacramento, dressed in a blood red dress and packing a .45 Colt Automatic loaded with four bullets strapped to her leg, she pulled out the gun, pointed it at Ford and pulled the trigger. Unfortunately for the hapless Squeaky, none of the bullets were actually in the firing chamber.

In the wake of the JFK assassination there was a 1965 special law covering assassination attempts on presidents. Fromme was convicted under this law and sentenced to life imprisonment. On 23 December she escaped from Alderson Federal Prison Camp in Alderson, West Virginia to see Charles Manson because she'd heard he had testicular cancer—which wasn't true. By Christmas she was back in custody and is now in the Federal Medical Centre, Carswell. She has always refused her right to a parole hearing.

Women seem to have had something against Ford. His second would-be assassin, mother-of-four Sara Jane More, had been involved with radical left-wing groups like the Symbionese Liberation Army, but had alienated them when she agreed, briefly, to become an FBI informant. Perhaps she felt killing Ford would be her passport to regaining credibility, although how she would have done so from inside a maximum security jail cell is puzzling.

At around 3:30 p.m. on 22 September, Moore took aim at Ford while he was on the corner of Post and Powell Streets in San Francisco. As Moore was about to fire her .38 calibre Smith and Wesson revolver, retired Marine, Oliver Sipple, spotted her, shouting 'Gun!' and striking her arm. The bullet ricocheted of a hotel wall and slightly wounded a cab driver. Moore pleaded guilty, received a life sentence and is still a 'guest' at the Federal Women's Prison in Dublin, California.

In a response to Ford's recent death, Moore seemed to regret what she had done: 'I know now that I was wrong to try … Thank God I didn't succeed.'

Ronald Reagan

It seems that something many failed presidential assassins have in common is mental imbalance combined with a personal agenda. John Hinckley Jr became obsessed with the movie Taxi Driver and its starring actress Jodie Foster. Somehow he came to the conclusion that killing Ronald Wilson Reagan would be 'the greatest love offering in the history of the world'. In a letter to Foster dated 30 March 1981, he spelled out his intentions:

> Jodie, I would abandon this idea of getting Reagan in a second if I could only win your heart and live out the rest of my life with you, whether it be in total obscurity or whatever. I will admit to you that the reason I'm going ahead with this attempt now is because I just cannot wait any longer to impress you.

At around 2.30 p. m.—two hours after he had written the letter—Hinckley fired six shots from a .22 calibre Rhom R6-14 revolver, loaded with exploding Devestator bullets, at Ronald Reagan just as the President was about to enter his limousine. Television cameras were following Reagan at the time and images of the assassination were transmitted around the world.

One bullet ricocheted off the car, entered Reagan's trunk under the left armpit and lodged in his left lung within an inch of his heart. Agents pushed the President into the car and sped him to hospital. Surgeons were able to remove the bullet and Reagan made a full recovery.

A Washington DC Police Officer, Thomas Delahunty, was hit in the back with the third of Hinckley's bullets. He made a full recovery and was later retired on a full disability pension.

Secret Service Agent Timothy McCarthy threw himself in front of the President, taking a bullet in the abdomen. He later made a full recovery, receiving the 1982 National Collegiate Athletic Association

Award of Valour. He continued to work for the Secret Service until his retirement in 1993.

House Press Secretary, James 'Jim' Brady, wasn't as lucky. He was hit in the left temple. The injury caused permanent paralysis and left Brady in a wheelchair. He has since worked as an active advocate of gun control. President Bill Clinton awarded him with the United State's highest civilian honour, the Presidential Medal of Freedom in 1996 .

Hinckley was found not guilty on his thirteen charges by reason of insanity and remains in St Elizabeth's Hospital in Washington DC. The current professional assessment is that his mental disorders are in full remission. He is even allowed out occasionally under the supervision of his parents.

Bill Clinton

Upholsterer Francisco Martin Duran's claim to fame is to have committed perhaps the dumbest presidential assassination attempt. On 29 October 1994 at 13:00 p.m. he stood at the White House fence and started firing from a Norinco semi-automatic rifle and a Mossberg pump-action shotgun at the presidential abode when President William Jefferson Clinton was in residence.

He didn't stand a hope in hell of killing Bill Clinton, but the White House and some trees did sustain some damage. Twenty-nine shots later authorities apprehended Duran after two passers by, Harry Racowski and Ken Davis tackled him to the ground.

At his trial his defence was that he was trying to save the world by destroying a mist connected to the umbilical cord of an alien being in the mountains of Colorado. Whether he did save the world will never be known, but he was sentenced to 40 years in jail for his trouble.

George W Bush

George Walker Bush has the distinction of being the only American president whose attempted assassination occurred while he was on foreign soil—it seems foreigners can hate American presidents too.

On 10 May 2005 Bush was giving a speech at Freedom Square in Tiblisi, Georgia, sharing the stage with Georgian President Mikhail Saakashvili. Vladimir Arutinian threw a Soviet RGD-5 hand grenade at the stage, but it fell about twenty metres short and failed to detonate, even after hitting a little girl. The grenade was old and Arutinian had wrapped a handkerchief so tightly around it that the firing pin didn't deploy fast enough.

Arutinian quickly quit the scene, but a manhunt soon captured the 27 year old. Georgian officials arrested him after a shoot out on 20 July 2005 in which a Georgian Interior Ministry official died. The Tbilisi City Court sentenced Arutinian to life imprisonment on 12 January 2006.

The Turn of the Millennium

No fewer than five presidents of Chechnya have died unnatural deaths. In fact all except the incumbent have been assassinated either in office or in exile, making the Chechen Presidency possibly the most dangerous political job on earth—with being a Sri Lankan MP a close second.

Assassinations seem to be in decline in the 21st century, perhaps because political killings now occur for the most part in the midst of civil war, rebellion and the like. Still, here are some notable exceptions.

The Bandit Queen

Phoolan Devi the dacoit 'Bandit Queen' and guerrilla fighter for the rights of India's lower castes spent most of her early adult life either liberating people or committing atrocities, depending on your point of view. She voluntarily surrendered to the authorities in February 1983 and spent the next eleven years in jail before she was eventually tried and then released on parole. She was twice elected as a Member of the Indian Parliament in spite of being illiterate and having little understanding of how parliamentary democracy works at the coalface.

Unknown assassins shot her dead on 25 July 2001, as she climbed out of her car at the gate of her house in New Delhi. A man called Sher Singh Rana confessed to her murder and was jailed despite there being doubt surrounding his guilt. In 2004 he escaped from Tihar Jail, present whereabouts unknown.

Sri Lanka and The Tamil Tigers

A relatively small country already, Sri Lanka has the misfortune of being split down the middle politically. From the outside the nation appears to be continually coming apart at the seams as ethno-political tensions between the Sinhalese and Tamils enter their umpteenth generation, and a situation that hit high gear in the mid-twentieth century is still going strong (and getting worse) in the twenty-first. Independence from Britain only seems to have made matters worse.

Solomon Bandaranaike was the Sinhalese Prime Minister of Sri Lanka when it was still known as Ceylon. Bandaranaike was an accessible Prime Minister and frequently mingled with the public. When he met Buddhist monk, Talduwe Somarama, Bandaranaike prostrated himself as a sign of respect and the monk shot him. The Prime Minister's bodyguards returned fire immediately, injuring Somarama. Although surgeons struggled for six hours to save him, Bandaranaike died the following day, 26 September 1959..

It transpired that Somorama was the fanatical tool of a conspiracy headed by Mapitagama Buddharakkitha, the Chief Incumbent of the Buddhist temple Kelaniya Raja Maha Vihara, and H Jayawardena, a closely associated businessman. The conspirators felt that Anglican Christian Bandaranaike was responsible for persecuting Buddhists. Ironically, Somorama converted to Christianity just before he was hanged. Vihara and Jayawardena received life sentences.

Bandaranaike was succeeded as leader by his widow, Sirimavo Bandaranaike. She was not only the world's first female prime minister, but she retained the leadership of her political party for 40 years, until her death. She was Sri Lanka's prime minister three times, and was in power for a total of eighteen years. She died on what was her last day in office anyway, shortly after casting her vote in the Sri Lankan elections on 10 October 2000. At the time of Sirimavo's death, her daughter Chandrika Kumaratunga was the Executive President of Sri Lanka.

Murderous monks aside, the real masters of political murder and, in some sense, the spiritual heirs of the Hashashin are the Liberation Tigers of Tamil Eelam (LTTE), better known to the West as the Tamil Tigers. They have been engaged in a decades-long war against the Sinhalese to establish a separate government for the Tamil majority of the north and east of Sri Lanka.

Since 1975 the LTTE have been responsible for about 30 assassinations, mostly of members of the Sri Lankan parliament. Their most high profile victim to date is the President of Sri Lanka, Ranasinghe Premadasa, who died in an LTTE suicide bombing in Colombo on 1 May 1993. Following the success of this action, according to British Journalist Jonathan Lyons, suicide bombers became the weapon of choice for the LTTE.

There are divisions within the LTTE as well. In 2004 the TamilEela Makkal Viduthalai Pulikal broke away from the mainstream LTTE in order to safeguard the interests of east Sri Lankan Tamils. Since then Tamils have begun to murder other Tamils. The plot thickens and so does the blood on Sri Lankan soil.

A Dutch anomaly

The charismatic, former communist and openly gay district councillor for Rotterdam, Wilhelmus 'Pim' Fortuyn, was hard to classify under the usual political classifications of left or right. He favoured the Netherlands' liberal drug policy, euthanasia and same-sex marriages, but he was also well known for his anti-immigration position, especially in regard to immigrants from the Middle East. Calling Islam a 'backward culture' didn't exactly endear him to the Muslim community, but this wasn't what killed him.

The Dutch general elections were only nine days away and Fortuyn was running for parliament. On 6 May 2002 he had just given an interview at a radio station in Hilversum, in the north of Holland, and was in the station's car park when animal rights activist Volkert van der Graaf shot him to death. Pym's driver Hans Smolders gave chase and the police were able to arrest the assassin shortly after, the gun still in his possession. Van der Graaf claimed that Pim Fortuyn was an 'ever-growing danger ... I thought I could solve it myself'. He was sentenced to eighteen years in prison for his approach to the problem. Fortuyn's murder was the first assassination in Holland in the modern era.

Theo van Gogh, film director and descendant of another Theo van Gogh—Vincent van Gogh's brother—was well known for his newspaper columns and his detestation of organised religion, especially Islam. He made a ten-minute film, *Submission*, which depicted naked women enshrouded in semi-transparent veils, kneeling in prayer and telling their life stories in conversation with Allah. After the movie's release in 2004 van Gogh received death threats.

He was in the process of making a documentary about one of only two politicians he ever had any respect for, Pim Fortuyn, when Mohammed Bouyeri shot him eight times with a Croatian HS 2000 hand gun in the streets of Amsterdam. Van Gogh died instantly, but Bouyeri slit the director's throat and plunged two knives into his chest, using one to pin a note to him threatening the governments of the West, the Jews and to the writer of *Submission*, Ayaan Hirst Ali, who had to go into hiding temporarily. A policeman shot Bouyeri in the leg. On 26 July he was sentenced to life in prison with no chance of parole.

Russia and Chechnya

If you want to look at mayhem on a grand scale, look no further than the former Soviet Union. Since the collapse of the USSR, democratic Russia and the former Soviet dependent states have, to varying degrees, become the basket cases of Eurasia. Of particular note is the regime of Vladimir Putin, with his alleged allegiances to organised Russian crime and his hard-line stance against Chechnya. Although he has been in power since 31 December 1999, it's only fair to say that the Chechen situation and the disintegration of law and order in Russia are problems that precede him.

The first president of the unrecognised Chechen Republic of Ichkeria, Dzhokhar Dudayev was blown up by two laser-guided missiles, on 21 April 1996, while he was using a satellite phone. A Russian reconnaissance plane informed base as soon as they detected his signal and two fighters launched the missiles within minutes.

His successor Zelimkhan Yandarbiyev actually survived his term, as did his successor Shaykh Maskhadov. However, on 13 February 2004, Yandarbiyev was assassinated in exile in Doha, Qatar when a bomb blew up his 4WD, himself and two bodyguards, and seriously injured his son. Mashkadov had abandoned the presidency to return to guerrilla warfare and died on 8 March 2005 when the Federal Security Service of the Russian Federation (FSB)—the successor of the KGB—carried out an 'operation' in the village of Tolstoy-Yurt.

Even Kremlin-backed presidents aren't safe in Chechnya. Akhmat Kadyrov was the target of at least a dozen assassination attempts before an explosion destroyed the VIP seating section at the Dinamo Soccer Stadium in Grozny while Kadyrov was watching a Victory Day parade on 9 May 2004. Two of Kadyrov's sons died soon afterwards in separate incidents, but since March 2006 his only surviving son, Ramzan Akhmadovich Kadyrov, has been the Prime Minister of Chechnya, with his own private army to prove it.

Sheikh Abdul-Halim Sadulayev, the fourth rebel president of Chechnya, died in a gunfight between his forces and a combined group of FSB and pro-Moscow militia in Argun on 17 June 2006. The Russians were investigating a Chechen safe house and apparently accidentally stumbled upon Sadulayev.

As of early 2007, the current Kremlin-backed President of Chechnya, Alu Alkhanov is expected to be succeeded by Prime Minister Kadyrov. In photographs, Alkhanov tends to look a little glum. Kadyrov, however, tends to look rather determined.

The troubles in Chechnya have created huge tensions in Russia and observers have credited a number of prominent deaths as being linked to the conflict.

The most striking in recent history is that of Anna Stepanovna Politkovskaya, human rights campaigner, journalist and staunch critic of the Putin government. In numerous articles in the liberal Russian newspaper *Novaya Gazeta*, she lambasted Putin, the military and organised crime. She maintained a high-powered rhetoric about human rights abuses in her country and the disintegration of anything resembling a rule of law. According to her editor, on the day of her death—7 October 2006—Politkovskaya planned to submit a long article about the torture practices of Chechen security forces.

Someone obviously wanted to shut her up. Politkovskaya was in the lift of her apartment building in central Moscow when someone, probably a professional contract killer, shot her four times with a Makarov pistol. After her murder, police seized her hard drive. The fate of the article remains unknown, as does the identity of her killer.

The assassination outraged many in Russia and the international community. The principle owner of *Novaya Gazeta*, billionaire Alexander Lebedev, offered a reward of 25 million roubles ($1 million) for information leading to her capture.

It remains to be seen whether we'll ever know the truth about this assassination, only one of many journalists' deaths in Russia.

The Great Survivors

There's something heartening about knowing that even though the target of an assassination has to be lucky all the time, and the assassin only has to be lucky once, some high flyers did manage a lifetime of luck.

It would be nice to end on a positive note. Of course the concept of 'positive' is relative in the subject area of assassination; but in a violent world, where it's so often a case of kill or be killed, it's comforting to know that at least some of history's leaders survived not only one or two attempts on their lives, but so many that history either lost count, or didn't record them. There's something heartening about knowing that, even though the target of an assassination has to be lucky all the time and the assassin only has to be lucky once, some high flyers did manage a lifetime of luck.

Apart from the presidents and various fortunate would-be assassinees we've already met, the following are worth mentioning:

Queen Victoria

Queen Victoria lived in an age when people were losing their faith in the divine rights of kings or queens—monarchs were becoming fair game. At the time of the first attempt on Victoria's life, she was 21 years old, recently married and pregnant with her first child, riding in a carriage with Prince Albert on Constitution Hill in London. Eighteen-year-old Edward Oxford tried to shoot her, but both bullets missed. In July 1840 he was found not guilty by reason of insanity, spent 27 years in mental hospitals and, in 1867, the authorities offered to discharge him if he agreed to leave the country. He went to Australia and disappeared from history.

Victoria survived three similar attempts on her life in 1842, then enjoyed a 45-year breather before authorities uncovered an Irish conspiracy, the 1887 Jubilee Plot, that came to nothing. In fact Victoria made it to her 60-year Diamond Jubilee and then some, dying in 1901 at the age of 81 in her bed.

Hitler

Of course, if you're looking for stories of habitual survival you need a leader with numerous enemies. German Reichskanzler Adolf Hitler survived what were probably hundreds of attempts to kill him. In some respects the whole of World War II was one long attempt to kill Hitler, which only succeeded indirectly.

The most famous direct failure was that of Catholic aristocrat Claus von Stauffenberg and his fellow conspirators. On 20 July 1944 Stauffenberg entered the briefing room at the military high command near Rastenberg, in what is now Ketryzn, Poland. He was ostensibly there to participate in a staff meeting, but also to meet his own agents.

The Wolfsschanze—the Wolf's Lair—was where Hitler felt the most secure, surrounded by his most trusted people. Stauffenberg, however, was carrying a briefcase filled with explosives primed with a ten to fifteen minute timer. He placed it under the briefing room table, while the meeting went on as normal. After a short while Stauffenberg excused himself, saying he had to make an urgent phone call to Berlin. He had waited until the last possible moment and a few minutes later a huge explosion let loose. Convinced that no one could have survived he made his escape. Four people had died and the rest were injured, but Hitler's physical injuries were only slight—the heavy conference table had shielded him.

Stauffenberg's plan called for a coup that his co conspirators had to implement, but Hitler wasn't dead. By the time Stauffenberg reached Berlin Hitler's men were ready for him and intercepted the conspirators. An impromptu court martial found Stauffenberg, General Freidrich Olbricht, Lieutenant Werner von Haeften and Oberst von Quirnheim guilty and they were executed by firing squad in the courtyard of army headquarters—the Bendlerblock—in Berlin. Ironically, the tribunal's head was also a conspirator, but General Freidrich Fromm was later found out and executed.

Another eight conspirators, including Claus' older brother Berthold von Stauffenberg, were hanged and died of slow strangulation on 10 August in Plotzensee Prison, Berlin. The Bendlerblock is now a memorial to the German Resistance.

Hitler's wounds from the blast were superficial, but the psychological effect was devastating. From that point on Hitler knew that he could trust no one. Sick as he was, the failed assassination made him sicker and the bomb was the beginning of the end. The true end came when he put a gun to his head in his bunker in Berlin.

Papal persistence

Of course even popularity doesn't protect you against everyone. In 1970 Pope Paul VI was attacked by Bolivian surrealist painter Benjamin Mendoza y Amor Flores, who lunged at the pontiff with a kris (a wavy bladed Indonesian dagger) at Manila Airport. The Pope's wounds were only superficial.

Pope John Paul II survived two assassination attempts. Mehmet Ali Agca, of the Turkish ultra-nationalists the Grey Wolves, fired four shots into the Pope's body at St Peter's Square on 13 May 1981. Two bullets lodged in his lower intestine, one hit his left hand and one his right arm. Although seriously wounded the Pope recovered. Agca claimed to be a mercenary hired by Abdullah Catli, the Grey Wolves' second-in-command, but his story was full of holes, often ranting and contradictory. He appeared to be a lunatic. In the spirit of his job, John Paul II forgave him. In July 1981 Agca was sentenced to life imprisonment, but Italian President Carlo Azeglio Ciampi pardoned him in June 2000. He was then deported to Turkey, where he was imprisoned for a murder that he committed in 1979. He was released on 12 January 2006 only to be reincarcerated eight days later.

John Paul II had to forgive another would-be assassin. On 12 May 1982, the day before the first anniversary of the previous attempt on his life, former Catholic Juan Krohn attempted to bayonet the pontiff while he was making a visit to Fatima, Portugal. Security guards overpowered Krohn before he could injure the Pope. The would be assassin claimed that he hated the Vatican II reforms and considered John Paul II to be a communist agent. Krohn served three years of a six-year sentence and was expelled from Portugal. He ended up as a lawyer in Belgium where he frequently behaved violently and erratically in courtrooms. In July 2000 he tried to climb the security railing at the Brussels Royal Palace in order to assassinate either King Albert II of Belgium or Juan Carlos of Spain. Krohn received a five-year sentence. Why he isn't getting any treatment for mental illness is anyone's guess.

The greatest survivor of them all: Fidel Castro

Fidel's name actually means 'faithful' and he has certainly been faithful to his cause, whatever *that* is, and faithful to his country. Above all else, however, communist and atheist Fidel must have been faithful to his own god of good fortune. On 25 April 2002 the BBC news feature 'Country Profile: Cuba' asserted that Castro has 'reputedly survived more than 600 CIA-sponsored attempts on his life'. Castro's former head of Cuban intelligence—therefore his chief bodyguard—Fabian Escalante, estimated the number to be 638 as quoted in Britain's Channel 4 documentary '638 Ways to Kill Castro'.

Perhaps these attempts could be regarded simply as the means to annoy him to death. They include: a poison syringe that looks like a ballpoint pen, a radio station booby-trapped with poison gas, a diving suit treated to induce a chronic fungal skin disease, placing thallium salts in his shoes to make his body hair fall out and even—believe it or not—exploding cigars.

The CIA have rarely been directly involved. For the most part they've trained Cuban exiles to carry out their dirty work. If even a small percentage of the claims are true then American taxpayers are really working hard to off Castro and they're not getting *any* value for money at all. The Cuban President himself has said that: 'If surviving assassination were an Olympic event, I would win the Gold Medal'.

Wouldn't that be fun?

Author's Notes

p.12 There are quite a lot of clues that this was the case. One of the Hebrew words for god and the third word in *the Bible*, 'Elohim', was actually a plural and could conceivably translate as 'they who are the objects of reverence'. Don't you just love these grammatical controversies?

p.32 The Rubicon itself no longer exists. The modern equivalent Rivers are the Pisciatello and the Fiumicino. A Starbucks franchise now claims to stand on the exact point where Caesar made his crossing.

p.211 $11.5 Billion in modern terms—cheap when you consider its oil reserves, oops, I meant its priceless value as pristine wilderness …

p.214 This very real hazard of the profession was the basis of Lewis Carroll's 'Mad Hatter' character in Alice's Adventures in Wonderland, published only months after Lincoln's assassination.

p.225 It took decades of advances in imaging technology but forensic investigator's were eventually able to confirm that photos of the prints on the gun did show that the prints were Oswald's.

Sources & Further Reading

Internet

en.wikipedia.org/wiki/Wiki

english.donga.com/srv/service.php3?bicode=040000&biid=2006060530608

jamestown.org/terrorism/news/article.php?issue_id=3059

members.aol.com/RVSNorton/Lincoln13.html

www.awionline.org/pubs/Quarterly/Fall2001/fossey.htm

www.espionageinfo.com/index.html

www.famouscanadians.net/name/w/whelanjamespatrick.php

www.law.umkc.edu/faculty/projects/ftrials/lincolnconspiracy/lincolnconspiracy

www.posner.com/book5.htm

www.timesonline.co.uk/article/0,,3-1393172,00.html

www.ucc.ie/chronicon/duncfra.htm

Printed works

Livy, *Ab Urbe Condita (From the Founding of the City)*.

Plutarch, *The Life of Numa Pompilius*.

Plutarch, *Lives of the Noble Greeks and Romans*.

Fetherling, George, *A Biographical Dictionary of the World's Assassins*, Robert Hale, London, 2002.

Spignesi, S J, *In The Crosshairs: Famous Assassinations and Attempts from Julius Caesar to John Lennon*, New Page Books, New Jersey, 2003.

Scarre C, *The Penguin Atlas of Ancient Rome*, Penguin, London, 1995.

The Truth About History, Reader's Digest, Sydney, 2006.

Acknowledgements

Thanks to my editors Belinda Castles, Kirsten Chapman, Sally Hills and Michael McGrath for doing their best on a rather difficult text.

Thanks, as usual, to the whole team at New Holland for their sterling efforts. It's always a real pleasure to work with you all.

About the Author

Xavier Waterkyn is the author of six books, including *Death Row* and *Women in Crime*. He lives in Sydney and is currently working on his next book.

Apart from writing and mentoring other writers, Xavier helps authors find publishers through Flying Pigs, the literary agency he manages with his business partner, ABC book reviewer Clare Calvet.